With Head and Heart

Other Books by Howard Thurman

THE GREATEST OF THESE

THE NEGRO SPIRITUAL SPEAKS OF LIFE AND DEATH

MEDITATION FOR APOSTLES OF SENSITIVENESS

JESUS AND THE DISINHERITED

DEEP IS THE HUNGER

MEDITATIONS OF THE HEART

THE CREATIVE ENCOUNTER

DEEP RIVER

THE GROWING EDGE

APOSTLES OF SENSITIVENESS

FOOTPRINTS OF A DREAM

MYSTICISM AND THE EXPERIENCE OF LOVE

THE INWARD JOURNEY

TEMPTATIONS OF JESUS

DISCIPLINES OF THE SPIRIT

THE LUMINOUS DARKNESS

THE CENTERING MOMENT

THE SEARCH FOR COMMON GROUND

THE MOOD OF CHRISTMAS

A TRACK TO THE WATER'S EDGE

THE FIRST FOOTPRINTS

FOR THE INWARD JOURNEY

WITH HEAD AND HEART

The Autobiography of

HOWARD THURMAN

A Harvest Book
Harcourt Brace & Company
San Diego   New York   London

Requests for permission to make copies
of any part of the work should be mailed to:
Permissions Department, Harcourt Brace & Company,
6277 Sea Harbor Drive, Orlando, Florida 32887-6777.

Library of Congress Cataloging-in-Publication Data
Thurman, Howard, 1899–1981
With head and heart.
(A Harvest book)
Includes index.
1. Thurman, Howard, 1899–1981
2. Baptists–Clergy–Biography.
3. Clergy–United States–Biography. I Title.
BX6495.T53A38   280'.4   [B]   79-1848
ISBN 0-15-697648-X

Printed in the United States of America
NPRSQO

*To the stranger in the railroad station
in Daytona Beach who restored my
broken dream sixty-five years ago*

Contents

Illustrations

Dr. Arnold Nakajima, and Ruth Acty. In the second row: Lynn Buchanan, Emory Mellon, Carolyn Threlkeld, George Acevedo, Sylvia Nichols, and Joseph Van Pelt.

Howard Thurman at the pulpit of the Church of the Fellowship of All Peoples, the first fully integrated church in America

Eleanor Roosevelt and Coleman Jennings, a close family friend, at a testimonial dinner given for Dean and Mrs. Thurman in 1944 as they were leaving Howard University to establish the Fellowship Church

Rabbi Alvin Fine of Temple Emanu-El in San Francisco greeting Howard Thurman at the Tenth Anniversary Dinner of Fellowship Church, 1954

At the Vassar College Commencement exercises, 1954, Adlai Stevenson gave the Commencement Address and Howard Thurman, the Baccalaureate Address. Sarah Blanding, president of Vassar, is at left.

Liturgical dancers and choir of Marsh Chapel, Boston University, 1960

Dr. Harold Case, president of Boston University, and Mrs. Phyllis Case greet the Thurmans in 1958. Dr. Thurman served as dean of Marsh Chapel and professor at the Graduate School of Theology.

Among those who gathered at Boston University in 1959 to commemorate the 175th anniversary of the death of Phillis Wheatley, the first recognized black American poet, were, from left to right, Meta Warrick Fuller, sculptor; Howard Thurman; Sue Thurman; Beth Ballard, secretary of Marsh Chapel; Mrs. Roland Hayes; Roland Hayes, tenor; and Georgia Douglas Johnson, poet

Dedication of the Howard Thurman Listening Room, the Cathedral Church of St. John the Divine, New York City, 1977. From left to right: Mrs. Amyas Ames, of the committee sponsoring the Listening Room; Yona Okoth, exiled bishop of Uganda; the Reverend Canon Mary Michael Simpson, Order of St. Helena; Dean James Parks Morton and the Reverend Canon Jonathan King, of St. John the Divine; and Howard Thurman.

The Thurmans on their thirty-fifth wedding anniversary in 1967

Grandchildren Emily and Anton Wong, and Suzanne Chiarenza

Howard Thurman's sister Madaline Thurman

The Thurmans' daughters, Anne Spencer Thurman and Olive Thurman Wong

Acknowledgments

I must express deepest appreciation to a group of friends who built the first fires under this pot and waited patiently for it to boil. They requested anonymity and of course they shall have it, but let them read here that I shall never forget them.

To Tina Wall and Joyce Sloan, staff of the Howard Thurman Educational Trust, who serve as our right hand and our left, my special thanks. They and a very kind volunteer, Dorothy Eaton, gave time and overtime, including many weekends, to typing, retyping, and valiantly trying to locate lost pages which at times I declared I had never seen.

My loving thanks to my sister, Madaline Thurman, whose memory and mine did not always agree, and to my daughter Olive Thurman Wong, who read much of the manuscript, making constructive comments and suggestions.

A special expression of spontaneous gratitude to my wife, Sue Bailey Thurman, whose sympathetic and caring heart did not protect me from the kind of tender and direct criticism that could only come from one who has companioned my life for forty-seven years.

My publisher, William Jovanovich, became during the long months of this writing that rare combination of critic, editor, and friend. His friendship has undergirded this entire effort and remains a priceless gift.

To my daughter Anne Spencer Thurman, who as collaborator and sounding board gave three years of her life to this project, bringing to it her training and experience as a critic and editor. Without her work this book would not have been published.

This book spans nearly four generations. It peeks in and out of a lifetime of people and events, yet it is by no means the whole chronicle. I have tried here to describe highlights of a career because it is impossible to describe a life. It has been a long time in the making—but now done I view it with some satisfaction and the hope that all who read it will share my journey with me.

                                                    H. T.

I

Beginnings

At the end of my first year at the Rochester Theological Seminary, I became assistant to the minister of the First Baptist Church of Roanoke, Virginia. I was to assume the duties as pastor during the month that the minister and his family were away on vacation. I would be on my own. On my first night alone in the parsonage, I was awakened by the telephone. The head nurse of the local Negro hospital asked, "May I speak with Dr. James?" I told her he was away. "Dr. James is the hospital chaplain," she explained. "There is a patient here who is dying. He's asking for a minister. Are you a minister?"

In one kaleidoscopic moment I was back again at an old cross-road. A decision of vocation was to be made here, and I felt again the ambivalence of my life and my calling. Finally, I answered. "Yes, I am a minister."

"Please hurry," she said, "or you'll be too late."

In a few minutes I was on my way, but in my excitement and confusion I forgot to take my Bible. At the hospital, the nurse took me immediately into a large ward. The dread curtain was around the bed. She pulled it aside and directed me to stand opposite her. The sick man's eyes were half closed, his mouth open, his breathing labored. The nurse leaned over and, calling him by name, said, "The minister is here."

Slowly he sought to focus his eyes first on her, and then on me. In a barely audible voice he said, "Do you have something to say to a man who is dying? If you have, please say it, and say it in a hurry."

I bowed my head, closed my eyes. There were no words. I poured out the anguish of my desperation in one vast effort. I felt physically I was straining to reach God. At last, I whispered my Amen.

We opened our eyes simultaneously as he breathed, "Thank you. I understand." He died with his hand in mine.

My father had died seventeen years earlier, in 1907. Those moments in the hospital had rekindled the new memory of the hurt and fear of a seven-year-old boy. Death was well known in our community. We did not know the cause or cure of typhoid fever. All we knew was that every summer there would be a regular death toll of typhoid victims. The course of the disease was as familiar as the distant but steady roar of the Atlantic Ocean, sounding across the Halifax River: first, the sick feeling and the depression; then, mounting fever; finally, the smell of the sickroom. Doctors could do little, but we used many techniques to break the fever. Sometimes we bathed the body with cold wet cloths, or wrapped it in large leaves stripped from the "Pomerchristian" plant. When all of these ministrations failed—as almost always they did—the word was whispered that "we will soon know one way or the other." A stillness pervaded the sickroom and settled round the entire house like a fog. Children were no longer permitted to play in the yard or in front on the street. Waiting. Waiting. Life came to a long moment of pause, for hours, sometimes days. Waiting. Waiting. Each was wondering, How long? How long?

At last, suddenly, the children would start to play again, communicating the joy of recovery, or one heard the crying and wailing of the women as their men stood mute. Either way, the crisis had passed. But parents had still other dangers to worry them. Which of us would drown in the quarry, where we were forbidden to swim? Who would be run over by the three o'clock train that came down the unprotected crossing, the shrill cry of the train whistle sounding too late? Who would be bitten by the ever-present rattlesnakes that lurked under the huckleberry bush where the biggest and most luscious berries grew? Death was no stranger to us. It was a part of the rhythm of our days.

My father, Saul Solomon Thurman, was a big man with a large frame. He worked on a railroad crew, laying the track of the Florida East Coast Railroad from Jacksonville to Miami, and would come home every two weeks. He was quiet, soft-spoken, and gentle. Sometimes I would pass the barbershop and look in. There he would be, getting a haircut and a shave before coming home from his two weeks' absence. He never wanted us to see him with his hair long, his face unshaven.

Suddenly one day, in the middle of the week, I heard him coming up the steps of our little house. The door opened and he fell inside. My mother and I struggled to get him to bed. He could hardly breathe and his body was racked with fever. He had pneumonia. Five days later he died. On the last day of his life, we could hear the death rattle in his throat. I sat on one side of the bed, Mamma on the other.

My young mother was a devout, dedicated praying Christian. My father was a good man, but the church was not for him. Even now I remember him sitting on the front porch, his legs crossed, looking into the distance, often with a book in hand that I could not read or understand. Sometimes I would crawl under the porch and lie on my back so that I could see his face without him seeing me. I wanted to see if he ever batted his eyes.

In the final moment before he died, my mother said softly and with utter tenderness, "Saul, are you ready to die?" Between great gasps for air, he managed to say, "Yes, Alice, all my life I have been a man. I am not afraid of death. I can meet it." With that, his body put forth one last great effort to breathe while we held him down in the bed as best we could. Then death. The long silence was broken only by the sound of our anguished weeping.

I helped my mother and grandmother bathe his body and "lay him out." In those days there were no Negro undertakers. There was one white undertaker in town, but the two races could not be embalmed or prepared for burial in the same place. Any embalming for us would have to be done in the home and, of course, it was almost never done.

The cost of the coffin was critical for the poor. When this sudden death visited our house, I was sent to our neighbors to ask them to help us by giving whatever they could. I was not self-conscious; there was no embarrassment. This was the way of life in our neighborhood. In sorrows, joys, good times and bad, this was the way we lived. We helped each other and we survived.

The burial and funeral arrangements were a serious problem, for in the eyes of the church he was a sinner. In the language of the time, he died "out of Christ." Our pastor therefore refused to

5

permit him to be buried from the church, and naturally was unwilling to take the ceremony himself. But to have it otherwise was unthinkable, hurtful, and also impractical, because there were no funeral parlors, and our homes were all too small to accommodate a group of any size. What were we to do? My grandmother, who took charge of the situation, did so in her customary manner. She went to the chairman of the board of deacons. "You cannot make the minister take Saul's funeral, but he has no right to keep him from being buried from the church. We hold the deacons responsible for this decision. Ministers come and ministers go, but the deacons stay here with us." Of course, he read her meaning quite clearly. At length, he agreed that my father should be buried from the church.

Our next hurdle was to find someone to preach the funeral. By chance—if there is such a thing—there was a traveling evangelist in town, a man named Sam Cromarte. I shall never forget him. He offered to preach Papa's funeral. He did not need to be persuaded. We sat on the front pew, the "mourners bench." I listened with wonderment, then anger, and finally mounting rage as Sam Cromarte preached my father into hell. This was his chance to illustrate what would happen to "sinners" who died "out of Christ," as my father had done. And he did not waste it. Under my breath I kept whispering to Mamma, "He didn't know Papa, did he? Did he?" Out of her own pain, conflict, and compassionate love, she reached over and gripped my bare knees with her hand, giving a gentle but firm, comforting squeeze. It was sufficient to restrain for the moment my bewildered and outraged spirit.

In the buggy, coming home from the cemetery, I sought some explanation. Why would Reverend Cromarte do this to Papa? Why would he say such things? Neither Mamma nor Grandma would answer my persistent query. Finally, almost to myself, I said, "One thing is sure. When I grow up and become a man, I will never have anything to do with the church."

I remembered those words years later, driving home in the darkening shadows of that day in Roanoke, when a man had died, his hand in mine, taking with him my urgent prayers for the peace of his soul. I remembered too the road over which I had come, and followed my spirit back to the beloved woods of my childhood.

When I was young, I found more companionship in nature than I did among people. The woods befriended me. In the long summer days, most of my time was divided between fishing in the Halifax River and exploring the woods, where I picked huckleberries and gathered orange blossoms from abandoned orange groves. The quiet, even the danger, of the woods provided my rather lonely spirit with a sense of belonging that did not depend on human relationships. I was usually with a group of boys as we explored the woods, but I tended to wander away to be alone for a time, for in that way I could sense the strength of the quiet and the aliveness of the woods.

A neighbor who also enjoyed berry-picking would go with me, but his primary purpose was to capture snakes for the local zoo, where they were a tourist attraction. I marveled at his courage. If we saw a rattlesnake, he quickly pinned the snake's neck in the sand with a forked stick. Then he would lift it carefully by the head and tail and drop it into the gunnysack I held open. We suspended the sacks from tree limbs. When we were ready to leave, we collected the sacks and strung them from a pole we held between us.

At home he would defang the snakes before taking them downtown to sell. He was fearless. He would even catch alligators and owned one as a pet.

Nightfall was meaningful to my childhood, for the night was more than a companion. It was a presence, an articulate climate. There was something about the night that seemed to cover my spirit like a gentle blanket. The nights in Florida, as I grew up, seemed to have certain dominant characteristics. They were not dark, they were black. When there was no moon, the stars hung like lanterns, so close I felt that one could reach up and pluck them from the heavens. The night had its own language. Sometimes, the night seemed to have movement in it, as if it were a great ocean wave. Other times, it was deathly still, no rhythm, no movement. At such times I could hear the night think, and feel the night feel. This comforted me and I found myself wishing that the night would hurry and come, for under its cover, my mind would roam. I felt embraced, enveloped, held secure. In some fantastic way, the night belonged to me. All the little secrets of my life and heart and

7

all of my most intimate and private thoughts would not be violated, I knew, if I spread them out before me in the night. When things went badly during the day, I would sort them out in the dark as I lay in my bed, cradled by the night sky.

The night has been my companion all my life. In Nigeria, at the University of Ibadan, at the end of the day after dinner and work, with the lights out, the darkness of the African night would float into my room and envelop me. I would listen to the various night noises. Here, too, the night was alive!

The ocean and the river befriended me when I was a child. During those days the beach in Daytona was not segregated as it was later to become. White and black had equal access to it. I was among the hundreds of people standing on the sand dunes behind the ropes as Barney Oldfield broke the world's auto racing record in 1910 on the great racing beaches of Daytona. Often, when the tide was low, more than a mile of packed sand lay where the races were run. Here I found, alone, a special benediction. The ocean and the night together surrounded my little life with a reassurance that could not be affronted by the behavior of human beings. The ocean at night gave me a sense of timelessness, of existing beyond the reach of the ebb and flow of circumstances. Death would be a minor thing, I felt, in the sweep of that natural embrace.

I was made keenly aware when a storm came sweeping up seemingly from the depths of the sea. First there was a steady quieting— a lull during which the waves seemed to lack the strength to wash fully up the shore; the sea grass along the top of the dunes was still; no wind blew in the treacherous quiet. Then a stirring like a gentle moan broke the silence. Suddenly, the winds were ferocious and the waves, now ten feet high, dashed into the shore. Again, the boundaries of self did not hold me. Unafraid, I was held by the storm's embrace. The experience of these storms gave me a certain overriding immunity against much of the pain with which I would have to deal in the years ahead when the ocean was only a memory. The sense held: I felt rooted in life, in nature, in existence.

When the storms blew, the branches of the large oak tree in our backyard would snap and fall. But the topmost branches of the oak tree would sway, giving way just enough to save themselves from snapping loose. I needed the strength of that tree, and, like it, I wanted to hold my ground. Eventually, I discovered that the oak tree and I had a unique relationship. I could sit, my back against its trunk, and feel the same peace that would come to me in my bed at night. I could reach down in the quiet places of my spirit, take out my bruises and my joys, unfold them, and talk about them. I could talk aloud to the oak tree and know that I was understood. It, too, was a part of my reality, like the woods, the night, and the pounding surf, my earliest companions, giving me space.

When I was growing up, Daytona had a population of about five thousand permanent residents. The number greatly increased in the wintertime when the tourists arrived. The wealthy, who were not interested in the social whirl of such centers as Miami and Palm Beach, found Daytona and its immediate environs to be an ideal setting. The Rockefellers, the Gambles, the Whites, and many other old rich families wintered there. For the most part, they employed local people, black and white, as servants and household retainers, while their chauffeurs and personal maids usually traveled with them, returning north at the end of winter. The tempering influence of these northern families made contact between the races less abrasive than it might have been otherwise.

Negroes lived in three population pockets. One was called Midway, the section in which Mary McLeod Bethune's school was founded and established. Midway was more progressive and more secular than either of the other communities. There were two pool halls there, as well as the single movie house open to us. The owners knew that if it were located in any other section, there would not be many customers. When I went from my neighborhood to Midway, I felt like a country boy going to the city. Next to Midway was Newtown, where the one public school for black children was located. The main street connecting Midway and Newtown continued into Waycross, the community where I lived. On the edge of Newtown and Waycross was the one source of recreation for all, the baseball park. The fact that it was so close to Waycross gave us children a certain pride of possession.

Waycross was made up mostly of homeowners. There was one restaurant, one rooming house, and the Odd Fellows Hall. The two churches, Mount Bethel Baptist Church and Mount Zion A.M.E.

Church, were on opposite sides of the main track of the Florida East Coast Railroad tracks which bisected the community. In our world, there were only these two religious denominations; and the line between the two was carefully drawn.

One of my aunts was a Methodist through marriage. She had a happy youthful spirit and we children loved her dearly. But there was an unspoken awareness that she was a bit queer because she was a Methodist. The son of the Methodist minister was the spokesman for the Methodist kids in arguments on the school playground, and I represented the Baptist kids. We would argue all the way home from school. The discussions usually turned on the efficacy of the rite of baptism. The Methodist boy would argue, quoting the Bible, that John said to Jesus, "I baptize you *with* water," meaning to apply; thus, the Methodists baptized by sprinkling. I would rejoin, "Yes, but the Bible says, when Jesus was baptized, 'He came up out of the water,' and that could only mean that Jesus had been *down under*."

Apart from these denominational frictions, the three neighborhoods formed a closely knit community of black people, surrounded by a white world. Daytona Beach (not Daytona itself) and Sea Breeze were exclusive tourist areas, located across the Halifax River from Daytona. I could work in Sea Breeze and Daytona Beach, but I was not allowed to spend the night there, nor could I be seen there after dark without being threatened. During those years, we were permitted to enjoy the beaches and to swim in the ocean—even these were later to be limited to whites only—but these areas were absolutely off limits after dark.

The white community in Daytona itself was "downtown," no place for loitering. Our freedom of movement was carefully circumscribed, a fact so accepted that it was taken for granted. But in Waycross, Midway, and Newtown we were secure and at home, free to move and go about our business as we pleased.

Thus, white and black worlds were separated by a wall of quiet hostility and overt suspicion. Certain white people could come into our neighborhoods without our taking notice. The sheriff often came on "official" business. And the insurance salesmen made their rounds. There was a group of Baptists from Michigan who occasionally came to worship at our church. The most frequent

10

white visitors were the people who regularly attended the gatherings at Mrs. Bethune's school.

In our tiny neighborhood within Waycross, we were what today is called an extended family. The children were under the general watch and care of all the adults. If we were asked to do an errand by any of the older members, it was not necessary for us to get permission from our parents. Reprimands were also freely given to the children by all the adults. Corporal punishment, however, was the exclusive prerogative of one's own parents. My father's death was only one of the many experiences I recall that bore the aura of caring of all, the sharing of all, during times of illness or suffering. The sick were cared for at home, for no hospitals were open to us other than the "pesthouse" on the outskirts of town, where smallpox victims were isolated. In every aspect of the common life, there was the sense of shared responsibility. Even the fast line between Baptist and Methodist yielded at this point.

For many years, my grandmother was a midwife. I cannot remember a time when she did not live with us. After Papa died, my mother supported us by cooking for white families. At first she and Grandma worked together washing and ironing for white families downtown. My job was to collect the bundles of soiled clothes from these families and from one of the large hotels. The laundry was placed outside the guest rooms, wrapped, and labeled. I collected these bundles and took them home in a large basket. Later I would deliver the clean laundry and collect the money.

There was one old family for whom my grandmother had done laundry for years. The man owned the only hardware store in town. In the fall of the year, I would rake their leaves every afternoon and put them in a pile to burn. The family's little girl, four or five years old, waited for me to come from school to do my job. She was a lonely child and was not permitted to play with other kids in the neighborhood. She enjoyed following me around in the yard as I worked.

One day, after I had made several piles for burning, she decided to play a game. Whenever she found a beautifully colored leaf, she would scatter the pile it was in to show it to me. Each time she did this, I would have to rake the leaves into a pile again. This grew tiresome, and it doubled my work. Finally, I said to her in some

11

desperation, "Don't do that anymore because I don't have time."
She became very angry and continued to scatter the leaves. "I'm
going to tell your father about this when he comes home," I said.
With that, she lost her temper completely and, taking a straight
pin out of her pinafore, jabbed me in the hand. I drew back in pain.
"Have you lost your mind?" I asked. And she answered, "Oh, Howard, that didn't hurt you! You can't feel!"

When I came home, I told Grandma about it. She was always
there. She was the receptacle for the little frustrations and hurts I
brought to her. Just as when, coming home from school, a classmate
began to bully me. I stood all I could and then the fight was on.
It was a hard and bitter fight. The fact that he was larger and older
than I, and had brothers, did not matter. For four blocks we fought
and there was no one to separate us. At last I began to gain in power.
With one tremendous effort, I got him to the ground and he conceded defeat. Then I had to come home to face my grandmother.
"No one ever wins a fight" were her only words as she looked at me.

"But I beat him," I said.

"Yes, but look at yourself."

My mother was a very sympathetic and compassionate woman.
There was about her a deep inner sadness that I could not, as a boy,
understand. It was not gloom, but a quiet overcast of feeling. She
had a shy sense of humor, yet was never a spontaneously joyous person. The daily care of her children—Henrietta, the oldest, Madaline, the youngest, and me—was in the capable hands of our grandmother. There were a few times in these beginning years when she
was able to be home with the family, though she worked long hours
away from home to keep us in food and clothing. Whenever she
could be with us there was a special moment that brought the day
to a close, when she knelt beside us by the bed and joined us in
saying the Lord's Prayer and "Now I Lay Me Down to Sleep."

Over the years I have learned very little about her life. She was
reticent by nature and never spoke of her youth and early life. We
children did not ask questions. I knew that Mamma was the seventh
or eighth child born to Howard and Nancy Ambrose. Her father
must have been quite a man to have left his stamp on the clan of
Ambroses, a clan spreading over central Florida, each one an unmistakable reflection of him. I was one of three or four grandsons

named for him, although he died before reaching his middle years, and none of his grandchildren knew him. He left his wife, Nancy, to care for this group of sons and daughters, some of whom were restless teenagers, which may account for her remaining a widow until her death at ninety-three. This was Grandma. She was fearless and embraced life with zest. Her devotion spilled over to every child in the neighborhood, many of whom, as midwife, she had helped into this world. As a boy I looked on with wonder and admiration as she hurried off with an anxious father (or frightened child) who came to summon her.

A communion existed between Grandma and Mamma so deep that there was never a discernible vibration of tension, or anger, between them. There must have been disagreements, but no discord affected the climate of our home.

She won the sobriquet Lady Nancy, and I am sure this was due in part to the black taffeta Sunday dress she always wore to church. It rustled elegantly as she moved down the aisle. I loved burying my head in that taffeta lap during the endless hours of the Sunday worship service. She spoke very little of her early life as a slave, except occasionally in poignant memory of a moment, the sharing of which would speak to the condition of her grandchildren. Never a word was mentioned about her Seminole Indian blood, but this was not unusual. There was much intermixing between the African slaves and Florida Indians before and after the Civil War, but in those days it was rarely spoken of. Among the scattered fragments of my earliest memory are the inscrutable faces of the Seminoles—one sitting very still under an oak tree, another passing by me silently on a country road.

The kindergarten in Daytona Beach was a gift to the community, made largely by a group of northern white people who were regular winter tourists. I do not know who they were, or why they made the gesture, but there was a kindergarten building with a big yard and a teacher named Miss Julia Green. One Monday morning, Mamma got me up early and dressed me very carefully. Worst of all, she combed my hair. My scalp was tender and my hair was thick. The ordeal was the scourge of my childhood. Whenever we were going out and it came to the inevitable hair combing, I would declare passionately, "Me don't want to go!" Undaunted, Mamma would put me on my stomach on the bed, a pillow on my back, her knee on the pillow to hold me down, and proceed to make me presentable. This morning was no exception. With my hair neatly combed, Mamma took me by the hand and delivered me into the hands of the teacher. She said to her, "I want my boy to learn." Miss Julia Green was a tall, very dignified lady, with large eyes and a warm, ready smile. In her eyes was a look of determination. She welcomed Mamma and me, gently told Mamma good-bye at the door, and led me in. With that, my formal education began. I well remember the trauma of that first day. I cried. I refused to have anything whatever to do with any of the games being played. But she would not let me sulk. She made me participate.

A few years ago I saw Miss Julia Green. She was bent with age, but she had the same fine face, the same sparkle, the same penetrating eyes. I knelt down by her chair to have our picture taken together. This was in 1963, when the mayor of Daytona Beach had declared a Howard Thurman Day. The fourteen-year-old boy whose broken dream was restored at that station some fifty years before returned with his family to receive the keys to the city. A brass band came out to meet us, and many friends from surrounding cities and the community of Bethune Cookman College attended the gala reception that evening, among them my kindergarten teacher. Seeing her again after so long a time and on that particular occasion was a high-water mark in my life. She helped to set me on my course, and she was there to receive me when I returned.

Mamma was a creative and imaginative cook. Though she did most of her cooking to earn a living, whenever she cooked for us she added a special touch. One summer, for some reason, the only vegetable to flourish in our garden was black-eyed peas. For days on end we had peas for supper, even on Sundays. One day she came home unexpectedly while we were eating. She must have sensed our despair. As soon as she put her things down, she brought a pot to the table and told us to empty our plates into it. She disappeared into the kitchen. After a short while she returned and refilled our plates with peas. Then from a large dish she took spoonfuls of fresh sliced onions and spread them over the peas. It was magic. The onions made the peas jump for joy.

Several times during the winter she would have a free Saturday afternoon. These were glorious hours. Sometimes she would make doughnuts fried in deep fat, or bake a huge lemon pie—thick, light, and tartly sweet. What she could do with mullet stew or chicken "purlo" seasoned with black pepper and onions defies description! After her death, my wife, Sue, discovered an old notebook in which she had written some of her favorite recipes and original concoctions. To this day, when any of the self-consciously fine cooks in our family produce a rare dish, we say, "It is worthy of Mamma Alice."

Mamma's second husband was a Mr. Evans who lived in Lake Helen, Florida, where the major employer was a large sawmill. My stepfather was a highly skilled operator of one of the machines in the mill. We lived in a house owned by the company. It was a short walk from the mill, so he always came home for his midday meal. This was the heaviest meal of the day, and Mamma took great pains to have a good hot dinner on the table when he arrived.

The second year we were in Lake Helen, in 1910, Halley's Comet appeared in our sky. I had heard Mamma and Mr. Evans talking about it. Some of the boys in the neighborhood had seen it, but I had not seen it myself because we children had to go to bed at sundown each evening. One day Mr. Evans brought home a small bottle of "Comet Pills." A traveling salesman had persuaded the owner of the mill to buy them. They would be protection, he said, against the conflagration sure to come when the comet fell to earth— the owner and his key employees would survive to start all over again if they took the pills. My stepfather was a key employee.

Mamma awoke me one night and urged me to dress quickly and come with her into the backyard to see the comet. We stood watching it together in silence. It was in its final phase, closest to the sun, its head barely visible, its tail spreading out in a shimmering fan-like shape over a vast section of the sky. I was transfixed. Quietly, I said, "Mamma, what will happen to us when that thing falls out of the sky?" I felt her hand tighten on my shoulder, and I looked up into her face. Her eyes were full of tears that did not fall, and her countenance bore an expression of radiance and peace such as I had seen only once before when, without knocking, I rushed into her room and found her kneeling beside her bed, in prayer. Finally, she said, "Nothing will happen to us, Howard. God will take care of us."

My stepfather was a very kind man who treated us with genuine fatherly concern. When he died, it was hard on Mamma. Mr. Evans had supported us, allowing her to be home with the children for the first time in many years. After his death, we moved back to our house in Daytona, and a few years later she married for the third and last time. Mr. Sams was a devout churchman. He had a clever and original mind and was engaged in several business ventures when he married Mamma. We children did not feel as close to him as to Mr. Evans.

My mother loved her church. Whenever she had jobs that made it possible for her to be home with the family on Sundays, we all went to church, morning and evening. Most often she was free to go to church with us only on Sunday night because her work required her to serve Sunday dinner. Yet my mother did not talk about religion very much. She read the Bible constantly but kept her prayer life to herself. I discovered the key to her inner religious life at the weekly prayer meeting, which she was always able to attend because it did not conflict with her work. The first time I heard her pray aloud in a meeting, I did not even recognize her voice. It had an unfamiliar quality at first; then I knew it was she. She spread her life out before God, telling him of her anxieties and dreams for me and my sisters, and of her weariness. I learned what could not be *told* to me.

I grew up in Mount Bethel Baptist Church. The church itself was a wooden building consisting of a sanctuary, without partitions, formed in the shape of a cross. All church meetings were held here. Sunday School classes met in separate sections of the same large area. The classes were conducted simultaneously, which meant we had to be sensitive to the presence of the others, and this sense of sharing was dramatized when the separate periods were over and we met as a group to listen to the review of the day's lesson, conducted by one of the deacons or by a visiting minister. Sometimes it was held by "jackleg" preachers. This term was applied to preachers who usually supported their families by working at secular jobs, but who had been "called" to preach and often were ordained. They assisted and sometimes substituted for the minister in emergencies. They were permitted to read the Scripture lesson, occasionally to give the morning's formal prayer in the regular Sunday service, and often they preached on the fifth Sunday night of the month. Sometimes they were the butt of insensitive jokes, and on the whole, they and their families were not treated with the respect they deserved. However, they endured and kept alive the flickering flame of the spirit when the harsh winds blew and the oil was low in the vessel.

Immediately after Sunday School there was a prayer service. At its conclusion, the minister and the choir appeared and the morning service began. The preachers in my church were not "whoopers"; they were more thoughtful than emotional. They were above average in schooling. Two of them had been college-trained. They were called "manuscript preachers." At the core of their preaching was solid religious instruction and guidance which augmented rather than diminished the emotional intensity of their words. One of these men, Dr. S. A. Owen, would later preach my ordination sermon. Under his guidance I preached my trial sermon, earning from the church a "license" that recommended me to the pulpit of any Baptist Church to preach but not to perform the rites of baptism, communion, or marriage. I was a freshman in college when I preached my trial sermon. My text was from one of the Psalms: "I will instruct thee and teach thee the way thou shalt go. I will guide thee with Mine own eye." When I finished and before the congregation voted, Reverend Owen said to me, "Brother Howard, I will pass on to you what was told me when I preached my trial sermon many years ago: 'When you get through, sit down.'" I never forgot this admonition, though at first it took some doing.

In the fellowship of the church, particularly in the experience of worship, there was a feeling of sharing in primary community. Not only did church membership seem to bear heavily upon one's ultimate destiny beyond death and the grave; more than all the other communal ties, it also undergirded one's sense of personal identity. It was summed up in the familiar phrase "If God is for you, who can prevail against you?"

The view that the traditional attitude of the religion of black people was, or is, otherworldly is superficial and misguided. "Take all the world but give me Jesus" is a false and simplistic characteriza-

17

tion of our religion. A "saved soul," as symbolized by conversion and church membership, gave you a personal validation that transcended time and space, because its ultimate guarantor was God, through Jesus Christ. It was nevertheless of primary importance to the individual living in "real" time and "real" space, because membership in the "fellowship of believers" provided the communal experience of being part of a neighborhood and gave the member a fontal sense of worth that could not be destroyed by any of life's outrages.

Hence, the "sinner" was a unique isolate within the generally binding character of community. It was this ultimate isolation that made the sinner the object of such radical concern in the church of my childhood. In the case of my father, the tensions existing between the two were never resolved. I was twelve years old when I joined the church. It was the custom to present oneself to the deacons, which I did. They examined me, and I answered their questions. When they had finished, the chairman asked, "Howard, why do you come before us?" I said, "I want to be a Christian." Then the chairman said, "But you must come before us after you have been converted and have already become a Christian. Come back when you can tell us of your conversion."

I went straight home and told my grandmother that the deacons had refused to take me into the church. She took me by the hand— I can still see her rocking along beside me—and together we went back to the meeting, arriving before they adjourned. Addressing Mose Wright, who was the chairman, she said, "How dare you turn this boy down? He is a Christian and was one long before he came to you today. Maybe you did not understand his words, but shame on you if you do not know his heart. Now you take this boy into the church right now—before you close this meeting!" And they did.

I was baptized in the Halifax River. On Sunday morning everybody met at the church after Sunday School. We did not hold the morning service in the church. Instead, a procession was formed outside. The candidates for baptism, in white robes, were led by the minister and the deacons, who were dressed in black waterproof clothing. At the rear of the procession were the members and all others who wished to witness the ceremony. Some rode ahead on bicycles to be at the riverbank when we arrived. This procession moved down the

middle of the street led by old lady Wright, who "sang" us to the
river. In full and glorious voice, she began:

"Oh, mourner, don't you want to go,
Oh, mourner, don't you want to go,
Oh, mourner, don't you want to go,
Let's go down to Jordan, Hallelu . . ."

Then the crowd picked it up:

"Let's go down to Jordan,
Let's go down to Jordan,
Let's go down to Jordan,
Halleluja . . ."

Verse after verse she sang all the way, until we turned the corner
and the river lay before us.

The candidates were then grouped before two deacons. One
deacon walked out into the water to stand near the stick that was
put down to mark the spot where the ceremony would take place.
The other led the candidates to this spot. The minister took each
candidate and, facing the people on the shore, spoke the great
words: "Upon the confession of your faith, my brother, I baptize
you in the name of the Father, Son, and Holy Ghost." Then he
dipped each one under the water. With the help of the assisting
deacon we would be raised to our feet again as the minister said,
"Amen." Then there was a chorus of Amens. This was repeated
until all the candidates were baptized.

Once you had joined the church, the next step in your validation
was to be placed under the tutelage of older members. Often there
were two, a man and a woman, who were spiritual guides assigned
to you. Every Tuesday afternoon, all the very young converts would
attend a prayer meeting. We were taught how to raise a hymn, to
pray in public, and to lead a prayer meeting. This took courage for
a beginner, but Tuesday after Tuesday we rehearsed thoroughly,
and slowly self-confidence developed. Finally, we were ready for
the final test, which was to lead an adult prayer service in the company of our sponsors. This done, the process of joining the church
was complete. With each learning step, your sense of your own
worth as a Christian was heightened. Your sponsor reinforced this
by reminding you of your confession of faith whenever your be-

havior warranted it. "Now that you are a Christian, you cannot behave that way. That was a part of your old life."

Unfortunately, I was soon tested and found wanting. Once or twice a week it was my regular routine to take orders for fish, catch them, and deliver them in time for supper. On the Monday after baptism, I was rowing my boat across the river to get to the pilings of the bridge closest to the channel where there was a plentiful supply of angelfish. Suddenly, a strong wind came up and it began to rain. I was pulling against the tide when the oar slipped, and I fell back, striking my head on the seat. I shouted a spectacular series of profanities; then I remembered that I had recently been baptized in those same waters. I cried all afternoon. "Let that be an object lesson to you," my sponsor said when I confessed to her. "Satan is always waiting to tempt you to make you turn your back on your Lord."

Looking back, it is clear to me that the watchful attention of my sponsors in the church served to enhance my consciousness that whatever I did with my life *mattered*. They added to the security given to me by the quiet insistence of my mother and especially my grandmother that their children's lives were a precious gift. Often, Grandma would sense this awareness beginning to flag in us. When this happened—even when we were not aware of it—she would gather us around and tell us a story that came from her life as a slave.

Once or twice a year, the slave master would permit a slave preacher from a neighboring plantation to come over to preach to his slaves. The slave preacher followed a long tradition, which has hovered over the style of certain black preachers even to the present time. It is to bring the sermon to a grand climax by a dramatization of the crucifixion and resurrection of Jesus. At such times, one would wait for the moment when the preacher would come to this grand, creative exposition. Sometimes he would begin in Gethsemane "with sweat like drops of blood running down . . ." or with Jesus hanging on the cross. But always there was the telling of the timeless story of the seven last words, the mother at the foot of the cross, the darkening sun, and the astonishment of the soldiers—all etched in language of stark reality. At the end, he would be exhausted, but his congregation would be uplifted and sustained with courage to withstand the difficulties of the week to come. When the slave preacher told the Calvary narrative to my grandmother and the other slaves, it had the same effect on them as it would later have on their descendants. But this preacher, when he had finished, would pause, his eyes scrutinizing every face in the congregation, and then he would tell them, "You are not niggers! You are not slaves! You are God's children!"

When my grandmother got to that part of her story, there would be a slight stiffening in her spine as we sucked in our breath. When she had finished, our spirits were restored.

Thornton Smith, my cousin, and Dr. Stockings were my masculine idols in those early years. As a young man, Thornton had been a semipro baseball player, but when I first knew him, he owned a restaurant in Midway, where I worked occasionally, churning ice cream in a large five-gallon freezer. In the summertime he would take me freshwater fishing on a large lake about fifty miles inland from the coast, a favorite place for Thornton because he had a friend there who kept boats and owned a large grove of orange and grapefruit trees. We fished for a panfish called "brims," and when we'd filled a washtub, we'd pack them in ice for the return to the restaurant.

Thornton always seemed to be his own man. Whenever Mamma needed personal advice, she turned to Thornton. Once or twice a month, he would come by on his bicycle just to have a few words with her. And he was a good businessman and a community leader. In addition to the restaurant, he owned property in various sections of Midway.

He was a wise man, unacquainted with fear. For many years the Ku Klux Klan was in control of local government. The best efforts of Daytona's "good citizens" could not get rid of them. During this period, Thornton was buying his restaurant supplies from a Mr. Armstrong, who headed the local reform movement. Thornton suggested to Armstrong that if the Klan was to be turned out, it could happen only if the local elections were open to Negroes. At first, Armstrong rejected such a radical idea out of

21

hand, but the next time they saw each other, he said, "Smith, we've talked it over and decided that we will give the local vote to all colored people who are property owners and taxpayers."

As Thornton had predicted, the Klan was voted out at the next election. A few days after the reform group was installed, Mr. Armstrong thanked Thornton for what he and his "boys" had done. Then he offered him an envelope full of money. Thornton refused. "We want," he said, "a new school building, and we want uniformed Negro policemen in Midway, Newtown, and Waycross." Within a few months we had both.

When he first came to town, Dr. Stockings lived at Mrs. Singleton's boardinghouse near our church. Mrs. Singleton was a quiet and gentle woman who lovingly provided a home for him as he slowly established his practice. He refused to join the church and it cost him: there was a feeling in our community that if a doctor did not belong to the church as a devout Christian, he was out of touch with the spirit of God. No one wanted to trust his or her life to such a person, however skilled.

One night our church held a food sale at the Odd Fellows Hall near the church. The first floor was filled with tables laden with food, including my mother's famous chicken "purlo," which consisted of rice cooked in broth made from chicken feet and giblets, seasoned with onions, black pepper, and some ingredients known only to her. We sold our "purlo" as others were selling meats, vegetables, baked goods, and homemade ice cream. Dr. Stockings did not come, but sat on the front porch of the boardinghouse across the street, observing the activity. Suddenly, into the hall walked the town bully, Paul Wells. He was a quiet man when sober but wild when drunk. He was just drunk enough to be mean; and he had a pistol in his hand. Everyone dove for cover. Then out of nowhere, Dr. Stockings appeared at the door. Silently he walked over to Paul and struck him one blow on the chin, knocking him down. Paul got up, put his pistol in his pocket, and walked out. After that, Dr. Stockings's medical practice flourished—though he still refused to join the church.

Dr. Stockings showed an interest in me from the beginning. He spent hours talking about the kind of service I could render if I gave myself to the study of medicine. He had little regard for the ministry and was genuinely distressed that I would waste my intellectual gifts on such a vocation. He was convinced my place was in medicine; he felt so strongly about this that he offered to see me through medical school if I would only make the choice. All through the years, until his death in 1963, I visited him whenever I went home. The last time I saw him he was dying and very weak. He did not ask me to pray, but he did want to hear me read a psalm. In farewell to my friend of fifty years, I read from my favorite, Psalm 139.

As a boy growing up in Daytona, I was of course familiar with how Mary McLeod Bethune started her school and I knew the mission she felt she was fulfilling. Very often she would come to our church, usually on the fifth Sunday night, and she would talk of her dreams for Negro youth. Often she would sing a solo. Always, the congregation gave her a collection for her work; and sometimes we attended her Sunday afternoon temperance meetings. The most memorable aspect of those Sunday afternoons was the lack of segregation in the seating arrangements. Many tourists attended, sitting wherever there were empty seats. There was no special section for white people. In that first decade of the century, Mrs. Bethune provided a unique leadership, involved in all the problems of Negro life in town, and at times she was the spokesperson on behalf of the entire Negro community. We attended commencement services at the school whenever Mamma could take us. They inspired me, even though it was a girls' school. Mrs. Bethune knew Mamma by name and whenever by chance she encountered me, she inquired about her. Though few local girls could afford to attend, the very presence of the school, and the inner strength and authority of Mrs. Bethune, gave boys like me a view of possibilities to be realized in some distant future. Later, both my wife Sue and I became involved in Mrs. Bethune's visionary crusade to uplift black women and young people. Sue organized and became the first editor of the *Aframerican Woman's Journal*, the official publication of the National Council of Negro Women, which Mrs. Bethune founded in 1935. Sue's mother donated the money to establish the museum and library archives of the council. When Mrs. Bethune died, it was my privilege to deliver her eulogy.

Public education for black children in Daytona ended with the seventh grade. Without an eighth grade, there could be no demand for a black high school; and if by chance a demand were made, it could be denied on the ground that no black children could qualify.

After I completed the seventh grade, our principal, Professor Howard, volunteered to teach me the eighth grade on his own time. At the end of the winter he informed the public school superintendent that he had a boy who was ready to take the eighth-grade examination and asked permission to give the test. The superintendent agreed to let me take the test, but only on the condition that he examine me himself. I passed, and a short time later the eighth-grade level was added to the Negro public school.

There were only three public high schools for black children in the entire state of Florida, but there were several private church-supported schools, the nearest to Daytona Beach being Florida Baptist Academy of Jacksonville. A cousin who lived in Jacksonville told my mother that if I enrolled in the academy, I could live with him and his wife, doing chores around the house in exchange for a room and one meal a day.

When the time came to leave for Jacksonville, I packed a borrowed old trunk with no lock and no handles, roped it securely, said my good-byes, and left for the railway station. When I bought my ticket, the agent refused to check my trunk on my ticket because the regulations stipulated that the check must be attached to the trunk handle, not to a rope. The trunk would have to be sent express but I had no money except for a dollar and a few cents left after I bought my ticket.

I sat down on the steps of the railway station and cried my heart out. Presently I opened my eyes and saw before me a large pair of work shoes. My eyes crawled upward until I saw the man's face. He was a black man, dressed in overalls and a denim cap. As he looked down at me he rolled a cigarette and lit it. Then he said, "Boy, what in hell are you crying about?"

And I told him.

"If you're trying to get out of this damn town to get an education, the least I can do is to help you. Come with me," he said.

He took me around to the agent and asked, "How much does it take to send this boy's trunk to Jacksonville?"

Then he took out his rawhide money bag and counted the money out. When the agent handed him the receipt, he handed it to me. Then, without a word, he turned and disappeared down the railroad track. I never saw him again.

The four years in high school were not easy years. There was never enough food and my health began to suffer. It was soon apparent that I would need extra money for food. As my mother could not afford to help me, I asked a few relatives for help. My cousin Thornton responded, sending me money every week to buy fresh eggs and extra milk.

At the end of my first year in Jacksonville, I learned that I could no longer board with my cousin in the fall. I would have to become a boarding student at a minimum of five dollars per month with the privilege of working out the rest of the cost. Somehow I would have to raise the money that summer at home.

One of my friends, Pierce Tucker, ran a shoeshine stand in Daytona, and he let me fill in for him during his vacation. Although I could keep all the money I made, I had neither the skill nor the manner to be a successful bootblack. I made very little money and my prospects for continuing my education dimmed. A few days before Pierce returned, two events happened that proved to be momentous. I was seated on the shoeshine stand thinking about my plight when, for some reason, I noticed the gables of a house directly across the river. They stood high above the trees. I knew it was the winter home of Mr. James N. Gamble of the Procter and Gamble soap company. He was well known in our community because of his generosity, particularly in making gifts to Mrs. Bethune's school. On impulse, I decided to write a letter to him asking for a loan.

I found writing paper immediately and, in my best penmanship, wrote the letter. I told him my age, where I was in school, my grades, and why I wanted to continue my education. It was then that I realized that I did not know his address. His summer caretaker was a member of our church. He could give me the address, but then he would question me about the letter, and this was a private matter. A local insurance agency handled the property, but of course they would never give me the address. Then, returning to work after lunch, I rode past the home of a very ill-tempered woman who came out of her front door just as I was riding by and yelled, "Boy! Come here." I put on my brakes and wheeled around. She scrutinized me for a moment, then said, "You look like a boy who can be trusted. Here, mail these letters."

I took the letters and was on my way. Just before I put them in the mailbox, I looked at them, and to my utter amazement, one was addressed to Mr. James N. Gamble, 1430 Union Trust Building, Cincinnati, Ohio.

Within a week there came a reply. It was the first typewritten letter I had ever received. It was addressed to Mr. Howard Thurman, 614 Whitehall Street, Daytona, Florida. He agreed to send me five dollars each month for nine months, beginning in September. For the rest of my high school and college years, he was a good and faithful friend.

When Pierce returned, I was out of a job, but a friend told me that Mr. Frederick Conrad, president of the Merchants Bank, wanted a trustworthy boy to live in his cottage on the beach, to protect the property, and to care for his two bird dogs. I went to see Mr. Conrad in his office and was thoroughly scrutinized again. At length he asked, "What's your name? Have you lived here all your life? Do you smoke? Do you drink? Do you run around with women? Are you going to school?"

My answers must have satisfied him, for he offered me the job on the spot, saying that he wanted me to move that very afternoon; the janitor of the bank would go with me and introduce me to the dogs as well as show me how to cook the dogs' food. I would have to learn to cook for myself. Fortunately, the janitor had once been a chef and taught me the principles of cooking meat, vegetables, and baking powder biscuits.

At first, Mr. Conrad came over only on weekends. When he discovered that I had learned to cook, he spent several nights each week, as well as weekends, at the cottage. A strong relationship developed between us—the factor of race seemingly irrelevant.

Among the men who came to visit Mr. Conrad on weekends was a Judge Fish from De Land, the county seat. One morning, he came into the kitchen saying, "Fred tells me you are in high school. What are you studying?" I told him my subjects.

"How much algebra do you know? What is $(a + b)^2$?"

I said, "$a^2 + 2ab + b^2$."

Whereupon he said, "Well, I'll be goddamned!"

Gradually Mr. Conrad became interested in my education. When I was hired, the agreement was that I would be paid in one lump sum at the end of the summer. There was no agreement on the amount. When the time came for me to return to school, he paid me generously, and he and Judge Fish gave me a large assortment of shirts, socks, and ties.

During the summer of 1918, the United States Government had a special Student Army Training Corps at Howard University in Washington, D.C. I was selected to represent my academy that summer. We lived in the dormitories at Howard and were sworn in as regular soldiers. Our officers were men from the black infantry and cavalry army units. The basic purpose of this summer camp was to train a number of select young black men with the skill and knowledge to qualify as sergeants when they were drafted into the regular army.

The majority of officers in the army and navy were southern white men, with many graduates of West Point and Annapolis. It was typical, for these men made the army their career out of economic necessity. The South had little regional industry. While it supplied raw materials, the factories and hence the economic power were in the North. Southern graduates of the military and naval academies tended to remain in the services. This meant that during the First World War, when thousands of men, black and white, were drafted, the black draftees would be at the mercy of southern white commissioned and noncommissioned officers, invariably leading to trouble. It was hoped, therefore, that the black men trained that summer at Howard would later be in direct charge of the black draftees in the segregated army.

When I returned to school, it became my responsibility to teach the men the drill regulation I learned at Howard. My duties were equivalent to those of a dean of men. I had to see that all lights were out in the dormitory at ten o'clock. I was not free to do my own studying until after that hour, and since I was carrying seven courses, I was up half the night studying. By Commencement time I was exhausted, but I was valedictorian of my class. The night of the junior reception for the seniors, while I was responding to the juniors on behalf of my classmates, I collapsed. My mother, who had come to see me graduate, was beside herself with fear and anxiety. She insisted on taking me home at once. I insisted on staying until Commencement Day, because I was determined to give the valedictory oration. She conceded, but immediately after the ceremony, Mamma took me home to Daytona. The next day Dr. Stockings ordered me to bed for an indefinite period of absolute rest. I was even forbidden to read. I stood as much rest as I could, then I quietly prepared to go to Jacksonville to get a job for the summer, to earn enough money to go to Morehouse College in the fall.

My cousin found a job for me in the freight department of the wholesale bakery where he was employed. I worked ten hours a day, six days a week, for eleven dollars a week. A part of that money was spent to realize a lifelong ambition to take voice lessons. I paid a dollar twenty-five for a half-hour of instruction. I did not learn to sing very well, but I did learn how to breathe effectively while speaking and singing. Incidentally, this training enabled me, years later, to make as many as five speeches a day during a visit to India, Burma, and Ceylon.

In the fall I went to Morehouse College in Atlanta. This time my mother did not try to persuade me to come back home. She wrote regularly to urge me to be careful of my health, and when the time came for me to be graduated, I insisted that she come to Atlanta to meet the president and all my professors. When she met President John Hope she was overwhelmed. I did not know what to expect, given how very shy she was. I could scarcely believe my ears when she said, "I just want to thank you for what you've done for my boy."

"Oh, no," he replied, "it was done by you, long before he ever came here."

From that time forward, whatever I was doing, I managed to get home once or twice a year. Each time I returned I would spend long hours talking with Mamma. Finally, she was able to stop working, and as the years of weariness melted away, she remembered facts about the family she thought she had forgotten, and began to enjoy her reminiscences. As for me, on each visit I would go to my oak tree to lean against it for an intense moment of past intimacy.

II

Years in Training

1. Morehouse

Morehouse College, where I enrolled in 1919, was founded for black men by the American Baptist Missionary Society and was originally called the Atlanta Baptist College. It was one of several colleges established by various Christian churches in the aftermath of the Civil War as an expression of conscience and concern for the education of freed slaves. Most were located in the South. The exceptions were Lincoln University and Cheyney Teacher Training School, both in Pennsylvania, and Wilberforce University in Ohio. Initially the colleges maintained affiliated secondary schools, because southern states made little or no provision for the public secondary education of freedmen and their children. By the time I entered Morehouse, however, its high school academy had closed, notwithstanding the fact that the first public high school for black children in Atlanta was not opened until 1923, the year I graduated from Morehouse, even though the black population of the city had climbed by that time to nearly eighty thousand.

Traditionally, any student graduating as valedictorian from a Baptist secondary school received a tuition scholarship to Morehouse, as I did. Without this aid, I would not have been able to attend college.

Bill James was the only student I knew when I arrived at Morehouse. He was a gifted violinist, called "Fiddler" by everyone. (Years after, on the faculty of Spelman College in Atlanta, he was director of music and one of the finest interpreters and composers of Afro-American music.) When I saw him the summer before school began, I expressed my hope that we might room together, for I was apprehensive about being far away from home, in an all-male environment for the first time in my life.

As it turned out, I had no choice as to roommates. I was assigned

Dick Richardson, a football player on campus, a man's man and tough. He had a kind heart and gracious spirit and we liked each other at once. He entertained me with football stories. "I threw that fellow so hard," he would say, "that he dug up potatoes 'way down in Macon County."

The routine of life in college was simple. There was a daily chapel, faculty presiding, from 9:30 to 10:00 A.M., Monday through Friday, and on Tuesday nights, immediately after supper, an informal religious meeting, led usually by senior students.

There was no student government, but there were several dominant student organizations. The student managers of the various teams were selected by the athletic association. There was strong competition for managerial jobs because managers could travel with the teams. Meetings of the athletic association were always lively and sometimes stormy, particularly during the annual meeting for the election of officers. The association had a faculty adviser, as did all the student organizations, but there was no mistaking the fact that it belonged to the students.

Another major organization was the Young Men's Christian Association. The student YMCA at Morehouse was a part of the national student YMCA and affiliated with the Colored Men's Division of the national organization. The student president of the YMCA was regarded as the religious leader on campus.

The Debating Society was small and prestigious. Morehouse belonged to a debating circle that included Talladega College in Alabama, Fisk University in Nashville, and Knoxville College in Tennessee. These four colleges debated one another annually. As a rule, one did not make the team until senior year. James Nabrit, now president emeritus of Howard University, and I were senior debaters; our coach was Benjamin E. Mays, now president emeritus of Morehouse College.

Although there was no student government, each class had its own elected officers. There was a monthly literary magazine, *The Athenaeum,* whose editor was regarded as an intellectual and a skilled writer. It was the dream of many students—I was one—to have a poem, a short story, or an essay accepted by *The Athenaeum.* I shall always remember the thrill of first seeing my name in print as the author of a little poem.

My class published the first senior yearbook in the history of the college, *The Torch*, in 1923. I was elected editor.

The informal life of the campus was rich and full of ritual. We had our meals together in the large dining room. Seniors were permitted to sit together at senior tables. The food was no better at the senior table, but the conversation certainly was. A favorite pastime at my senior table was a word game. Each day, at our midday meal, one of us would use a new word in a sentence. The rest of us tried to guess its definition, either lexically or from the context in which the word was used. The competition was in deadly earnest: our vocabularies increased with each meal. The library was small by any present standard. Many of the books had been given to the college by retired northern white ministers. Jim Nabrit and I undertook to read every book in the library. He started at the top shelves and I at the bottom, and we worked our way across. We did in fact read every one.

I was profoundly affected by the sense of mission the college inculcated in us. We understood that our job was to learn so that we could go back into our communities and teach others. Many of the students were going into the ministry; many were the sons of ministers, which accounted in some measure for the missionary spirit of the place. But over and above this, we were always inspired to keep alive our responsibility to the many, many others who had not been fortunate enough to go to college. Almost every student taught a Sunday School class in one of the city's churches. There was no formal worship service on Sunday morning in the college chapel; instead, an early Sabbath service of about twenty minutes took place. After that, we were free to scatter throughout the city to participate in the religious services of the various black churches. These churches welcomed us not only because, as Morehouse men (and some of the pastors had been Morehouse men), we provided leadership and inspiration to the youth, but also because our presence was sometimes an inspiration to the congregation as a whole.

Pervading all was the extraordinary leadership of two men, President John Hope and Dean Samuel Howard Archer. John Hope was a graduate of Worcester Academy and Brown University. His Phi Beta Kappa key, worn from a chain on his vest, was the first I had ever seen. Finally I knew what my high school teacher had meant by the "gold key." He was the first black man to become president of Morehouse College. Genteel, scholarly, decorous, he talked to us in chapel every Tuesday morning. This constituted perhaps our greatest single course of instruction in the four undergraduate years. His talks spanned the entire field of contemporary life. Although a layman, John Hope was an important churchman. He traveled widely and always brought back to us news of the winds that were stirring in the world far beyond our campus.

He always addressed us as "young gentlemen." What this term of respect meant to our faltering egos can only be understood against the backdrop of the South of the 1920s. We were black men in Atlanta during a period when the state of Georgia was infamous for its racial brutality. Lynchings, burnings, unspeakable cruelties were the fundamentals of existence for black people. Our physical lives were of little value. Any encounter with a white person was inherently dangerous and frequently fatal. Those of us who managed to remain physically whole found our lives defined in less than human terms.

Our manhood, and that of our fathers, was denied on all levels by white society, a fact insidiously expressed in the way black men were addressed. No matter what his age, whether he was in his burgeoning twenties or full of years, the black man was never referred to as "mister," nor even by his surname. No. To the end of his days, he had to absorb the indignity of being called "boy," or "nigger," or "uncle." No wonder then that every time Dr. Hope addressed us as "young gentlemen," the seeds of self-worth and confidence, long dormant, began to germinate and sprout. The attitudes we developed toward ourselves, as a result of this influence, set Morehouse men apart. It was not unusual, for example, to be identified as a Morehouse man by complete strangers, because of this subtle but dramatic sense of self.

Dr. Hope put his signature on us in another way. No man could get a degree from the college until he had conceived and memorized an original oration. We were required to write one each year for four years and were not permitted to graduate until we had given our orations in Friday chapel in front of the student body and the faculty. Occasionally a man would come to his senior year without having delivered the earlier orations. He would then be required to write and deliver all four original discourses during his last year. We were thus trained in public speaking before what was the most critical audience in the world for us—our classmates and professors. If we forgot our lines, there was no prompting. We would have to try again the next week, and the next, until we were able to deliver the speech effectively and well. We learned to think on our feet and to extemporize. Later, during my early postgraduate years, members of the audience would frequently come up to me after one of my talks to say, "You're one of John Hope's men, aren't you?" The Morehouse training was unmistakable.

During my senior year, Dr. Hope invited me to go with him to an interracial meeting at the Butler Street branch of the YMCA (Colored). Present at the meeting, together with a small group of black leaders from the colleges and the wider community, were a handful of southern white liberals. One of these men reported on his efforts to change the seating in the city auditorium on the occasion of a concert by Roland Hayes. Traditionally, Negroes sat only in the balcony or at the very back of the auditorium. This man had persuaded the city fathers to change the seating arrangements so that the line separating the races would be vertical rather than horizontal. The center aisle would be the demarcation line upstairs and down, whites on one side and we on the other. I was so impatient and disgusted with this bit of racial legerdemain that I walked out of the meeting. Dr. Hope followed me. He put his hands on my shoulders and said, "Thurman, I know how you feel about what is going on in there, but you must remember that these are the best and most liberal men in the entire South. We must work with them. There *is* no one else. Remember." I did remember, and his advice helped me grow in understanding.

Dr. Hope's whole tenure as president was accented by such touches. While attending an international missionary conference in Jerusalem, Dr. Hope became friendly with the Anglican bishop of Uganda. They arranged for a Ugandan student of the bishop's choosing to come to Morehouse for four years on a full scholarship, the bishop to be responsible only for round-trip transportation.

Several years later the bishop chose such a student, arranged passage for him to New York, and advised Dr. Hope when he would be arriving so that a representative of the college could meet him. The letter was misdirected. As a result no one met the young man and he was held on Ellis Island until his passage could be booked to Liverpool and back to Uganda. Weeks later, Dr. Hope underwent major surgery and decided to convalesce on a cruise to Europe. It happened that the ship on which he was traveling was the very one carrying the young African back on the first leg of his long journey home. Dr. Hope had the custom of walking through third class whenever he traveled, to see if there were any black people among the passengers. The two met during one of these walks. Dr. Hope asked him where he was going. The young man said, "My name is Balamu Mukasi. I am returning home in disgrace because a Dr. Hope in America has betrayed my bishop." Then he told the story. Arrangements were made for Mukasi's return to America by the next ship. His education at Morehouse was assured. Such a man was John Hope.

If Dr. Hope was the guiding mentor of Morehouse, Dean Archer was the wise, supportive father. He stood over six feet tall and exuded vitality, tempered by a glowing warmth of spirit. The men of the college honored and liked President Hope. They revered and loved Dean Archer. Wherever Morehouse men of his period come together even today, each one has his special story to tell about "Big Boy," as we called him.

Dean Archer was a great teacher. Not only did he plumb the mysteries of mathematics and the intricacies of the syllogism (he taught mathematics and logic), but he helped us define the meaning of the personal pilgrimage on which we were all embarked. One incident, also involving an African student, reveals perhaps better than any other the great heart of this beloved man. The student was supplementing his small scholarship by working in the college kitchen. His supervisor was the steward, a difficult and overbearing man. Tensions between the two had intensified to such a degree that the young man broke under the pressure.

One evening during supper, he came into the dining room armed with a pistol, asking for the steward. He went directly to the faculty table. As if by a single command, everyone, students and faculty alike, ducked under his own table—everyone, that is, except for one professor who was known for his starched collar and cuffs and highly dignified demeanor. Nevertheless, when he discovered that he alone faced the student's gun, he also scrambled under his table. The story goes that as he did so, he shoved one of his female colleagues aside, saying, "I'm sorry, but you're a lady, he won't shoot you. We'll have to exchange places!"

At length, the young man was persuaded to put his weapon down and was sent to his room. A discipline committee was formed on the spot, which voted then and there to expel him. Big Boy asked them to reconsider, and when they refused, he asked which of them would take responsibility for paying the student's fare back to Africa. There were no volunteers. Big Boy then invited the student to his home, where he and Mrs. Archer gave him the care he so badly needed. They fed him and put him to bed on the sleeping porch. After a few days, his emotional balance restored, he returned to the dormitory. The incident was soon forgotten by everyone—except that troubled student, who would never forget the kindness of Dean Archer.

How we loved him! Another student, whom Big Boy had expelled for cause, said to me as he was leaving the campus for good, "Before I leave, I must say good-bye to Big Boy. I don't want him to think I hold it against him because he had to send me home. I don't think Big Boy would do anything to hurt anybody."

During my senior year, I had a disciplinary encounter with Big Boy myself. One evening at supper I was suddenly overcome with loathing for the grits and gravy on my plate. I walked out. As if by prearrangement, all the men at my table followed me out of the dining hall. The revolt was spontaneous, yet I was reported to the discipline committee as the ringleader, with a recommendation that I be suspended. I was not advised of this until the next day, when the dean invited me into his office. He said, "Mr. Thurman, you have gathered mud on your escutcheon," and told me about the action of the committee. "Suppose you tell me exactly what happened." I told him, he asked no questions, and I never heard of the affair again.

Hope and Archer—what a team!—were pioneers in education: they undergirded the will to manhood for generations of young black men, tapping out the timeless rhythm of "Yes," which

39

countered all the negatives beating in upon us from the hostile environment by which we were surrounded.

E. Franklin Frazier, the eminent sociologist, began his celebrated teaching career at Morehouse during my undergraduate days. He was a graduate of Howard University, regarded at that time as the capstone of Negro education in America. To be a graduate of Howard University was to be a crown prince. Frazier had very little, if any, experience of the Deep South. Not only was he a graduate of Howard, but he had earned his master's degree from Clark University, in Worcester, Massachusetts. He had his own classroom, a section of which he converted into a small study. It was lined with shelves that held what seemed to us at the time to be an enormous number of books for one person's exclusive use. The sight of Frazier at work in that study day and night was a visible example of scholarship for all of us.

Frazier was independent and straightforward. At the end of a football rally, during my senior year and Frazier's first year at the college, the first chords of "Morehouse College, Bless Her Name" were struck. The singing of this college anthem was the emotional zenith of any assembly at Morehouse. We stood as a man, students and faculty alike. Frazier remained seated. We were outraged. That afternoon an ad hoc committee went to see him to protest his sacrilegious behavior. He listened, and when we had finished, he said, "At the present time, the only thing that Morehouse means to me is a job, nothing more. I am not a hypocrite. When the time comes that this college means more than this to me, I'll stand for the anthem, but not before." We were frustrated by his response but impressed. I had never before encountered such unabashed honesty.

Frazier did not participate in the religious services of the college. In the classroom he exercised absolute authority. His lectures were conversational in tone, but highly persuasive. He did not indulge in flights of oratory, but spoke in simple language. He was spellbinding. I had never had a teacher quite like him before. (I had taken a course in municipal government at Columbia University the previous summer and had signed up early for Frazier's course in Social Origins. My self-image was inflated by the fact that I had earned an A grade in the summer course at Columbia, and had in fact excelled in all my college courses. To put it plainly, I was a nuisance, though I saw myself at the time only as a conscientious student, eager to learn.)

One memorable morning, after Frazier had called the roll, he turned to me in complete exasperation and said, "Howard Thurman, if Dean Archer wanted you to teach this course, you would be standing where I am and I would be seated where you are. Since he has not made such a decision, I am the teacher and you are the student. From this day forward you are not to speak a word in this course, not even to answer 'present' when the roll is called. Understand?" With that, he proceeded with the lecture.

I wrote all the papers and the final examination. My term paper was a study of the profit-sharing system of Hart, Schaffner and Marx, the manufacturers of men's clothing. Frazier gave me an A for the paper, the final exam, and the course. From that time until his death, we were good friends, serving together for some years on the faculty of Howard University. Neither of us ever referred to this incident, but I shall be forever grateful for the lesson. Humility is taught by such as he.

Both E. Franklin Frazier and Benjamin Mays were young faculty members in their late twenties, not much older than many of us in the student body. I was twenty-three when I finished college. This was the average age of my classmates, though some upperclassmen were older by several years. All of our teachers were not young men from eastern and northern colleges, however. There were many seasoned men who were also inspiring teachers, touching us at a place in ourselves beyond all our faults and all our virtues. They placed over our heads a crown that for the rest of our lives we would be trying to grow tall enough to wear. This was a gift far greater than the imparting of information and facts.

One such teacher was Gary Moore, who taught sociology and conversational French. He was perhaps the first Morehouse man to have his B.A. degree validated by Columbia University. The validation of degrees was necessary at that time because most of the black colleges were not accredited; therefore, students receiving undergraduate degrees at these institutions were required to take a fifth undergraduate year at an accredited college before being accepted for graduate study. Moore was a bachelor and lived in one of the dormitories. He seemed to have time to visit with any student who knocked on his door. He even maintained a small emergency loan fund for students. We could always borrow a dollar or two from Professor Moore to help us over a rough spot. Most of us were in such financial straits that this fund often stood between us and calamity.

Lorimer Milton guided me through my major in economics. He was a graduate of Dunbar High School in Washington, D.C., and received his A.B. and M.A. degrees in economics from Brown University. He was short in stature, with a slight hesitation in his speech. This gave the listener a split second to race ahead and try to complete the word or sentence before Milton could. The result was that one's mind rarely strayed from Milton's lectures. We became friends instantly. We came from vastly different worlds, but we met above the timber line where the language of the mind and spirit become universal. Much of my spare time was spent in his dormitory room, where our conversations ranged wide and deep. He had very little interest in religion and social issues as such, but he opened to me exciting possibilities in the world of business and economics and urged me to consider a career in business. He considered me an apt student, so much so that when he became seriously ill for several weeks, he asked me to take over his classes during his absence. Milton was such a brilliant teacher that I have thought, in the years since, that even with his amazing success as president of the Citizens Bank and Trust Company in Atlanta, his final full-time commitment to business and finance was a serious loss to education. Nevertheless, through the years since that far-off time, he has been peripherally involved in the education of our youth, climaxing this aspect of his career by serving as chairman of the board of trustees of Howard University for more than a decade.

Each instructor at Morehouse made his special contribution to the direction our lives would ultimately take. Had it not been for Benjamin Mays, for example, it is doubtful that I would have journeyed north to Columbia University to take the course that resulted in the youthful arrogance that so exasperated E. Franklin Frazier. Mays first awakened in me a keen interest in philosophy. At that time, Morehouse offered a course in logic and a course in ethics, neither of which was strictly in the field, and no courses whatever in formal philosophy. I do not think this was accidental. In the missionary colleges of the South, few (if any) courses were offered in the formal study of philosophy. I believe that the shapers of our minds, with clear but limited insight into the nature of our struggle for survival and development in American life, particularly in the South, recognized the real possibility that to be disciplined in the origins and development of ideas would ultimately bring under critical judgment the society and our predicament in it. This, in turn, would contribute to our unease and restlessness, which would be disastrous, they felt, for us and for our people.

By the end of my sophomore year I was determined to take such a course wherever I could find a college that would admit me to a summer school. Gary Moore had often talked about the summer school at Columbia. I sent for a bulletin and discovered that I could take at least two good courses in philosophy—"Reflective Thinking" and "An Introduction to the Study of Philosophy." I calculated the cost of tuition and figured a minimum cost of fifty-five cents a day for food, plus round-trip train fare. Then I set about to win all the cash prizes to be awarded at Commencement. This would be a giant step toward my goal. I won them all.

Two problems remained. The first was where and how to live between the end of the school year in May and the opening of summer school at Columbia in early July. The second was to find living accommodations in New York. I had an uncle living in Cleveland who agreed to let me live with him during that interval if I would do chores for the family. In Cleveland, on the first Monday, I located the 79th Street branch library and presented myself to the librarian and asked for her help in preparing the courses I would begin in July. "I want to be able to understand what the professors are saying in their lectures. I have never read a book on philosophy. Can you help me?"

She examined my face for a long time, then she said, "Come with me." We went to the large reading room, where she had the custodian find a bookshelf, a chair, and a table for my use. "When you come back tomorrow, I will have on this shelf all the books in our branch that may be of help to you. When you finish them, I will get books from the main library." Every day, Monday through Friday, I went to the library and read what she had selected for me, trying to become familiar with the vocabulary and the terms and propositions of the subject. Most of the reading was in Greek philosophy, but there were also contemporary books on the history of European philosophy and a volume by William James.

When the time came to go to New York, I persuaded one of my closest student friends at Morehouse, George Van Buren, to share a room with me for six weeks. George had collected insurance on the death of his brother in the First World War, and some of this money went toward our rent. We had a comfortable room on West 131st Street, within walking distance of the campus. I found an excellent creamery where I could get an inexpensive breakfast. I took my second meal on the campus.

Perhaps the most significant single course I ever took, certainly during this critical period of my life, was the course in reflective thinking, taught by a young Ph.D. graduate in philosophy, E. A. Burt. In later years he became one of the great teachers at Cornell University. He had graduated from both Union Theological Seminary and Columbia University. We used two basic texts, John Dewey's *How We Think* and an anthology called *An Introduction to Reflective Thinking*, which had been the formal outline for a course that had been given as a team-teaching experiment in the Columbia Colleges. It was an analysis of the structure of reflective thinking as process. It examined a basic methodological approach to problem-solving in all fields of investigation, from simple decision-making to the understanding and treatment of disease and the most confused patterns of human behavior. This course established for me a basic approach that I would use not only in my subsequent work as a counselor but also in thinking through the complex and complicated problems I would encounter in my personal life and as a social being. As a tool of the mind, there is no way by which the value of this course can be measured or assessed.

Each Sunday during that summer I attended services at the Fifth Avenue Presbyterian Church, never dreaming that one day I would preach a sermon from that very pulpit. The summer minister was Dr. Hugh Black, the great Scottish preacher, then a professor at Union Seminary. He was tall, gaunt in appearance, with reddened cheeks showing from a hollow face. His long bony fingers would lace his shock of gray hair at certain moments of high drama in his sermon.

I had never entered a church like Fifth Avenue Presbyterian. To my young eyes it was vast and ornate and, above all, awe-inspiring. The first few pews in the front were slanted so that one could look up into the face of the preacher without straining. The ushers wore cutaway coats, with a flower in the lapel, and gray-striped trousers. They seemed to me the essence of dignity. The pews had little name plates on them. I had no idea what they meant, so when I arrived on that first Sunday I took a seat in a pew, two from the front. Presently an usher came down to speak to me. Since I was seated in a family pew, he assumed that I was a servant of the family. I explained who I was and why I was there. He seemed pleased that I wanted to hear the famous preacher and assured me that because the family was away for the summer, it would be all right for me to sit in that pew each Sunday.

The mind of Hugh Black roamed over the vast areas of biblical thought and gave listeners glad and dramatic tidings from the heart and spirit. All this, and his delightful Scottish brogue!

My vocational choice was settled by the time I reached my senior year. The college offered me an instructorship in economics and would have given me assistance in validating my B.A. degree the next year at the University of Chicago. I decided against it. I wanted to go to seminary, of this I was certain. I was less sure of the ultimate expression the religious training would take.

From high school days, I had heard about the Newton Theological Seminary in Newton, Massachusetts. The school carried an attractive advertisement in the *Watchman Examiner*, a Baptist journal that I had seen in our little academy library in Jacksonville. I wrote a letter to Newton Seminary inquiring about admission. In reply, I received a very cordial letter from the president expressing his regret that the school did not admit Negroes, and referring me to Virginia Union, a Baptist missionary college in Richmond, Virginia. The letter wished me well. It assured me that at Virginia Union I would be able to secure the kind of training I would need to provide religious leadership for my people.

45

2. Rochester

In the spring of 1926, I applied to the Rochester Theological Seminary in Rochester, New York. Certain things commended the school to me. Dr. Charles Hubert, a graduate of Rochester, taught a course in religion at Morehouse and was a solid, pervasive influence on the life of all the college men of my generation. Mordecai Johnson was also a graduate of Rochester. Morehouse men had established a reputation for high scholarship there that challenged those who followed.

In due course I was accepted. The letter of acceptance made it clear to me that I was privileged to be included in the new class. I knew that it was the policy of the seminary to have no more than two Negroes enrolled in any given year.

When I entered seminary, I experienced the most radical period of adjustment of my life up to that moment. I was living for the first time in a totally white world. The impact of this fact alone was staggering. All my professors were white men, who seemed quite old to me, compared with the more youthful teachers of my Morehouse days. These men were stereotypical "professors." They were devout and formal. Each class session began with prayer. All students were addressed as "mister." At daily chapel we were addressed either by one of them, or by a distinguished visitor of whom I had never heard. The order of service was stylized in a manner outside the context of my experience.

At the first meeting of each class, students were given a long reading list, an outline of the course requirements, and information concerning the reserved shelf of books for each course, to be found in the library. Then a schedule of term papers, along with due dates, was distributed. And finally the aim and the scope of the course were specifically described. The summer at Columbia

46

had given me a foretaste of this. But the general atmosphere at Rochester contrasted sharply with the more personal and responsive ambience of Morehouse College.

The majority of my classmates were from eastern and midwestern colleges, with Colgate University, Denison University, and the University of Rochester having the largest representation. At first my classmates seemed more broadly educated than I, and more widely read, and I felt intimidated by this. But as the weeks wore on I discovered that this was not the case and I could hold my own very well; my anxiety diminished.

The library was my refuge and my joy. The librarian, a middle-aged woman with beautiful gray hair and a warm and sensitive spirit, took a special interest in me. She responded to my eagerness, which I made no effort to conceal. For the first time I had hundreds, nay, thousands, of books at my disposal, with open stacks and magazines of every description, many of which I had never seen before. My earlier exposure to the vast library resources at Columbia University had been limited by my status as a summer school student, which prevented me from feeling completely at home in my use of the facility. I had taken full advantage of the library in Cleveland, but its resources were limited, to some extent. But now, at last the world of books was mine for the asking. I spent hours each week wandering around in the stacks, taking down first one book, then another, examining the title, reading the foreword and the table of contents, leafing through the pages, reading a paragraph here and there, getting the feel of the book and familiarizing myself with writers across centuries who would in time become as closely related to me as my personal friends.

Friday afternoons I would take my book bag to the library. My friend the librarian placed no limit upon the number of books I could take out at any given time. She allowed me to use books on reserve from Friday evening until Monday morning when the library opened. I developed a system for doing as much reading as possible. I kept certain books in the bathroom. Others I read only during the ten-minute intervals between classes. Inasmuch as all the classrooms were in the same area, as soon as one professor ended his lecture, I would hasten to the next classroom, take my seat, and read until the lecture started. Once a week I went across town on the streetcar for a group meeting at the YWCA, and I read coming and going. All of this in addition to regular reading and study times in the afternoons and far into the night. During my first year especially, my professors would often make references that were unfamiliar to me. When this happened I would ask for details and further references at the end of class. Often my professors would make suggestions to me for supplemental reading. I felt I had much to overcome because of a restricted literary background, but it was not long before I realized that most of my classmates were in no way better equipped than I to deal with ideas, though in one particular way they seemed to have an unyielding advantage. They were at home in this world, and I felt a stranger. Whether they were gifted intellectually, or mediocre, the fact remained that this world belonged to them. My sense of alienation was reinforced by the attitude of certain professors and visiting lecturers. Any discussions about broad church policy or programs assumed that I was innately a person apart.

One day I was invited to talk before a district missionary meeting of Baptist women. I asked Dr. Barbour, president of the seminary and himself a great preacher, what I should talk about.

"I would describe a Negro camp meeting. The ladies will find that most interesting."

Now I knew very little about Negro camp meetings, but it was obvious to Dr. Barbour what my one area of expertise must surely be. We were from different worlds, to be sure. But the differences not only had to do with the general social climate, but were grounded in the inner prism of spirit and mind through which we gazed out upon the external world.

The city of Rochester itself seemed fabulous to me. I enjoyed window shopping, looking at all kinds of beautiful things—chinaware, furniture, linens, clothing. There were several excellent restaurants that served foods deliciously foreign to my palate. Generally, I was not troubled by the question of race; I was never refused service or otherwise insulted in any of the stores. By planning my time very carefully, I was able to see one movie each week. Every Friday I attended orchestra concerts at the Eastman School of Music. Rochester was the first stop of the Metropolitan Opera Company on tour. The Little Theater at the Eastman School gave chamber music concerts, and at the Eastman Theater I heard for the first and only time the entire "Ring" cycle.

There was a small black community in the city. Whenever possible I attended the Baptist Church. The minister there was a graduate of Howard University, as well as Rochester Seminary. These kind people opened their homes to me. I made many friends among them and began to feel a sense of belonging that slowly found its way back into my life in seminary.

The YWCA there had a colored branch; not so the YMCA. At the YWCA I was invited to teach in the adult education evening school, sharing what I had learned of books and letters with black people, most of whom worked as domestic servants by day.

I began to get many invitations to speak at the Sunday evening services of the churches in the surrounding towns and communities of western New York. Usually I spoke on some religious subject, but increasingly I was asked to discuss the race question. Often, before the meetings, I would be the guest of the minister's family at dinner. Most of them had never had any contact with black people before. The experience was always educational and sometimes awkward for us all. If there were little children in the family, I was delighted, because very early in my career I learned that if I made friends with the children in an atmosphere of total acceptance in the family, a tie would be established that time and circumstance could not alter. One evening I was scheduled to speak at the annual meeting of the men's club of a small church. The chairman invited me for dinner beforehand. His five-year-old daughter and I became friends instantly. At dinner she insisted on sitting next to me rather than at her usual place. About midway through the meal I thought I heard her whisper, "Stop, nigger! Stop!" More conversation followed around the table, and then I heard it again, and this time I was certain. Finally, her mother said, "Why don't you take him out into the kitchen and be sure to close the door so he can't come in and bother us," whereupon the child reached down, picked up a large black cat, and proceeded to the kitchen. At that moment I realized with a start that the family was unaware of the implications of the incident.

During the middle and late 1920s the Ku Klux Klan flourished in western New York. This surprised me, when I learned of it, because I had grown up associating the Klan with the persecution of Negroes in the South. I was all too familiar with the cross-burning, night-riding violence of the Klan.

But there were few black people in western New York during this period. The primary targets of the Klan, therefore, were Jews and Catholics. One of my roommates pastored a Baptist Church in a nearby town in which most of the men were Klan members. My roommate and the Methodist minister were the exceptions. It was the minister's custom to preach a sermon each month against the Klan. One night the Methodist Church was burned to the ground. The congregation then began to meet each week at the Baptist Church building, alternating between morning and evening services.

The first Sunday evening that the Methodist congregation gathered in the Baptist Church building, Klan members filled the church. At the offering, the Kleagle presented the minister with a rawhide bag filled with coins. The minister accepted it and offered a prayer of thanksgiving. The next day, when my roommate remonstrated with him about this, his reply was classic: "The Good Book says, 'The earth is the Lord's and the fullness thereof.' Sometimes the fullness gets into the Devil's hands and the sooner I take it out the better."

During my first year there, I spoke in almost every town in the area around Batavia and Rochester. After my last scheduled talk of the year, a man came up to me saying, "Well, this is your last talk until next fall because seminary closes this week. I have heard practically every sermon you have preached since last fall. I know where you went, what your subjects were, and how many people were in your audiences." He took a small notebook from his pocket to show me that he had such a record. Instantly, I knew him to be a Klansman, and my mind traveled back to another encounter I had had with the Klan that year.

I had been scheduled to preach at a church whose minister I did not know. The arrangements had been made by correspondence. The Saturday afternoon before I was to preach he appeared at my door at seminary to explain to me that there was considerable resistance to my coming. He wanted me to know this so that if I wanted to withdraw I could, and if I appeared I would be prepared for the situation. I asked, "Do you want me to come or to stay away? It makes no real difference to me, but you must live there after tomorrow."

He wanted me to keep the engagement. The next morning he met me at the Interurban station and we drove directly to the church. The building was located a hundred yards back from the street; a cement walk led directly to the entrance. When we arrived, men were lined up shoulder to shoulder on both sides of the walk. We ran the gauntlet, and violence was in the air. The minister was so upset that he walked to the pulpit without removing his coat or hat. My sermon text for that occasion was "Not by might, nor by power, but by My spirit, says the Lord."

It was not until I returned to the seminary in the afternoon that the reaction set in and I became so anguished that I lost my appetite and took to my bed until Monday morning.

By my second year, new vistas were opening up before me at many levels. Until I went to Rochester I had accepted the fact that I was a Christian, a practicing Christian. I believed sincerely in the necessity for loving my fellow man. It was a serious commitment; however, it had not ever occurred to me that my magnetic field of ethical awareness applied to other than my own people. Therefore, at Rochester, I found this commitment to brotherhood severely tested. Slowly I was drawn to certain of my classmates and they to me. My room became the gathering place. Now it happened that across the hall from my room was a suite for three students which was occupied by only two men. The two men, Red Mathews and Dave Voss, both a class ahead of me, invited me to move out of my single room and join them. Instinctively, I knew that if I were to make the move I could never be as I was before; a lifetime of conditioning would have to be overcome. I asked for time to think it over so that we could be sure that this was what we wanted. I knew also that if I moved in with them we would be breaking the long-established separate housing policy of the seminary. When I mentioned this to Dave and Red they said that they knew of no such policy and would, in any case, ignore it.

I moved in. The men in the dormitory took it in stride as far as I could ascertain. The authorities at first did not take kindly to the idea, but there was nothing that could be done about it. Officially, not a word was said directly to me, but both my room-mates were called to the office; they did not discuss with me the substance of their interview. And that was that.

My two roommates were very different in temperament and personality. Red was an extrovert, with a cheerful countenance and easy grace, the kind of man who would become a good pastor greatly beloved by his parishioners. In conversation, he always had the precise word and the completely adequate gesture, simple in itself but always effective. With red hair and lively eyes, he was a man easy to love. Our friendship lasted until the time of his death. I was delighted but not surprised to learn that he had named a son for me.

Years later his health failed and he gave up his ministry and moved to Southern California. I visited him in Los Angeles. We had not seen each other since my graduation. We talked of many things. He knew that his illness was terminal and so did I, but this was a zone of quiet held sacred between us. At the end of our visit he took me into his library. It was there that he broke the silence and spoke of his approaching death. He took down two volumes and gave them to me. "I will not need these books again; I want you to have them. This *Pastor's Manual* I bought in semi-nary, and it has been my companion ever since. In its margins are all my special notes and scribbles. I'll be happy knowing that it will now be your companion." The other book was a one-volume commentary of the Bible. "So much of what I did not learn about the Bible in seminary I have found in these pages," he said. It was our final meeting.

My other roommate, Dave Voss, had little interest in becoming a pastor or in the preaching ministry. By nature he was a teacher, with the instincts of the hunter when it came to the origin and the evolution of words. He seemed happiest when tracing the deriva-tion of words and marking the point at which their definitions were expanded by different cultures and generations. No word was accepted by Dave for its current usage alone. He had to know its journey and the relatives it had picked up along the way.

Dave was also an avid chess player. During our two years as roommates, he played chess by correspondence with a former classmate. Once a week the postcard with the move would arrive. Dave would take out his small chess set immediately, arrange the pieces, study carefully, make the move, write it on the card, and take it to the mailbox, all within the hour!

Dave and I maintained our correspondence through the years. He retired from his teaching career but continued his intellectual pursuits; until his death in 1978 he was among the most consistent supporters of the work of the Howard Thurman Educational Trust.

Rochester seemed to me to have the most consistently cold weather in the world. I had not experienced snow and ice before, not to speak of the bitter winds. I had seen snow only once, and that for about a half-hour in the winter of 1917 in Jacksonville. In the middle of the morning a light snow began falling, and classes were dismissed temporarily so we could run outside and enjoy it. But that first winter in Rochester found me ill prepared; I was unable to get winter-weight clothing before I arrived. But I made it through the year without contracting a single cold. It was a miracle. I had read somewhere that skiers and mountain climbers often wore heavy paper, tightly wrapped around their bodies, under their clothing, as a shield against the wind. I tried it—and it worked! I also found that if I ended my morning shower with cold water and rubbed down with alcohol, I could withstand the cold somewhat better. Before the end of that first year I met Jack Schooler, who, with his brother, owned Cornwall Men's Clothiers. They sold "seconds" of well-known clothing manufacturers. Jack and I became friends soon after our meeting, and for the rest of my days in Rochester and for more than ten years after graduation, I bought all my suits from Jack. He was a thoughtful friend and a wise merchant and he gave me good advice. "Howard," he would say, "I won't sell you this suit because it won't stand up to constant wear and you can only afford one suit. Buy something more durable."

The relative proximity of Rochester to New York City made it possible for me to take advantage of many of the cultural opportunities uniquely available in that city. I gained my first exposure to the New York theater during those three years. I managed to see Walter Hampden in the entire Shakespeare repertoire,

Blanche Yurka perform in her Ibsen series, and Pavlova dance in *Swan Lake*. I never missed an opportunity to go to the theater. If I could not find overnight lodging with a friend, I would sleep on a bench in Grand Central Station. This was an exhilarating time for me, full of rewards and possibilities. So many times I found myself quoting a poem by an unknown author I had learned many years before.

> I am tired of sailing my little boat
> Far inside the harbor bar—
> I want to go out where the big ships float
> Out on the deep where the great ones are.
> And should my frail craft prove too slight
> For waves that sweep those billows o'er,
> I'd rather go down in the stirring fight
> Than drowse to death by the sheltered shore.

Several teachers influenced my growth, but three stand out as being profoundly influential. Dr. Conrad Moehlman, professor of the history of Christianity, introduced me to the vast perspective of the Christian movement through the centuries, and the struggle for survival of the essential religion of Jesus. He exposed me to the issues surrounding the great creedal battles of the church. His acute observations, massive scholarship, and authentic sense of humor made historic movements seem contemporary, as very often they were.

Dr. Henry Burke Robins, silver-haired and somber, let us listen to the movement of the springs of his own spiritual landscape. He communicated the awe, the mystery, and the glory of the Presence. His course in the history of religion revealed a new world to me and prepared me for many encounters in my own journey.

The professor who had the most significant influence on my thought and my life was Dr. George Cross. He was a Canadian and had received his doctoral degree from the University of Chicago Divinity School. He taught systematic theology, an advanced course available only to students in the second semester of the middle year.

His lectures were concise and meticulously constructed, but he was not without his quiet humor. One day our class met immediately after chapel, where we had listened to a guest lecturer who made a point of telling us that he read more than two hundred books each year. As we took our seats in class, Dr. Cross opened his remarks with these words: "Two hundred books a year. Piffle. Let us pray." Dr. Cross had no reserve shelf in the library for reference books. What we did not get from his lectures he expected us to research independently. He dismantled the structures of orthodoxy with scrupulous scholarship. At first he seemed to me both pious and iconoclastic, ruthlessly dethroning our inherited orthodoxies. I was by turns fascinated and outraged by what seemed to me to be his supreme self-confidence.

His classes were governed by stern etiquette. For instance, no student was permitted to raise a question in class if he could not state his query with well-reasoned clarity. Dr. Cross would not permit us to criticize any conventional or orthodox position unless we could also make an equally persuasive case *for* the position we sought to undermine.

Very early in his course I developed the habit of reserving a page in my notebook, directly opposite the one on which I took notes of his lecture, to write the questions that were raised in my own mind by the lecture. Each Saturday morning whenever it was possible, which was often, I had a conference with him in his office during which we discussed these questions and I had a chance to air any disagreement or frustration. With the utmost patience and understanding, he would reduce my arguments to an ash. At the close of each conference I would leave, thoroughly humbled, only to reappear the following week, armed and ready for combat.

One of the first papers I wrote for him was a study of the doctrine of original sin in *The Confessions of St. Augustine.* I researched the subject thoroughly. Over the Thanksgiving recess I wrote my paper, working day and night. The final draft, with documentation and bibliography, ran to well over seventy pages. I could hardly wait to turn in my assignment. In a few days it was returned to me with a long note from Dr. Cross saying that the paper was completely unsatisfactory and would have to be rewritten. I was hurt and angry; I went to see him to express my utter confusion. When I had finished, he said to me, in a tone only slightly above a whisper, "Mr. Thurman, that paper is not worthy of your mind and ability. For some other men in the class the paper would be more than satisfactory, but from you, it is not enough. I insist that you start over again and give me a paper that is worthy of you!"

Dr. Cross encouraged his students to explore new ground. If we did not wish to select one of the topics on his suggested list for term papers we were permitted to submit our own topic and our reasons for the choice. Then if, in researching the topic, we could not identify suitable reference materials, Dr. Cross would suggest several titles, and these we had to use.

As I said earlier, the first two summers that I was a student at Rochester, I worked with the First Baptist Church of Roanoke, Virginia. The minister, Reverend A. L. James, had been the pastor of our family church when I was a little boy in Daytona, and was a close family friend. Cousin Arthur, as we called him, invited me to share in the work of the church and live with his family during the summer months. When I arrived, he told me, "The church does not know that I have arranged for you to assist me this summer. I am depending on you to prove yourself and to be so helpful in every way that they will suggest to me that I compensate you. Do you think you can do it?"

I was not prepared for this, but the challenge was exciting and completely irresistible. I worked in the Sunday School and directed a Daily Vacation Bible School for about three hundred children between the ages of seven and twelve. In addition, I shared all of the ministerial functions of the church with Cousin Arthur. I participated in everything from morning worship service to funerals.

I learned to drive an automobile during that first summer, a Hupmobile. After two attempts, and two failures, I passed the driver's exam and secured my license. But I found it next to impossible to keep my mind on the road when I drove. I would drive all around town in first gear, a trail of exhaust following behind. Before long my driving became notorious. No one in his right mind would ride with me. When I took burial ceremonies at the cemetery, cars would line up—all of them full to capacity—while my five-passenger car stood empty, save for me, the driver!

The climax came near the end of the summer. There were few

signal lights in town, but there were traffic officers at the busier intersections, one of which was two blocks from the church. One day, as I crossed this intersection, my mind wandering, I suddenly saw a huge figure jumping frantically to the side, out of the path of my car. The jumping figure was a policeman, and when I heard the blast of his shrill whistle, I stopped. "Oh! It's you again," he said, approaching the car. "I am going to have this out with Dr. James. He has got to take you off the street. You are going to kill somebody one of these days." He was as good as his word. After that, and for the rest of the summer, I drove only in authentic emergencies.

In my second and final summer in Roanoke I applied to my church in Daytona Beach for permission to have the Roanoke church ordain me for the ministry. The minister there refused, so it became necessary for me to join the First Baptist Church of Roanoke. This done, I applied for ordination. The date was set for convening an ordination council, made up of the delegates of the various churches. I invited my long-time friend, Dr. S. A. Owen, who gave me my preacher's license while I was still in college, to give the sermon of ordination. Not only did he agree to come, but he traveled at his own expense from Memphis, Tennessee.

I had no idea of the procedure for ordination as set forth by the churches of Virginia. I asked for permission to prepare and read a statement of faith. It was highly irregular, I was told, but my request was granted. Then I brashly announced that I did not want the laying on of hands during the prayer of ordination. This custom was altogether too old-fashioned, I argued, with all the arrogance of youth. At this point Cousin Arthur balked. "There will be the laying on of hands or there will be no ordination."

The day came. Dr. Owen arrived before noon. We gathered in the sanctuary. After all the delegates had been duly registered, the presiding minister turned the meeting over to an officer of the council, who served as the "catechizer." I read my statement of faith, which was preceded by an announcement that this was an unusual procedure and was granted as a special favor to the host minister. Then the questions began, running the gamut of religious doctrine within the scope of Virginia Baptist orthodoxy. The hours dragged on. After more than four hours of questioning, we were all exhausted and irritable. Finally, the secretary of the council, a young pastor who was a student and not much older than myself, raised the question of evolution. The Scopes trial was being held at the time. He spoke at length before coming to his question. "What does this young man really think about the inspiration of the Holy Scriptures? What he read from that piece of paper about the word of God could be said about Bryant's *Thanatopsis*." But he had talked so long to make his point that before I could respond, a motion was made to dismiss me, that my case might be discussed and a vote taken. It was duly seconded, but on the "question" the eldest minister said, "I would like to ask our younger brother only one question: When did God the Father and God the Son and God the Holy Spirit meet for the first time?" When I replied to the catechizer, in weariness and frustration, "I don't know, because I wasn't there," everybody laughed. Looking straight into my eyes, he answered his own question. "It was at the baptism of our Lord. I pray that They may see fit to meet in your heart." His words ended the meeting.

The ceremony of ordination was held at eight o'clock in the evening, and the moment of transcendent glory was for me the laying on of hands, which I had so strongly resisted. During the performance of this ancient and beautiful ritual "the heavens opened and the spirit descended like a dove." Ever since, when it seems that I am deserted by the Voice that called me forth, I know that if I can find my way back to that moment, the clouds will lift and the path before me will once again be clear and beckoning.

In early September, before the beginning of my senior year, I joined with a group of students from several schools and colleges to attend a retreat in Pawling, New York. The convenor was Grace Elliot, student conference secretary for the national board of the YWCA. We rented the facilities of an old hotel that had closed for the winter and ate at a small restaurant operated during the summer months by two teachers of home economics at Teachers College, Columbia University. They agreed to delay their closing in order to accommodate us. A Canadian, Hugh MacMillan, who was en route to a university in China to teach religion, was the discussion leader. The program was informal and unstructured.

The entire morning, after chores and breakfast, was given over to informal discussion. At the time I was impressed by the fact that the theological students from Union, Yale, Oberlin, and Rochester were raising essentially the same questions raised by the undergraduates from Wellesley, Barnard, and Holyoke. As we stretched out on the floor or leaned back in comfortable chairs there was a sense of relaxation and community that encouraged the most searching questions of minds and hearts to surface.

The men occupied the first floor, the women the second. We drew lots for roommates. There was one double bed in each room. I chose the single odd number, which meant that until the one person who was yet to come arrived I would have the room to myself. The afternoons were free for reading, hiking, and other forms of recreation. These were the times when personal relationships deepened into friendships unbroken throughout the intervening years. The evenings were memorable. This was a time for the sharing of treasures: poetry, dreams, and memories from the past. My introduction to Olive Schreiner came one evening when Shorty Collins read "The Dream of the Hunter."

One afternoon I took a long hike with Grace Loucks, of the national staff of the YWCA, responsible for the program of all their summer conferences, which resulted in my involvement with the Student Christian Movement for the next two decades and beyond.

On the third night, long after I had retired, I was awakened by a sound and turned on the light. There stood Allen Hunter. He was as shocked to see me as I was to see him. We managed to introduce ourselves. At that time Allen was a student at Union Theological Seminary and had recently returned from the Near East, where he had served a stint as a Congregational missionary. With frank simplicity he told me that although he had been unaware of harboring any racial prejudice until that moment, he also had never faced the prospect of sharing a bed with a Negro. Social relationships with Negroes were beyond the scope of his experience. We explored our souls together that night and helped each other exhume ghosts of racism each of us had considered forever buried. We talked until early light, and then we went to sleep. When we awoke, our lives were bound together in friendship and affection which the years have crowned with a shekinah that remains undimmed.

During the winter of my senior year I was invited to preach at Mount Zion Baptist Church in Oberlin, Ohio, and later to become its pastor. I accepted. I was eager to have responsibility for my own church and the position at Oberlin was especially attractive because my sister was a student in the Conservatory of Music there, and several of my Morehouse classmates were in the Theological Seminary. I also felt that there was substantial creative potential in a church in a small college town, where "town and gown" could worship together.

At the end of my senior year, Dr. Cross and I had a final conference. I told him that I had been invited to become the pastor of a Baptist Church in Oberlin. It was my hope, I said, to study New Testament with Dr. Edward Increase Bosworth and Old Testament with Dr. Kemper Fullerton at the theological school. He was smiling and enthusiastic as I told him my plans. Presently his demeanor became sober, even grave. What followed astounded me. He told me that I had superior gifts and that he felt it probable that I would be able to make an original contribution to the spiritual life of the times. That said, he went to the heart of his concern. "You are a very sensitive Negro man," he said, "and doubtless feel under great obligation to put all the weight of your mind and spirit at the disposal of the struggle of your own people for full citizenship. But let me remind you that all social questions are transitory in nature and it would be a terrible waste for you to limit your creative energy to the solution of the race problem, however insistent its nature. Give yourself to the timeless issues of the human spirit," he advised. When I did not reply, he said, "Perhaps I have no right to say this to you because as a white man I can never know what it is to be in your situation." I pondered the meaning of his words, and wondered what kind of response I could make to this man who did not know that a man and his black skin must face the "timeless issues of the human spirit" together. But before I could speak he said, "Next year I take my sabbatical leave, and I plan to spend the time in England and on the Continent. I will find a teacher for you there who can guide you in your development, so that you may go abroad to complete your studies. We will keep in touch."

At the end of our time together he cautioned me about my reading. "Do not waste your time on superficial books. Any book you can read more than fifteen pages an hour is not worth your time. Read today for what you will be thinking and preaching ten or twenty years from now. Do not preach out of a lunch basket."

I never saw Dr. Cross again. When he returned from his sabbatical leave, I received a letter from him saying that he had found my mentor and had completed arrangements for my journey to Europe to study in the fall. We set a date for me to visit him in Rochester, but before I could see him, he died suddenly. He had not shared his plan for me with anyone. I have often wondered where and with whom he had arranged for me to study, but the answer to my question died with him. What difference would it have made? I wonder, but can never know.

III

Launching a Career

1. Oberlin

Kate Kelley and I were married June 11, 1926, one week following my graduation from seminary. Katie, the oldest of the brood of Frances and Charles Kelley, Sr., had completed what was then known as the Teachers' Professional Course at Spelman. Katie, her sister, and her three brothers were considered birthright "grandchildren" of Morehouse and Spelman. They had all attended these institutions, as had their mother and father. Katie took further training at the New York School of Social Work. She had won high praise for her service as director of the new community center in Morristown, New Jersey, and had completed two years in the field at the time of our marriage.

We chose an early morning ceremony at her home in La Grange, Georgia, attended only by our immediate families and closest friends. I well remember the softness of the rising sun reflected in the mysterious beauty of Katie's eyes. After a family breakfast following the ceremony, we took the train immediately for Oberlin, Ohio, so that we would arrive in time for my first pulpit appearance on Sunday morning as pastor of the Mount Zion Baptist Church.

When I assumed the pastorate of Mount Zion, I was on my own for the first time in my life. I was no longer a student, depending for guidance in times of emergency on my professors, or my mother, or grandmother. Now, others would look to me for support, strength, and for guidance. The situation was dramatized for me when Kate and I went to a local physician so that she could have a checkup because she had become ill shortly before our marriage. While Kate's examination was in progress, the receptionist asked me to fill out a medical questionnaire, then asked to what address I would prefer to have the bill sent. Curiously, I heard her query as, "To whom do I send the bill?" and realized for the first time the scope of my responsibility to my new wife, my new church, and myself.

The membership of Mount Zion was small but substantial. Many of the old families in the town were pillars of the church. They had lived in Oberlin for generations, and they had maintained the church throughout the years. At this time there were two primary black churches in Oberlin—the Methodist and the Baptist. A few members of the Old First Church of the college were black, and minority students were free to attend any or all of the white churches in town.

At first my congregation consisted of townspeople, with a scattering of black students from the college. As a result of my work— just beginning—with the annual summer student YM-YWCA conferences at Lake Geneva, Wisconsin, more and more students from Oberlin and the neighboring colleges began to attend our morning worship. I found I could meet the demands of the growing congregation. My confidence in myself as a preacher began to grow.

Slowly, I was developing a style. I thrived on the experience of interpreting Christianity for my "flock" as I began to grow, as it seemed to me, in my own spirit. Initially, the temptation was to try to educate and re-educate my congregation in the light of my own learning and my own process of understanding. I was eager to put at the disposal of my congregation the riches that had come to me in my quest for truth. As I saw it, we were together engaged in an adventure of mind and spirit. Occasionally, my zeal offended their sensibilities—and they did not hesitate to let me know it.

One Sunday morning in the fall of that first year, I read the Scripture lesson from Moffatt's translation. As soon as the service was over, the wife of a senior deacon, a vocally explosive but compassionate woman, came to me and said, "Reverend, that was not the real Bible you read this morning. It was some man-made version, not the true word of God. You cannot bring that kind of thing into this church." I launched into a discourse on the scholarly uses of the various translations of the Bible to no avail.

When she walked away, obviously dissatisfied with my response, I decided to use my time at the weekly prayer service for a group study of the Sermon on the Mount. To prepare for this, I ordered copies of Goodspeed's translation of the Sermon on the Mount from the University of Chicago. We used these as texts, comparing the translation with the King James Version, section by section. By the time these sessions ended, I was able to use modern translations of the Bible in our services without offending the congregation, and I had gained a healthy respect for the traditionalists among them.

It was during the two years at Oberlin that I discovered that, for me, the most creative method was a sermon series, which I used in the Sunday evening service. The morning service was attended variously by a cross section of the community and the regular congregation, including visitors; on the other hand, the evening congregation consisted primarily of the membership itself, so that many of the same people came Sunday after Sunday. My first series followed the theme from I John: "Perfect love casteth out fear." I took the liberty of substituting "knowledge-understanding" for the word "love." Some of my illustrative material came from a two-volume work published by the American Medical Association, *Nostrums and Quackery*. It was an exposé of bogus claims of snake-oil salesmen for potions and pills, promising to cure tuberculosis, liver disorders, asthma, and rheumatism, among other dread diseases. I met with considerable opposition because, as I soon discovered, some of the nostrums discussed in the book had for years been household remedies for many of the congregation. Nevertheless, I made the volumes available, and a surprising number of our church members took advantage of the opportunity.

The practice of the church was to have communion on the first Sunday evening of every month. From my early childhood experiences in Daytona Beach and the summers in Roanoke, I knew that I would have to come to terms with the meaning of this important celebration for this, my first congregation, and for myself for all the remaining years of my ministry.

In many of the black churches, going far back into history, the communion ceremonial became the occasion to "right personal wrongs against each other," otherwise the unworthy recipient drank "damnation unto his soul." In preparation for the service, members held the customary covenant meeting, at which time they witnessed to the successes and failures of their own Christian journey and confessed to ill feelings harbored in the heart. It was a wonderful catharsis for pent-up spirits, often involving dialogue between sisters and brothers, husbands and wives, parents, children, neighbors. With these preliminaries concluded, all members in good standing were deemed worthy to break bread together at the communion table. But the outsider was excluded, there being not even the hint of ecumenicity among the churches of that day. Even a visiting minister from another denomination would be denied the "Lord's Supper."

As a youngster, though I took the bread and wine regularly after joining the church, the ceremony remained separate from my perception of the pain and pathos of the crucifixion itself. Now for the Mount Zion service I sought to create with my congregation a new interpretation of the sacraments, whose practice had both united and separated thousands of communicants in the Christian world.

In seminary I had researched the roots of the celebration in the history and evolution of society. I discovered the pre-Christian origins of the practice. To eat the body and drink the blood of the sacred totem of the tribe in special ceremony meant sharing the life and partaking of the essence of the sacred object—in so doing, one became like the object. Thus, one became what one worshipped. This made structural sense of the communion service. As applied to Jesus, it became symbolically an experience of total surrender to or a taking into one's self of His spirit and His life.

In preparation for this first communion service I explained the sense in which the celebration had its ancient roots in the early memory of the race and the unique significance given to it in Christian tradition. In keeping with the spirit of the Master, participation in the service would be open to all who wished to become one with His spirit. The communion service in this small church became a high moment of dedication and commitment and, though at the time I did not know it, it served as a model for future services in my ministry to two large American university communities and ultimately the Church for the Fellowship of All Peoples.

I was distressed by the isolation of the young black people of

Oberlin. They had few examples to follow and little inspiration in their lives. It was not until my first year there that the first local black man in recent memory was graduated from the college, and only a handful of young women from the community had graduated from the school.

I decided to encourage the young people of my congregation to select one of their number to attend the annual YMCA student conference meeting at Kings Mountain, North Carolina. Then, an incredibly trivial circumstance took its toll on me. The group had decided to order Schrafft's candy to sell in the community, using the profits to pay the expenses of their delegate to North Carolina. I ordered the candy and paid for it with the understanding that I would be reimbursed when the candy was sold. With a salary of less than fifty dollars a week, I could not afford to subsidize the whole project, though I wanted to.

By the time I reached the church, having been told the candy had arrived, ready for distribution, the young people had taken over the sanctuary and were standing on the pews exchanging spitballs. To the horror of the adults, the grape juice for communion had been consumed and the bottles filled with water. I was outraged and started into the sanctuary, when suddenly I remembered that these young people had to sell the candy that week, and that my own money was tied up in the project. I knew that if I offended them, I would have all the candy on my hands, and I could ill afford the loss. When I realized the compromise I was about to make, I overreacted. The explosion that followed left me spent and completely overwhelmed them. They literally fled from the church. Five days passed before they came back for the candy. When they did, we talked, and from that time on the young people and I worked together. Against the background of my analysis of the meaning of the communion celebration, the use of water instead of grape juice did not create a religious problem for the congregation. Indeed, the incident drew young and old closer together.

It seemed natural that my congregation should be going to "school" when college opened for the fall. Therefore, I organized various classes which met at the parsonage. These sessions covered Negro history, current social and political problems, selected texts from great writers, books of the Old Testament, and the life and teaching of Jesus.

Meanwhile, I enrolled for postgraduate studies in Old Testament with Dr. Fullerton and New Testament with Dr. Bosworth at the Oberlin School of Theology, for I could learn much from these two remarkable men. Dr. Fullerton invited me to do a special study of the suffering servant in Isaiah. We met at his home. Our time together was a great creative adventure for my mind and spirit; I have never since lost sight of the far-flung mystery and redemption of the sacrament of pain.

I was acquainted with Dr. Bosworth through his books and the generations of Oberlin students whose lives he touched. He was a man with relaxed and quiet eyes, dapper in appearance, yet saintly in manner. I met him one day in the town haberdashery while he was selecting a necktie. I stopped by the counter for a word of greeting. "I am trying to select a necktie," said he. "I believe that a man is under moral obligation to give to people who look at him as completely satisfying an experience as possible. The clothes a man wears are also a part of the sacrament of living." He was meticulous about his obligation, in this small matter of clothing as well as in great matters. Once, I held a long conversation on prayer with a man who had spent some twenty years as a YMCA secretary in China. The conversation turned to Dr. Bosworth. The man said, "When my daughter was in her early teens, she was having a very tempestuous time with her emotions. My wife and I were living in China and felt helpless. I thought of Dr. Bosworth and decided to write to him and ask if he would include our daughter among the persons for whom he prayed each day. I received an immediate reply in which Dr. Bosworth expressed his concern. He said that it was impossible for him to include our daughter in his list, because his list was full. Then there followed a most amazing comment. As nearly as I can remember it, it was this: 'I do not think that I should have more people on my list than I can attend to thoughtfully and prayerfully in the period of my day that is specifically set aside for that purpose. A man must mean business with all of the powers of his mind and spirit when he lifts another person in prayer to God. When there is a vacancy on my list, I will include Mary.' "

For many years, it was customary in the village for the churches and the college to unite in a Thanksgiving service in Old First Church. After the sermon, there was a period given over for testimonials, when individuals, as the spirit moved, rose to express their thanksgiving to God. One morning, a very elderly Negro lady rose to speak. She had learned to read when she was sixty-two years old so that she might read the Bible. She was overcome with emotion; at length she recovered her bearing and said simply, "I know that my redeemer liveth for He liveth in my soul. Glory, Hallelujah!" When she sat, there was a breathless silence. Into the stillness came the quiet voice of Dr. Bosworth. "What the sister has just said is the final word that the human spirit has to say about the meaning of life and the meaning of God. I rejoice to be in her fellowship, and I can only repeat her words. 'I know that my redeemer lives, for He lives in my soul. Glory, Hallelujah!' "

As a pastor I learned at close range that the human spirit is capable of great nobility. Often, I was not certain whether that nobility was a special grace or a gift of the spirit. No matter. During those early years I learned the difference between dealing with one's personal problems and sharing in the vicissitudes of other lives. One day I was asked to visit an old man, how old I could only guess. I had not met him before. I walked into the stillness of his small bedroom, and there he was. The most vital part of him was the smoldering fire in his eyes. He was frail, and the odor of old sickness filled the room. He said, "You are looking at a man who cannot die." While I struggled to understand that statement, he continued, "Not long before the war over slavery I barely escaped from the plantation with my life. I was accused of doing something I had not done. The master himself had me dragged to the empty smokehouse. I was stripped to my waist and my hands were tied to one of the crossbeams. I was beaten until I fainted, then revived with buckets of cold water and flogged again. The next thing I remember was the darkness of the night and someone was cutting me loose and helping me to dress in fresh clothes that hurt my skin. Oh, Reverend, how it hurt! Whoever this was helped me to escape into the woods. Finally, I came to the river and got across to Ohio. Ever since I have been kept alive by hatred for the man who beat me. I suppose he has long since died—at least I hope he was killed

71

in the war. The only thing I know is I cannot die until I forgive him. Now, don't waste your prayer and your words on me." I sat until the upheaval in me subsided. We did not pray, but we spoke together quietly for a while, and then I left. As the weeks passed I would drop by for a few minutes from time to time just to chat. One morning when I came to see him he greeted me with great excitement. "It happened last night! It happened!" For a swirling moment I could not make the connection, then I knew. In a few days he was dead.

Later, I received a phone call from a hospital in Steubenville saying that one of our members en route to Oberlin with her brother had met with an accident and was asking for me. When I arrived at the hospital, the nurse told me that the woman's brother had been driving the car and had been killed instantly, and she urged me not to tell her at this time because she was too weak to sustain the shock. I entered her room. She was completely bandaged except for her lips and one eye. I had to lean close to hear her. She asked me to read certain Scriptures to her. Afterward, I prayed with her. Finally, she asked me, "How is my brother? Is he dead?" I said, "No, he is not dead. He is here in the hospital." She drifted off and I left.

All the way home I agonized. Suppose she dies, I thought; how could I have betrayed her at such a moment by lying to her, whatever the apparent justification? As Sunday approached, I felt a need to share the burden of my guilt with my congregation. I prayed that God would understand and forgive; I felt that He would. But I needed the reassurance of my congregation that they, too, could forgive what I had done. On Sunday, just before the morning's prayer, I said to the congregation, "Let each of us ascend his own altar stairs in his own way. I must do this for myself and I do not feel that I can lead in prayer today." The congregation sat surrounded by the silence.

I did not preach the usual sermon. Instead, I reminded them of one of the incidents in Henry Van Dyke's *The Other Wise Man*, in which he told a lie to the Roman soldier to save the life of a little Jewish boy. Then I recounted in naked detail what had happened in Steubenville. I shall never forget the sense of strength that came to me from a supportive congregation. Person after person said, "I am praying that she may live so you can tell her what you told us today." She did recover. As soon as I called to see her, before I could say one word beyond the greeting, she said, "There is something I must tell you. I knew somehow that my brother had been killed, but I was comforted that you were willing to do what you did for my sake. I thank you for your kindness and understanding."

As time went by, I accumulated experiences of this kind and my capabilities and my confidence grew steadily, slowly. I began to explore my inner regions, and to cultivate an inner life of prayer and meditation. The experience of religion became increasingly central to my development. This was revealed to me in the gradual change in my attitude toward leading my congregation in public prayer. From the beginning of my ministry I tended to be highly self-conscious in public prayer. I found it difficult to express, in public, utterances of the inner spirit. My felt needs were so profound that at first there seemed little room for the other and possibly unconnected needs of my congregation. But as I began to acquiesce to the demands of the spirit within, I found no need to differentiate human need, theirs and my own. I became more and more a part of the life of my people and discovered that at last I was able to pray in public as if I were alone in the quiet of my own room. The door between their questing spirits and my own became a swinging door. At times I would lose my way in the full tide of emotions as a sense of the love of God overwhelmed me. At such moments we became one in the presence of God. At the same time, my preaching became less motivated by the desire to "teach"; it became almost entirely devoted to the meaning of the experience of our common quest and journey.

One afternoon a Chinese gentleman came to see me. I had seen him in church each Sunday morning for many weeks. Always he slipped away quietly without speaking to anyone. Now he introduced himself, saying that he was returning to China and wanted to tell me good-bye and express his appreciation for the experience of worshipping with us each Sunday morning. "When I close my eyes and listen with my spirit I am in my Buddhist temple experiencing the renewing of my own spirit." I knew then what I had only sensed before. The barriers were crumbling. I was breaking

73

new ground. Yet, it would be many years before I would fully understand the nature of the breakthrough.

As much as I doubted the value of time spent at meetings of the associations and conventions to which my church belonged, I had one experience that proved to be critical to the direction of my spiritual journey. I attended a state religious education convention in a town not far from Oberlin. Ever impatient, I decided to return to Oberlin before the conference ended. As I was leaving the church, I noticed a book table near the door. The sign said, "Your choice for 10¢." I bought two books, *The Life of Mary Baker Eddy* and a little book entitled *Finding the Trail of Life*, by Rufus Jones of Haverford College. I was intrigued by the title and sat on the steps of the church and began reading. I did not move until I had read the entire book. When I finished I knew that if this man were alive, I wanted to study with him.

As soon as I returned home I learned what I could about Rufus Jones and Haverford College. I was sure that the college did not admit Negroes. Later, I told one of my Quaker friends of my encounter with *Finding the Trail of Life*, and how I longed to study with this wonderful philosopher-mystic. As it happened, he and Rufus were friends of many years and had once been neighbors. He said that he would talk to Rufus. A short time later I heard from Rufus Jones himself, asking what I had in mind. After I sketched my background and my education, I told him that I was a black man who was unfamiliar with the racial policies of Haverford College. Significantly, in his reply he did not comment on whether I would be admitted, but rather expressed interest in my plan. Though he had not done this kind of directed study before, he welcomed my coming, and went on to say that while I had applied too late to receive graduate aid, I could live in Graduate House—and there would be no costs for tuition. I knew then that I would have to leave Oberlin.

Two major personal events marked the brief interval in Oberlin. The first was the birth of our older daughter, Olive Katherine. Now, despite my imagining that I fell far short of my dream of what a responsible man should be, I was a father, a strange and exciting experience. In the conception and physical birth of a child, the man is an outsider, the instrument of the creative process

74

of life itself, but never one with it. Only a woman becomes a part of the experience of creation; only she sees the perimeter of the self fade into the life force and reappear, and again fade and reappear. She knows a secret that the father can never quite experience. Nevertheless, with my firstborn, there soon came to me a sense of possession, and a swelling pride of parenthood. We named our daughter for Olive Schreiner, whose creative spirit had so long been an inspiration to me.

Our joy was short-lived, because the doctors felt Kate should return South immediately for treatment of an illness she had contracted during her years of social work, and remain there to convalesce with her family. Our Oberlin family had to be broken up for a time. Kate and the baby went to La Grange, and my sister Madaline, who had been living with us, moved to the college dormitory. I resigned from the church to study with Rufus Jones.

It was a time of far-reaching change. I missed my small family, so many miles away, and during the months that followed I was able to visit them only at long intervals and for too short a time.

2. Haverford and Morehouse

The invitation from Rufus Jones put to rest once and for all the question whether or not I would pursue the Ph.D. degree. The life of the scholar as such did not appeal to me, however much I reveled in pursuits of the mind. I sensed somehow that if I were to devote full time to the requirements of a doctoral program, academic strictures would gradually usurp the energy I wanted so desperately to nourish the inner regions of my spirit, which was even then clamoring for attention. I was recommended by Dick Edwards, the executive director of the National Council on Religion in Higher Education, to be appointed a Fellow. Though a primary function of the council was to enable men and women to pursue the doctoral degree, an exception was made in my case. The grant from the council made possible my independent study with Rufus Jones.

In early January 1929 I arrived at Haverford College. Rufus decided that I would attend all his lectures in philosophy and become a member of a special seminar on Meister Eckhart for teachers of philosophy at several colleges and universities in the Philadelphia area. The seminar was exciting and stimulating beyond anything I had known before. On my own initiative, I attended the Wednesday meeting for worship in the Haverford Meeting House, at which Rufus almost always spoke; and I had weekly conferences with him. These were seminal times; Rufus was utterly informal and his discussions ranged over the broad expanse of his thought and experience. His discourses were often anecdotal, sometimes whimsically reflective, but always directed toward opening before my mind a stretch of road down which I was invited but never urged to travel. At these sessions, especially in the general field of mystical religion, he gave me carefully selected reading assignments and later listened to my reactions to the reading and discussed them with me. I wrote several papers, one on Spanish mystics, particularly Madame Guyon, and another, a definitive study of the mysticism of St. Francis of Assisi.

My study at Haverford was a crucial experience, a watershed from which flowed much of the thought and endeavor to which I was to commit the rest of my working life. These months defined my deepest religious urges and framed in meaning much of what I had learned over the years. During the entire time with Rufus, issues of racial conflict never arose, for the fact of racial differences was never dealt with at the conscious level. The ethical emphasis in his interpretations of mystical religion dealt primarily with war and peace, the poverty and hunger of whole populations, and the issues arising from the conflict between nations. Paradoxically, in his presence, the specific issues of race with which I had been confronted all my life as a black man in America seemed strangely irrelevant. I felt that somehow he transcended race; I did so, too, temporarily, and, in retrospect, this aspect of my time with him remains an enigma.

Rufus Jones was a prolific writer, an inspiring teacher, an engaging preacher. He had the gift of intimacy, which allowed him to go to the heart of his personal experience without causing embarrassment to his listener or himself. He was not self-conscious, nor did he presume to give advice. One day he told me that it had been his lifelong habit to take a nap after lunch. I smiled, the reaction of youth to what seemed to me to be a waste of time. He responded by saying, ever so gently, "The time will come when you may wish you had been wise enough to have developed this habit while you were young." Toward the end of my stay at Haverford, he stopped me on campus to say that he had actually forgotten to meet his class. With a tone of muted sadness he said, "Now I know that it is time for me to retire."

The spring of the year was marked by three important events. The first was the death of my friend and teacher Dr. George Cross. The second was an invitation to speak at Tuskegee Institute, of which I had heard a great deal but had never visited. There I met Dr. George Washington Carver. To the end of my years I will carry in memory his face as he sat in his special pew in chapel, looking intently into mine as I preached the morning's sermon. There was the customary rose in his lapel, a Bible in his lap, and a light in his eyes that seemed to be controlled by some inner dimmer switch. Dr. Robert R. Moton, the principal of Tuskegee, invited me to take the chaplaincy there, but I was already committed to teach at Morehouse and Spelman that fall.

The third event was a meeting with Dr. John Hope, during which he told me of the long-range plans for the development of the Atlanta University system of colleges, which he would organize as its president. He deeply regretted having to yield the presidency of Morehouse and was anguished over the possible consequences of its becoming a part of the larger system and losing a measure of autonomy. Yet, he was sure of his goal. I shall never forget his voice, or the sadness in his eyes. "It may kill me," he said, "but I must do it. It will assure the future of Morehouse."

My appointment was made jointly by Morehouse and Spelman. At Morehouse I taught philosophy and religion, and at Spelman I taught the Bible as living literature and served as religious adviser to students and faculty. I took chapel services several times during the month, often for a week at a time. I had no responsibility for Spelman's Sunday vespers because, by tradition, the president of the college presided and a local minister (usually from one of the white churches) gave the sermon. This tradition at Spelman provided the largely white faculty and administration of the college with their only direct contact with the outside world in the city of Atlanta.

My first formal presentation concerned the religious insights of Negro spirituals and was given during five successive daily chapels at Spelman. This marked the beginning of a long quest into my own past as the deep resource for finding my way into wholeness in the present. These studies finally culminated in the Ingersol Lecture on Immortality which I gave at the Harvard Divinity School in 1947, and the publishing of *Deep River* in 1955. The required courses allowed me to explore fully with the students the mind of Jesus as found in the Gospels. Strangely, we did not study the life of Jesus from the distinct point of view of the disinherited. Instead, the girls and I found ourselves on a personal quest for a sense of our own worth, using the life of Jesus as example. The racial climate was so oppressive and affected us all so intimately that analogies between His life as a Jew in a Roman world and our own were obvious. I believe, looking back, that my contribution to the students was not made in the classroom or even in the chapel services, but more in the personal encounters we had in individual and group counseling. It was here that the small miracles were wrought. Again and again, I was privileged to observe a student grow into awareness, then into self-esteem, and finally into the confidence to begin a quest in her own right.

There were only three men on the staff. All the rest of the administration and faculty were women. Miss Florence Read, the president, was a Mount Holyoke College graduate whose early orientation was service to the Rockefeller Foundation. A woman of strong will, courageous and dedicated, her university training was limited, but she had a commitment to the education and development of young black women that stood in somewhat sharp contrast to earlier Spelman administrators. In the early days of her administration, she exposed Spelman students to outside academic and social currents with an openness her predecessors would have deemed unthinkable. The atmosphere came alive because of it. She herself was spirited. One day in downtown Atlanta she saw a man beating his horse. Without hesitation, she ran out into the street, caught the horse by the bridle, and held on while berating the man for his cruelty. She was also generous. I shall always be grateful for her opening a wing of the McVicar training hospital on Spelman's campus, making it possible for Kate to spend many months there in her fight for her life against tuberculosis.

Yet, my professional relationship with her was doomed from the beginning because I deeply resented the fact that, since its founding in 1881, Spelman had been presided over by white women presidents. Miss Read, for all her qualities, was yet another. She could be sensitive in her interpretation of topical events, in her chapel appearances, or in talking with the students. What worried me was that the Spelman girls lacked models for themselves as black women; there was no one whom they could emulate or admire on their own terms. Almost imperceptibly at first, the breach between Miss Read and me widened; then two things happened that brought my feelings out into the open. I had just begun to speak at chapels in eastern and northern white colleges. One weekend I went to Mount Holyoke, Miss Read's alma mater. Although I had no weekend responsibilities at Spelman, Miss Read insisted that I let her know in advance whenever I was going out of town. I considered this personal business, and left for Mount Holyoke without telling her. When I returned, we had a bitter exchange, opening a conflict that was unresolved to my final day at Spelman.

The other incident revealed what seemed to be an intolerable, if subconscious, patronage on her part. The famous president of Mount Holyoke, Mary Woolley, was retiring after a long and distinguished career, during which her name became synonymous with that of the college. I asked Miss Read if she had considered applying for Miss Woolley's position. I was shocked by her response. "No, Mr. Thurman, I do not have the academic equipment to be president of Mount Holyoke"—clearly indicating in her emphasis that while she felt perfectly competent to preside over a college for young Negro women, she was sure this level of competence was not nearly sufficient for her to preside over a white women's college. The implications about Spelman College and black people in general infuriated me and strained our relationship as long as we were associated. Years later, it must be said, we developed a certain equanimity. After her retirement to a quiet life in Princeton, she was one of the warmest and most enthusiastic greeters whenever I came to Princeton University to speak, and she usually invited her friends to a dinner at which I was guest of honor. The years diminished the friction between us somewhat, but the gulf of misunderstanding was never fully bridged.

At these two colleges, which were so strategic to the higher education of our youth at that time, I began in earnest to learn how to teach. At Morehouse, I chose not to use a textbook; instead, I would take a basic concept, such as the relation between the universal and the particular, or the timeless and the temporal, or the infinite and the finite, and would challenge a single student to work through the definition and limitations of such a concept. There were times when I would spend the entire class period in dialogue with one student.

During my first year, I lived in an apartment in one of the dormitories. It was then that I began the practice of inviting groups of students to my rooms for Saturday night discussions. For refreshments, I roasted a peck of raw peanuts. Then I made a special concoction, consisting of two and one-half quarts of lemonade churned in the freezer until frozen bits began to gather inside the churn, to which I would add the beaten whites of several eggs, pouring them into the semi-frozen mass and churning again furiously until the entire mixture expanded into a fluffy and delicious sherbet.

When the men came we would sit on the floor in a circle, with the huge pile of freshly roasted peanuts in the center. Each man would have his own piece of newspaper for the empty shells, and we would help ourselves to the sherbet. No subject was forbidden, and the discussions ran the entire gamut of our interests and concerns, although they were inevitably related to our survival in a society that seemed to have no room for our young dreams and longings. Most often we came around to the central problems of self-realization as black men in American society. Invariably, we asked, Why are we in college? What are we trying to find? How can we immunize ourselves against the destructive aspects of the environment? How manage the carking fear of the white man's power and not be defeated by our own rage and hatred?

I was then only in my late twenties, but I could insist that neither they nor I could consider ourselves educated until we were able to relate what we had learned to our daily lives. I had majored in economics, but I could not be said to understand the modes of production and consumption until I was able to predict their effects on my own environment, that of a black man in America.

During my second year on the Morehouse faculty I was asked by the president to take full responsibility for daily chapel. At that time, attendance was compulsory for all students, except seniors. There was resentment that it was required at all. I felt that the burden of proof was on the college itself. The services ought to be so interesting that the men would want to attend for their own sakes, their own enrichment.

In keeping with Religious Emphasis Week, which is still featured on many church-related campuses, I selected a theme, and then invited members of the faculty to state from their own particular disciplines those ideas that seemed relevant to that theme, and to share those ideas at chapel service. The theme chosen for the first year was "Man and the Moral Struggle." My chapel talks centered on examples in the lives of Job, Jesus, and Paul the Apostle. I invited, as guest speaker for the week, A. Philip Randolph, who was then locked in a struggle with the Pullman Company to organize the Brotherhood of Pullman Car Porters. At first, the invitation to Mr. Randolph threatened to be an embarrassment, because the college was in the midst of its first major financial campaign, and Randolph's courageous crusade was considered controversial. But President Hope and I were able to resolve this problem and the program went forward as planned. As a climax of the week, on Friday night, the college presented Shakespeare's *Macbeth*. Under the direction of Dr. Anne Cook of the Spelman faculty, we produced an excellent student performance. The power of that presentation was overwhelming. As if by magic the entire chapel audience was enveloped in an experience of transcendent encounter between person and power.

During the fall of my second year in Atlanta, we knew we were losing the battle for Kate's health. Medical techniques then known were to no avail. She died in December, on the first day of winter. Kind, comforting friends from the Atlanta colleges traveled with me as we took her home for burial in La Grange. My mother came to Atlanta to live with me and care for the baby, while I finished out that painfully tragic year.

A few days after Kate's death, I received from Red Mathews, my former roommate at Rochester Seminary, and Evelyn, his wife, the one and only Christmas package he ever sent me. It was a package full of all kinds of holiday goodies. I had not shared my personal crisis with him. But the package came, its timing perfect, with the simple signature, "Red and Evelyn."

When June came, I was physically and emotionally exhausted; I needed to get my bearings on my future, personally and professionally. I could think of nothing better than to return to the sea for solace and restoration. I would take a sea voyage to Europe. My sister Madaline, who had recently graduated from Oberlin College, offered to take the summer off to care for my little daughter.

I knew no one in Europe. My first days were spent in London.

Even then I had difficulty finding accommodations. I discovered there what I had known so well in America, that the places least likely to discriminate against race or color are the more expensive hotels, which are usually out of reach of the traveler of modest means. There were, here and there, hotels which catered primarily to students. In the end, I was able to find adequate facilities in a small hotel in Gower Street, where many of the foreign students, particularly East Indians, lived. For days, I learned London through the soles of my shoes.

From London I journeyed to Scotland, where I had been invited to live as a paying guest on a large estate about five miles beyond the town limits of Pitlochry, just north of Edinburgh. The owner of the estate raised sheep on his land; shepherds lived with their families in stone cottages scattered over the huge acreage. When I arrived, I was met by a shepherd in a two-wheel cart and driven out to the estate, where I lived as a guest for more than a month. Each morning after breakfast I packed a lunch and tramped the moors, hour after hour. At midday I ate my lunch and then took a nap in the fields. I returned in time for dinner, after which I visited with his family. For the first time, I was part of a texture of life foreign to me.

Without knowing when or how, I moved into profound focus; the direction of the future opened wide its doors. My life seemed whole again and the strains of an unknown melody healed my inmost center. It was glorious. When I returned to London and went on to Paris and Geneva, I was aware that God was not yet done with me, that I need never fear the darkness, nor delude myself that the contradictions of life are final. I was ready now for my journey.

3. Howard

It was a special grace that brought back into my life at this time a friend of former years, Sue Bailey. Her wisdom and sensitivity surrounded me during those difficult days of crisis following Katie's death and the reorganizing of my life in adjustment. Slowly it became evident that despite the difficult experiences of the recent past, our love for each other provided a foundation upon which together we could build an extraordinary new life. Sue was at this time a traveling collegiate secretary for the national board of the YWCA. She and I shared a circle of friends during her final year in the college preparatory department of Spelman College while I was a student at Morehouse. Sue and her friends would read aloud to each other the letters they received from their boyfriends at Morehouse, and we would do the same with the letters from the Spelman girls. It was a friendly and creative rivalry.

Sue brought into our coming together a rare beauty of person, a clear and analytical mind, a sensitive imagination, and a fresh enthusiasm of heart that only love could inspire. In a manner that after forty-seven years remains a mystery, she related to me as a person, as a man, giving to me at my center a life of heart that made the whole world new. In the realm of ideas and dreams, she continues to be an active "tennis player." We play the court, bouncing the balls back and forth until there emerges a unanimity both of mind and of plan.

She was the daughter and last living child of the Reverend and Mrs. Isaac G. Bailey of Arkansas. Her father had been a member of the Arkansas legislature, and his father before him had founded in 1840 a church that still exists in Arkansas City. Sue's father entered the ministry at the time of his marriage to Susie Ford, a teacher in the southeast Arkansas schools. Together they moved from Pine Bluff, home of the Branch Norman College and birthplace of all their children, to found an academy at Dermott, which at that time was one of the bare handful of high schools for black youth throughout the state of Arkansas. After graduating from Spelman, Sue received two degrees from Oberlin—one from the College of Arts and Sciences and the other from the Oberlin Conservatory of Music. She taught at Hampton Institute in Virginia for two years, and then joined the national staff of the YWCA to serve colleges on the eastern seaboard and in the Deep South.

One of her accomplishments in her last year at this post was to organize the annual June conference of YWCA students, which usually met at Talladega College in Alabama, into a joint session with the YMCA student conference at historic Kings Mountain, in the Piedmont hills of North Carolina. Early each summer young men from black colleges all over the South gathered here. In a climate of acceptance—and in the absence of all the traditional academic or athletic rivalry—there came men from as far north as Howard University, and Morgan College in Baltimore, and Lincoln University in Pennsylvania. Faculty members of these colleges and academies also participated. The guiding forces in the early 1920s were the national student secretaries of the Colored Men's Division of the YMCA in America, among them Max Yergan and Frank T. Wilson. Leaders of American religious and political thought, black and white, also met with the students here; they included Reinhold Niebuhr, A. Philip Randolph, and Channing Tobias.

Sue and I decided that Kings Mountain was the fitting setting for our wedding. A place hallowed by the circling currents of the springs of our common past. The date was June 12, 1932. This would be Sue's final conference as a national YWCA secretary; and I was leaving the Deep South for a new assignment at Howard University. The invitations were printed by The Press in the Forest, in Carmel, California. We chose the weekend following the close of the conference so that many of our mutual friends could share in the ceremony. They rented a large farmhouse where they lived and readied themselves for the wedding. They were to be the bridal chorus, not because they could make fine music with their voices, but because we felt that each had the perfect instrument—the singing heart—to rejoice with us in the adventure we had won.

The ceremony was scheduled to take place on a hillside sacred to us because of the vesper services held there each year, from which students beyond number had gone forth to live out the visions that had visited them in that place. But, barely an hour before the service was to begin, the rain came down in sheets. We worked like quick-change artists with an expert crew to prepare the refectory for the ceremony. We gathered hillocks of laurel leaves and wildflowers which were banked behind tall pinewood candelabra, forming the altar, with a center aisle of Queen Anne's lace down which the bridal party would come. We did not realize then the symbolism of that moment—that in a thousand instances, we would spend the rest of our lives turning refectories into chapels. Sue left with a smock on, returning alone to an empty dormitory to dress for the wedding. Within the hour she returned, utterly transformed. With a soft pink satin bridal dress shimmering shyly through a network of lace—the whole picture accentuated by the bridal veil—her entrance marked a moment of utter bewitchment. Afterward one of those present commented to me, "She was poised and beautiful; a vision of utter loveliness." It was as if she had never been involved in the turmoil of less than two hours before, when all plans had to be changed and the complete transformation of the refectory had taken place.

The wedding proceeded in three parts. First, I read poems and prose passages, sharing with those present some of the beauty that Sue and I had discovered together in the growing fullness of our love and friendship. Then came the bridal procession, the chorus singing the words and music from *Lohengrin*, followed by other long-time favorites of the bride and myself. My daughter, Olive, was a charming little flower girl and Sue's only attendant. She spread blossoms along the path as Sue walked alone to join me. I took her hand and we knelt at the altar in front of lighted tapers. I said a prayer and we pledged our love and said Amen as one. From the audience, one of our friends, Reverend C. J. Gresham, gave the conventional blessing and pronounced us man and wife.

I had moved from Atlanta to our new home on the campus of

Howard University by July 1. Sue, who had been living in New York City, joined me a few days later.

Our return to Washington held significance for both of us. She had spent two years in elementary school in the District of Columbia and graduated from the eighth grade at Lucretia Mott School. Her brother, Isaac G. Bailey, Jr., a Howard graduate, died in Washington while serving as chief clerk of a selective draft board during World War I; and, of course, I had spent a summer on the campus as a part of the special army program in my third year of high school.

I spent the first night in our new home alone. When I came downstairs to greet the morning, I saw a young man seated on the steps with his suitcase between his legs. He said, "Mrs. Bailey sent me here. She said that when I got here, you and Miss Susie would see to it that I get an education. My name is Phillip Miller." He was a gifted teenage artist who finished Dunbar High School and later graduated with honors from the art department of Howard University. This marked the beginning of a long line of young people, inspired and helped by Sue's mother, to leave the small town of Dermott to seek an education in the large world beyond. There was scarcely a year during the entire period of our tenure at Howard University that three or more students (with the mark of Mrs. Bailey on their brow) did not share our life, either on that campus or another to which we were able to send them.

I was no stranger to Howard University. President Mordecai Johnson had been a steady source of inspiration from my own high school days. Also, for several years I had visited the campus as Week of Prayer preacher and during that time I had made many friends. I was caught up in Mordecai Johnson's vision to create the first real community of black scholars, to build an authentic university in America dedicated primarily to the education of black youth. For many years, this was regarded as a pretension and, in some important ways, it was a creative mixture of fact and fiction. However, Howard University to this day holds unique magic for many black youth, and is internationally recognized as one of the finest American universities.

Because Howard University was sponsored by the federal government, the doctrine of the separation of church and state gave a secondary position to any emphasis on the place of religion in the academic community. The university was (and continues to be) under the patronage and sponsorship of the federal government, although it is a private institution. As Dr. Rayford Logan points out, in his *Howard University: The First 100 Years, 1867–1967*, the physical plant of the university is located on a federal reservation rather than in a state, and its government appropriations cannot be used to support religious institutions on campus—neither the School of Religion nor the Andrew Rankin Memorial Chapel.

My first appointment was to the faculty of the School of Religion, and later to the chairmanship of the university Committee on Religious Life. While I was on leave as chairman of the Delegation of Friendship to India, Burma, and Ceylon, I was appointed dean of Rankin Chapel. The designation of chapel dean had been made only twice before on any American university campus, and for a long period thereafter there were only three such appointments in American education—at the University of Chicago, at Princeton University, and at Howard.

When we returned from the year's absence in India, I embarked on what was substantially a new career as dean. In the first place, the gulf was wide between faculty and students. Students were seldom invited to faculty homes, because the majority of the faculty lived a distance from the campus, and their social ties were made in communities in other areas of the city; further, there had been no precedent for student-teacher exchanges outside the classroom. Most of the black faculty members were graduated from eastern and northern universities where they were that tiny minority whose lives were peripheral to the mainstream of the white campus life. Only rarely were they guests in a professor's home, the exceptions being an occasional gathering for a seminar or class. During my entire three years at Rochester I do not recall ever being a guest in a professor's home, not even that of Dr. Cross. It simply was not done. So there was nothing in the background of the professors at Howard that would make any such informal coming together seem normal. This was doubly true of the white faculty, of course.

Sue and I, because of our years of work with young people,

were used to the flow of students in and out of our home. It was our conviction that the ministry of the dean of the chapel was wholly encompassing, extending far beyond whatever transpired in Rankin Chapel on Sunday mornings at eleven o'clock. The first step was to secure a group of ushers to serve at the public religious services. I discovered after the first Sunday that the ushers were not volunteers, but were paid at the same rate as ushers for any other public function of the university, such as Commencement or Charter Day exercises. When, on the Monday afternoon following my first Sunday, the spokesman for the group came to see me to make formal arrangements for compensation, I was shocked. It was my first dramatic student confrontation. There was no provision in the small budget for such an outlay, but I was opposed in principle to remuneration for chapel ushers. After some two hours of discussion, and several cups of coffee, we came to an agreement. The ushers would not be paid but would be formally organized and given full responsibility for the service each Sunday. In addition, the group would meet in our home once each month for dinner and a general discussion. During the month of May, before finals got under way, there would be a dinner at our residence to which each man could bring his date. The men would select the menu, help shop for the food, and prepare it; after dinner, they would also share in the clean-up. In other words, they would be at home. This was the first opportunity these men had had for free and easy access to a faculty home and a faculty family. The word spread quickly that the Thurmans had an open-door policy. Sue and I soon came to know intimately a broad cross section of student friends.

Ivy-covered Rankin Memorial Chapel, built in 1894, was the only auditorium or assembly hall on campus. Concerts, lectures, and general campus-community meetings were held there. This meant that the Sunday morning service had to compete, in the minds of the congregation, with memories of other events that had taken place in this structure, which represented, for many, the essence of Howard University itself. I spent long hours of quiet in the empty chapel, listening to the silence and gazing through the rose window at sunset, until slowly it was clear to me what I would have to do.

The order of service was completely redesigned. A sense of worship emerged through the leadership and inspiration of the choir directors, Miss Lulu V. Childers and, later, Dr. Warner Lawson, the organist, the choir, and the board of ushers. They worked together as a team of singular dedication. Along with the order of service and announcements, poems or prose selections were printed on the back of each program, which further enriched the spiritual tone of the service. Gradually, Sunday morning service at Rankin Chapel became a watering place for a wide range of worshippers, not only from within the university community, but also from the District of Columbia. Despite the fact that the District at that time was as segregated racially as Atlanta or Jackson, the Sunday chapel service provided a time and a place where race, sex, culture, material belongings, and earlier religious orientation became undifferentiated in the presence of God.

Fortunately, it was well established before I joined the faculty that stipends were provided for guest preachers and speakers. These men and women came primarily from the academic world, our funds permitting us to invite them from distances as far away as the Midwest, the Deep South, and New England. Without any formal expression of intent, I excluded from consideration speakers from any institutions whose policies discriminated against black or minority students. There was one notable exception, Patrick Malin. Malin taught economics at Swarthmore College and was working almost single-handedly to change the racial policy of that Quaker institution.

The pulpit was open to anyone within the Judeo-Christian tradition. During that period, I was beginning to feel my way beyond that limitation to include speakers who represented other world religions. Our pulpit was often filled by rabbis. Invitations were also extended to black ministers who received few, if any, offers to preach before a congregation such as Rankin Chapel.

During the twelve years we were at Howard University, our residence was located on campus. As the university had no guest facilities in those days, visiting preachers usually were guests in our home. Sue and I invited both faculty members and students to have dinner with our visitors on Saturday night. Slowly, these became important occasions for the university, for the discussions were often tense, penetrating, and even painful. In the end, however, harmony would be restored, and with it would come a tolerance, if not understanding, that had not existed before.

On one occasion there was a gala reception for the minister of the Haitian legation, his family, and his staff. This occasion also launched the formal organization of the university faculty and administrative wives. The year was 1938.

Sue had called together a group of concerned faculty wives, proposing that such an organization, so much needed on campus, be established around an exciting international event to include all faculty and administrative officials.

The Haitian legation was the only black legation in Washington at that time. Their appearance as guests of honor at the reception marked a significant first in the capital city. That night also marked the first appearance in concert of Katherine Dunham, the young dancer who had recently returned from a tour of study and research on the dances of Haiti. Miss Dunham came from Chicago for the occasion.

Years followed, with black embassies growing by the scores in Washington. Katherine Dunham later formed her own troupe from which came most of the great dancers of the black American community. Sue, a founder of the Howard University Faculty Wives Club, has been invited back several times to celebrate the years of continued service of this group, one of the finest women's organizations on any American university campus. Dorothy Burnett Porter, as curator, has kept their historical records in the Moorland-Spingarn Center at Howard University from their first international venture to this day.

The depression influenced the thought and life of us all. The New Deal, the dynamism of the Roosevelts, the upheaval deep within the inner processes of the federal government, gave deeper stirrings to my own mind and emotions. When the dust in the streets of my spirit needed settling, I would go out to the old section of the Rock Creek Cemetery. There was a semicircular granite bench there, in front of the famous Saint-Gaudens statue over the grave of the wife of Henry Adams. On it sat the life-size figure of a woman, draped in a cowl from head to foot, her chin supported by her right hand as she leans slightly forward, looking directly into the distance. Her countenance is drained of all emotion, her eyes exhausted from tears—she is at once alive and dead. To sit there alone surrounded by the silence, a slight wind sometimes stirring the leaves of evergreens overhead, gave me a sense of the ancient vision of Jacob and the ascending and descending of angels before the throne of God. I shared this experience with many of our visiting preachers early on Sunday mornings before the formal activity of the day began.

On campus the growth of the daily religious life was not sponsored by any existing student organizations, despite the fact that the first student YMCA to be organized at a black institution developed at Howard University. From my ministry of the chapel, a new undergraduate religious organization developed, known as the Fellowship Council. This was the vehicle through which much of the chapel's religious program would be realized. Its immediate purpose was to establish nurturing relationships between student and student and faculty and student. Its two annual faculty-student dinners were the only occasions, aside from Commencement itself, that involved the coming together of faculty and students from all the departments.

Mindful of the loneliness of the holidays through the years when we ourselves could not go home, Sue and I opened our house to all the students who remained on campus at Christmas. We invited everyone for Christmas breakfast. My reputation as a cook was spreading far and wide, and I delighted in it. I knew that breakfast would be, for some, the only festive meal of the day, so I concocted a specialty of chicken à la king, full of meat and vegetables and delicious seasonings, served with rice, a variety of breads, and plenty of coffee, followed by fruit and hard candies. The students did the serving and helped to restore order following the meal. Then we joined Sue at the piano and sang carols at the top of our voices. In time they would leave, and we would settle down to our own family Christmas.

At Howard, I began to experiment with forms of worship other than usual religious services. The sermon was not always the centerpiece. Within the regular order of service, I provided stretches of time for meditation, a quiet time for prayers generated by silence. I also wanted to develop a service that would permit greater freedom for the play of creative imagination, a vesper service; these were called Twilight Hours. Each Twilight Hour was different in form and texture. I knew there was a felt need in the congregation, with its diversity of religious background, for a sense of the majesty of Holy Writ. The very first service was devoted to "The Ancient Heritage of Man's Quest for God," using both Old and New Testament passages that addressed this theme, some dramatically, some even rebelliously, and others, as in the great Psalms, with a sublime sense of redemption. These selections were typed and mimeographed as a single connected story. As shadows gathered in Rankin Chapel, after an organ prelude, I began to read aloud, the tones of the organ weaving in and out in muted accompaniment. There were periods of silence here and there to allow the inspiration of the words to hold full sway. When the service was over, I left the pulpit, but the audience remained in their seats, in total silence, for several minutes. When they rose to leave, the ushers gave each of them a copy of the reading.

One of the most daring of these Twilight Hours was the introduction of dance as a spiritual ritual. This was a hazardous experiment, because the general attitude toward dance was that it might be art but it was also entertainment. The physical education department had long taught creative dancing for women, but no one related this to worship. Sue shared my interest in the use of the arts in the Twilight Hours and introduced me to a young dancer who taught in a Catholic institution in Baltimore. She was attempting to use dance as an act of Christian worship, and was greatly enthusiastic when I invited her to give a solo dance vesper in Rankin Chapel. I selected four of the universal moods of the human spirit: Praise, Thanksgiving, Contrition, and Faith. Readings were selected to accompany each dance—several taken from the Bible—and selections of music were chosen by the dancer to be played by the university organist.

Every effort was made to prepare the community for the vesper. There were carefully designed announcements, with comments in the Sunday bulletin, and we never missed an opportunity to discuss the event during our daily rounds on the campus. At last the Sunday arrived. The chapel was packed for the service, even the standing room area at the rear. I could sense the mixture of confused anticipation, skepticism, honest curiosity, and for many, eagerness to find yet another way to reach the highest altar. Dressed in flowing robes, the dancer entered, and the moment was hers, like the instant just before the first finger of dawn moves above the horizon at the break of day. Would the sun appear or would it be hidden by morning mist and cloud? Suddenly it was as if the walls separating each of us from the other were removed, and we became a worshipful people united by a single rhythmic beat. It was magnificent. Here was a young Caucasian woman, Roman Catholic by religious faith, sharing an experience of profoundest spiritual significance with a group made up predominantly of black Protestant worshippers in a university religious service. What happened was its own authenticity.

An even more dramatic expression of the Twilight Hours was one that in time became a chapel tradition at Christmas. This was the staged presentation of "Living Madonnas," posed to replicate great paintings. I selected six European masterpieces that seemed appropriate for this presentation and sent for reproductions. The idea was to render in tableaux a life-size reproduction of each masterpiece, giving careful attention to composition, color, and costume. I discussed my choices with the fine arts faculty and the director of the university art gallery. At first, the idea seemed to be a staggering undertaking, impractical for a chapel stage. But I was convinced that if we could re-create these pictures with living subjects, perfectly lighted, at intervals of several minutes, the congregation could experience the breathtaking beauty and spiritual depth of the famous originals. To enhance the visual experience, it occurred to me that an "Ave Maria" by one of the great composers could be played or sung. This was the School of Music's special contribution. Under the auspices of the department of drama and home economics in the College of Liberal Arts, a large picture frame, nine by five feet, was built, stretched with theatrical gauze, and placed in the center of the chapel platform. Lights were arranged at all sides of the frame, and velvet curtains hung from the side walls.

It was considered a great honor to be chosen a Madonna. I always got a warm reception whenever I visited the women's quadrangle of dormitories, but my popularity increased by leaps and bounds just before selection time. I had an advantage over the original artists. The colors of my models were alive and various, and ranged from ivory to burnt umber. They were more beautiful than any painting.

The night of the performance, as the lights were brought up slowly to full illumination of the tableaux, and the music of the "Ave Marias" filled the chapel, the effect was electrifying. In the interval between each reproduction, there was utter silence; it was what Otto calls "the numinous silence of waiting." The congregation and the participants were fused in a single moment of spiritual transcendence. I discovered, again through worship, that an experience of unity among peoples can be more compelling than all that separates and divides. This type of vesper was later re-created at several colleges throughout the country.

Our younger daughter was born during the early years at Howard University, and she was named for the poet Anne Spencer, one of our oldest friends. Sue and I had spent many contented hours during our honeymoon at her home in Lynchburg, Virginia. We enjoyed her carefully tended rose garden, which we shared with another visitor, James Weldon Johnson, who loved it as we did. At the end of our visit, we told Anne Spencer that if we had another daughter, she would bear her name. Later, when Anne was already our daughter's namesake, we had but one choice as godmother. Our cherished friend Dr. Marion V. Cuthbert came down from New York to be the "Madrina" for the new baby.

Our family was now complete. Partly because we lived on a campus, with a constant flow of faculty and students through our home, our daughters felt secure in the world bounded largely by the life of the university. Their horizons were enlarged by acquaintance with guest ministers from all over the world. However much we wanted them to be at home in a world of diverse cultures and creeds, we knew that this was possible only if they were centered in their own heritage. Hence great care was given to their orientation in the family idioms and ethnic roots out of which Sue and I had come and which we shared. Each summer, therefore, we left the campus and the girls became a part of Sue's family in Arkansas and my family in Florida.

After her husband's death, Sue's mother moved into the life

of the total community by working closely with the Women's American Baptist Home Mission Society. She was the lung through which the community breathed—always the teacher, always the counselor, always the friend during crises of living, and the consoling companion to the gates of death. To everyone in Dermott, white and black, she was "Mrs. Bailey," an illuminating presence in her town. The large library in her home was filled with good books to inspire and kindle the imagination of the local youth. She subscribed to *Crisis*, the official organ of the National Association for the Advancement of Colored People, the Afro-American periodicals, *St. Louis Argus* and *Chicago Defender*, and at least two widely read national weeklies, which gave a contemporary picture of the cross section of life in the black world and beyond. "Reading circles" met in the afternoons at her home to conduct studies of a wide range of subjects, including Afro-American history. She used her home as a community center and the large acreage around it as a playground for the children of the town. She lived by the Sermon on the Mount and was a careful student of its teachings. After breakfast each morning there were family devotions which included all in her house. During the long hot summer days, I was able to relax completely. I read all of Mark Twain for the first time, and the children's favorite Peter Rabbit tales, and many other books that had not been available to me in my youth. For our daughters, Dermott added another dimension to a sense of their own worth, so central to the psychic health of minority children growing up in an environment that often denigrates and diminishes their self-esteem. Dermott also gave them a sense of abiding home place, which balanced the transitory quality of university life where associations are of necessity short-lived and often tenuous.

The journey to my hometown, Daytona Beach, provided a different experience. Here they became the youngest members of a larger family unit, consisting of my mother and stepfather, my grandmother (their only living great-grandparent), and several aunts and cousins. In comparison to the small inland community of Dermott, Daytona Beach was a bustling city, its life and character influenced by the sea. My mother lived in the house in which

I grew up as a boy. In this seacoast community was my own sense of place.

On one of our visits to Daytona Beach I was eager to show my daughters some of my early haunts. We sauntered down the long street from the church to the riverfront. This had been the path of the procession to the baptismal ceremony in the Halifax River, which I had often described to them. We stopped here and there as I noted the changes that had taken place since that far-off time. At length we passed the playground of one of the white public schools. As soon as Olive and Anne saw the swings, they jumped for joy. "Look, Daddy, let's go over and swing!" This was the inescapable moment of truth that every black parent in America must face soon or late. What do you say to your child at the critical moment of primary encounter?

"You can't swing in those swings."

"Why?"

"When we get home and have some cold lemonade I will tell you." When we were home again, and had had our lemonade, Anne pressed for the answer. "We are home now, Daddy. Tell us."

I said, "It is against the law for us to use those swings, even though it is a public school. At present, only white children can play there. But it takes the state legislature, the courts, the sheriffs and policemen, the white churches, the mayors, the banks and businesses, and the majority of white people in the state of Florida —it takes all these to keep two little black girls from swinging in those swings. That is how important you are! Never forget, the estimate of your own importance and self-worth can be judged by how many weapons and how much power people are willing to use to control you and keep you in the place they have assigned to you. You are two very important little girls. Your presence can threaten the entire state of Florida."

But the time for visiting with our southern families was limited for me because much of the summer vacation was committed to conferences, on both coasts. For many summers I was a staff member of the national YWCA, working in their annual summer school held at Asilomar, California. On one of these Asilomar assignments I visited San Francisco for the first time. When I disem-

97

barked from the Oakland ferry and walked down Market Street, I had a sense of coming home that I had never felt any place else in the world.

At this point in my chapel ministry I was eager to provide opportunity for exchanges between the students of Howard University and other institutions. I wanted to begin the exchange with students from a college that did not admit Afro-Americans. A way opened to initiate an exchange with Vassar College. For several years previous to my going to Howard, I had served as guest preacher at Vassar. In those days the visiting preacher was not only the guest of the president, but his time was also shared by a special student committee. They were the official escorts with whom the speaker had his meals, and they assumed responsibility for arranging group meetings other than the Sunday service. I discovered in one of the luncheon discussions that some of the girls in the group were a part of a committee concerned over the admission of Negro girls to Vassar. There were several members of the faculty who shared their concern, as well as a few alumnae. The president participated in our discussions.

The following spring I invited five Vassar girls to visit Howard University for a weekend. I knew that it was important that they come as guests of the women students of the university. The first step was to invite President Henry MacCracken to be the pulpit guest in our chapel. This accomplished, the date was set for the visit of the Vassar students. Our dean of women agreed that they would live on campus, and an equal number of Howard girls were asked to be their hostesses. The guests with their hostesses had dinner at our home when they arrived. After dinner and a lively discussion, the Howard group invited their visitors to be their roommates for the weekend, having arranged for their regular roommates to move into other quarters. The Vassar girls promptly invited their new friends to be *their* guests at Vassar at the time when I would be speaking there later in the spring. The Howard girls returned the visit, and the door was opened for much that followed. Finally, the activity of the Vassar committee had effect. The application to Vassar of a black graduating senior from a public school in New York City was accepted. The committee raised a special scholarship fund for her and met her during the spring session so that she would not be a stranger when she entered college in the fall. This student had a brilliant four years at Vassar and later entered the medical profession. She broke ground for the hundreds of black women who followed.

IV

*Crossing the Great
Divide—India*

In 1935 the national YMCA and YWCA International Committee, acting on behalf of the World Student Christian Federation, invited me to be the chairman of a delegation of Afro-Americans on a pilgrimage of friendship as guests of the Student Christian Movement of India, Burma, and Ceylon. The delegation would consist of four members: Reverend and Mrs. Edward G. Carroll, my wife, and myself.

The idea of such a delegation was at that time audacious; nothing like it had been undertaken before. India, Burma, and Ceylon were still colonies of the British Empire. Gandhi had been imprisoned several times and was in a life-and-death struggle for freedom against an established imperialism. The vast Indian masses were being stirred by the invasion of a hope that steadily contradicted the grimness of their present reality. Gandhi was a symbol of that hope.

The presumptuousness of our pilgrimage was made clear when the International Committee sought visas for the delegation to enter and to travel in those colonies for a period of four months. Such an application could not be handled as a routine matter by a consulate but had to be referred to the Home Office in London. At the time it was reported to me by a member of the committee that the representative of the British government in New York had remarked, "You do not know what you are asking. If an American-educated Negro just traveled through the country as a tourist, his presence would create many difficulties for our rule—now you are asking us to let four of them travel all over the country and make speeches!" Yet the way was cleared for us to go.

My central concern was whether I could in good conscience go to India, or any other missionary field, as a representative of the

Christian religion as it was projected from the West, and primarily from America. I did not want to go to India as an apologist for a segregated American Christianity, yet how could I go under the auspices of the Student Christian Movement without seeming in fact to contradict my intention?

Suppose I refused and stated my basis for so doing, would this abort what initially had been a good idea, a tremendous contribution to creative human relations transcending boundaries—national, international, racial, cultural, and religious? How clear a case could I make for the religious grounds of my objections? If I could not represent American Christianity in foreign countries, how could I continue to be part of it in my own country?

Sue and I spent many hours discussing all the issues. A great gift in my life has been the companion who meets me at the gate in any arena where I am called upon to do battle and who with great compassion finds the weak points in my idea or contention without in any way diminishing me. For an entire weekend the struggle was on. Finally, we came to a place of calm and decision—I must refuse the invitation. This I did in a letter in which I made it clear that I did not think I could go to India and speak my own mind, interpreting Christianity as I felt it and thought it. I was sure that I would be bound by assumption to interpret Christianity from within the framework of *American* Christianity, which, from my point of view, lacked much that was fundamental to the genius of the faith itself.

Instead of replying to my letter, the New York committee sent Winifred Wygall, a good friend of ours, who was a national YWCA secretary, to Washington to talk the whole matter through to see if there could not be a meeting of minds. She was empowered to speak for the committee, and whatever understanding was reached among the three of us would be binding on the committee. We talked far into the night.

Among us emerged the kind of communication that is possible only in a climate of honesty and trust. It was clear to her what our objections were, but she argued that these did not make a real handicap. On the contrary, as a member of the committee she was sure that it was precisely because of the objections I had expressed that the committee had chosen me as chairman and included Sue in the delegation. We were now of one mind that the trip was right for us at this time, and so advised the committee.

We did not know intimately the young couple making up the other half of the delegation. I knew Edward G. Carroll from previous meetings, but at the time of their selection I had not met his wife. How fortunate we all were to have come together in such a crucial and exacting undertaking! They were just married and several years younger than we were. He was well trained for his vocation, a graduate of Morgan State College in Baltimore and of the Yale Divinity School. As the son of a Methodist clergyman, he was closely acquainted with some of the amoral aspects of highly structured Christian organization. He had come through this organization carefully nurtured by his father, a dedicated Christian minister, and a wise, sensitive mother. He grew up seeing the institution without blinkers and of his own choosing became a clergyman in the church of his father. With all of this he was blessed with a spontaneous gaiety that prevented him from taking himself too seriously. His wife was a college graduate, equally committed in faith, personable, quick-minded, and blessed with a joyous laugh that carried its own contagion. As couples, we soon enjoyed being together as though we had known each other many years.

During the fall before the India journey, Miriam Slade visited New York City for a period of five days. She was the Englishwoman who had given up her life in England in order to become not merely a follower of Gandhi but also to live in his ashram as a member of the family community of which he was the center. As soon as I learned of her visit, I knew that it was most important that two things happen while she was in this country. In the first place, it seemed urgent that we should have a chance to meet and talk. From her I was sure that it would be possible to get a feel of the life, the mood, and the people of India that reflected much of the quality of Gandhi himself. Her situation was unique because she was a woman of the upper class and had given up her way of life, abandoning many of the goals of her peers, including wealth and status. I was curious to understand how she had been energized to take such a step. For me, it was inevitable that I would see the Mahatma through her eyes and be affected by the feeling tone which emanated from her concerning the people of the country and their aspirations. In the second place, it was important that she should have exposure, in a primary way, to American Negroes, in order that her reaction be shared with the Mahatma. This would be a prelude to our journey and, however limited, it would be equivalent to firsthand information for Gandhi himself.

After many telephone calls I was able to speak to her directly. I extended to her a personal invitation from the university to be our overnight guest and to address a special assembly of faculty and students. I told her that as Howard was the only Negro university of its kind in the United States, her experience there could not be duplicated anywhere else in the world. It was my sure feeling that the Mahatma would expect her to do this once she had such a unique opportunity. Of course, because of his experience in South Africa, Gandhi was acquainted with African people, but he had no opportunity to know Afro-Americans firsthand. My final argument was that my wife and another couple were going to India in the fall to make a pilgrimage of friendship to the students of India, Burma, and Ceylon. She was convinced, rearranged her schedule, secured the cooperation of her manager, and four days later came to visit Howard University.

The problem of getting an audience to attend a public lecture in the middle of the week (or any other time) was formidable. Besides, there was little general knowledge of the vast subcontinent of India. Here and there were a few people who knew Indian students or lecturers who had come to this country, but that was all. On the other hand, there was keen interest in the struggle of freedom from colonialism between Gandhi and the British government. There was a stirring in the wind that we recognized. Finally, President Mordecai Johnson, again and again, in public addresses, paid authentic tribute to the journey into freedom charted by this "little brown man."

Miriam came. It was a part of her agreement through her manager that she be booked into the Willard Hotel, the capital's most prestigious guest house. When I met her in the lobby, I was overwhelmed by her appearance. She was tall and elegant in bearing. Her sari was made of khadi cloth; she wore a greatcoat against the winter winds, over her shoulders a rather elongated cloth bag, on her bare feet a pair of simple sandals which, I discovered later, were made from the skin of an animal that had died a natural death. She greeted me, looking directly into my eyes, then smiled as she said, taking in her surroundings in one sweeping glance, "Miriam, what are you doing in a place like this?"

The subject of her address to the assembly was in itself a bold, almost arrogant, challenge, but not quite so: "He who has more than he needs for efficient work is a thief." The essential point was quite clear and convincing. There is no moral justification for having food and a surfeit of creature comforts at one's disposal while numberless people all over the world in every country are without the necessities to survive. Hers was a quiet, undramatic delivery, but the intensity of her passion gathered us all into a single embrace, and for one timeless interval we were bound together with all the people of the earth.

For days afterward, half in jest but with an undertone of seriousness, one student would say to another, "You are a thief, look at your clothes!" Or "Are you a thief? You must be, with all that food on your plate!" Ultimately, the effect of her address could not be measured, but its impact that night was sure!

The next day she came out to visit the university before returning to her hotel. She was profoundly affected by the dogs in the kennel at the Medical School. I can see her now even more clearly than I can hear her words: "Of course, these dogs are kept for experimental purposes in the course of which they will be killed." Then she entered into a discussion about the total meaning of reverence for life and the relevance of the doctrine of ahimsa.

When I spoke of our plans to visit India in the fall, she said, "You must see Gandhiji while you are there. He will want to visit with you and will invite you to be the guests of the ashram. I'll talk with him about it upon my return and you will hear from him." Sure enough, when we arrived at Colombo there was a postcard from him inviting the delegation to be his guests at the ashram.

It was in the late spring of the same year that Muriel Lester was touring the West Coast during one of her periodic lecture tours in the United States. She was well known among pacifists and religious leaders all over the world. Many of her years were spent, as

107

a young woman, working in the slums of London. From this experience she emerged with a sense of world mission to fulfill the true destiny of the children of men, now thwarted by poverty, violence, and exploitation. She had been our guest at the university, and I knew of her established friendship with Gandhi and the Indian movement.

When she discovered through a mutual friend in Los Angeles the purpose of our mission to India, she urged him to invite me to meet her in Berkeley the following weekend so that we would have a full day to talk. She said that a friend had made it possible for her to defray all expenses for my trip. I arrived in Berkeley by train on a Sunday morning. We spent most of the day walking and talking in the Berkeley hills before returning to the railway station in time for me to get the train back to Chicago the same day.

The burden of her conversation had to do with sharing her knowledge and feelings about Gandhi, the Indian situation, and her embarrassment that her country, England, was the great offender. Above all else, she wanted to tell me about the students and the general mood of the Indian people as she knew them. It was important for me to correct her information concerning our situation in America and to reveal to her our mood and attitude toward both American Christianity and Western Christianity in general. The exchange was most profitable. Her greatest contribution to my thought was the insight she shared into the Anglo-Indian mentality.

How arduous it was to take a leave from Howard University for an entire year! I had been on the faculty only three years. As chairman of the university's Committee on Religious Life, I was responsible not only for the Sunday services in the chapel but also for the total unstructured religious witness in the university community. My teaching in the School of Religion was opening up a whole new range of exploration for my mind. We had just begun to find our way in the confusion, paradoxes, and secularism of the only recognized Negro university in the country.

President Johnson recommended my leave of absence from September 1935 until September 1936, without salary. This was an overwhelming hardship because I was still paying off an indebtedness of several thousand dollars incurred during the three traumatic years of Kate's illness.

By securing a loan on my life insurance I was able to make the necessary financial arrangements. As far as the university was concerned, it only remained for me to arrange for someone to take my place as acting chairman of the committee and to preside at the university chapel services. I was happy in the choice of Oscar Lee, to whom we gave the use of our furnished residence, which made the transition easier.

We could not take our two small daughters with us to India. But we were able to get my sister Madaline to accompany all of us as far as Geneva, Switzerland, where, in addition to acting as surrogate parent to our daughters, she could continue her study of the Dalcroze School of Music's method of teaching. The five of us set sail for Europe in September on the *Ile de France.*

It was the second crossing of the Atlantic for Sue and me, but the fall of the year was new to us; the mood of the sea is restless then and wary of all objects of whatever size that are not denizens of its waters. There were days and nights when the sea was in pure rage. The ship was sealed against the wind and the waves as it was flung recklessly up and down and from side to side—passively—as if at last we would be swallowed up or be demolished. I loved it all. The very roots of my being were exposed by the raw energy of the sea, as it tried to dislodge the huge steel intrusion into its vital parts. Not once did I sicken, not once did I miss a meal, although during the critical periods I was practically alone in the huge dining room. It was necessary to quiet the fears of our girls, particularly Olive, who was well aware of what was happening and had to be constantly reassured. Anne needed attention, because she had been given her last series of inoculations after we set sail from New York. She had to face two demons simultaneously—the pain of the needles and the heaving and plunging of the ship. Fortunately, because of her age, her fears and discomforts could be diffused with the amusements we devised. I shall always remember the quivering muted whimper of terror that came from the children's lips when the huge vessel shuddered, and everything around us, including the floor and the bunks, seemed to go into an uncontrollable spasm.

But when the sun shone and the sea was calm it was pure bliss to experience as a family those moments when the seemingly endless water reached to a circled horizon and made us feel that we and the whole sweep of the world were undifferentiated in a moment of time. Such moments on deck in the good clean brisk air cleansed our nostrils of the subtle stench of the toilets that made one think of rivers of urine. By journey's end it seemed that the odor was tangible, despite constant and persistent scrubbings and fumigation.

Sue was occupied during most of the crossing with creating and putting together by hand a little green velvet dress for Anne's birthday, which, with Olive's, would be celebrated in Geneva on the evening we were scheduled to leave Geneva for Marseilles. Fortunately, several years before I had spent part of a summer in Geneva and lived at a Quaker hostel. Mrs. Redpath, the director, and I became quite good friends and we had kept in touch with each other during the interval. She helped us find a good place for Madaline and the girls to live, thus easing a critical problem for us in leaving them behind in a strange city.

On arriving at the railway station in Geneva, I carried the baby in my arms as I made arrangements for our trunks to be brought out. Suddenly I realized that she was becoming more and more excited, but I could not understand the reason because she was looking over my shoulder in the opposite direction. When I turned around I noticed some twenty-five or thirty people following us in animated conversation and excitement because of the communication they were having with this strange, beautiful, happy brown baby. It was her introduction to Geneva, Switzerland—and variations of that experience took place during the entire stay in that unique European city.

Olive joined the children of many nations attending the International School for Children in Geneva. She had been Sue's companion in Mexico the previous spring, so this was her second international adventure. Madaline had arranged for her own studies at the Dalcroze School of Music before we left the United States. We took a night train to Marseilles after celebrating the birthdays of our girls, both born in October. We had a small family party, watched the candles burn down, and then quickly, silently, took our leave for an unknown country on an uncharted pilgrimage. For long hours Sue and I sat in the carriage watching the darkness, here and there a few stars, lights from houses and towns through which we passed—each of us with his own thoughts and questions. There was no time for words—all the words had been said and the heart could only commune with itself, the pure language of silence. At last we shared assurances with each other and were comforted. Our children were closer to India, being in Switzerland, than would have been the case had they remained in America. And they were with the one person besides ourselves who, on all counts, meant more to them than anyone else in the world. Our travail was quieted.

We joined the Carrolls in Marseilles, to begin the long sea voyage. There would be some days to wait in this most fascinating of French ports before taking ship to Colombo, the capital and port city of Ceylon. We could well use this period of time together in defining the meaning of the venture as a whole and the responsibility of each individual for the several assignments in the tentative schedule that we had in hand.

Sue had earlier been part of one of the first faculty-student Tours of Friendship to eight student centers in Europe under the auspices of the International Student Service. Further, as a national traveling secretary of the YMCA, she had worked with women and girls on college and university campuses and in wider communities throughout the United States, with occasional staff visits to Canada. Anticipating the India assignment, she had spent several months in Mexico, studying the history and culture of the people. It was decided that, as a social historian in the field of Afro-American life and history, she would speak at college assemblies and meet with women's groups that at that time were spreading a vital influence in the three countries to be covered on the tour.

Phenola Carroll had only recently graduated from college with a major in education and had begun teaching in Virginia. She was especially interested in those methods of teaching in the educational system of India based on British precedents. It was decided she would visit schools and speak particularly to young people's groups.

111

Reverend Carroll would share much of the preaching with me, especially on Sunday morning, and would address the college and university chapel services so prominently featured in the program.

That left me the heavy assignment of speaking almost nightly in all places visited, at what was called the public meeting, with all four members of the delegation present. These were to be important occasions, bringing together broad segments of the total community, including the several religious faiths of India, various denominations of the Christian church, government officials (British and Indian), civic organizations, and, of course, college and university faculty and students.

The trip across the Mediterranean, through the Suez Canal and into the Indian Ocean, provided long days in which there was time for the four of us to become a unit. By journey's end we were a family and the purpose of our journey was clearly felt and thought through.

We arrived in Colombo after twenty-one days of ocean travel. We were scheduled to spend ten days as the guests of the student movement of Ceylon, but there was some trepidation about our being able to land because we were not sure that the government would honor our credentials. Our ship passed the breakwater to the harbor; at last we were in smooth waters. The monsoons were exhausted; only the high spray of the tides remained as they dashed against the breakwater. The ship was surrounded by narrow skiffs carrying only one man apiece—they seemed like a spill of toothpicks that some giant had spread on the surface of the sea.

Our first encounter with the British government was the customs officer at the large table in the middle of the first-class saloon, who questioned us carefully. He told us to step aside until our hosts arrived to take us off the ship. Then abruptly he changed his mind and gave us landing permits. As the customs officer inspected our luggage, he said, "You come as bearers of peace; we do not suspect you."

It was a totally new world to us. Suddenly I realized that the most subtle reaction was stirring in me. At first I did not know what was happening. There was the strangeness of the dress, the unfamiliar language, the faint aroma of spices mixed with a medley of smells that did not quite agree. Even when we were settled in

112

our rooms and were acquainted with our schedules there was this inner stirring that could not be defined.

Suddenly what had been eluding my mind came to me. The dominant complexions all around us were shades of brown, from light to very dark; and more striking to me even than this were the many unmistakable signs that this was *their* country, their land. The Britishers, despite their authority, were outsiders. I had never had an experience like this. I did not know until that awareness came to me what a subtle difference this fact made in my reaction to my environment.

Ah! The first meal—how can I forget it? On board ship we were served an occasional curry dish as a foretaste. But now we were face to face with the hottest curry dishes to be found in the whole subcontinent. The curries were so hot and we so unaccustomed to the taste that it was not possible to get beyond the heat to savor the food itself. To top it all off, with our first meals we were served a glass of clear pepper water. That did it.

My first major engagement was at the Law College. The chairman of the Law Club wanted me to address the assembly on the aspects of civil disabilities under states' rights. The subject was phrased technically as he presented it. I told him that I knew much about the subject experientially, but the group would have to transpose my observations into legal jargon.

At the end of my lecture there were two questions—one about an exhibit in the Scottsboro trial, and the other about the lack of black Americans in jury service. Both questions were posed by young men who had never traveled beyond the borders of Ceylon.

At the end of the lecture, the chairman invited me for coffee. When we were through, and the service was removed, he faced me directly and said, in effect:

"I had not planned to ask you this, but after listening to your lecture I am convinced that you are an intelligent man. What are you doing here? Your forebears were taken from the west coast of Africa as slaves, by Christians. They were sold in America, a Christian country, to Christians. They were held in slavery for some two hundred years by Christians. They were freed as a result of economic forces rather than Christian idealism, by a man who was not himself a professing Christian.

"Since that time you have been brutalized, lynched, burned, and denied most civil rights by Christians, and Christianity is unable to have any effect upon your terrible plight.

"I read a clipping from one of your papers giving an account of how one of your community was being hunted down by a mob on a Sunday night. When the men in a nearby church heard the news they dismissed the service and joined in the manhunt. When the poor man had been killed they went back to resume their worship of their Christian God.

"I think that an intelligent young Negro such as yourself, here in our country on behalf of a Christian enterprise, is a traitor to all of the darker peoples of the earth. How can you account for yourself being in this unfortunate and humiliating position?"

In reply, I told him that I was not there to bolster a declining or disgraced Christian faith, nor did I come to make converts to Christianity. "It is far from my purpose to symbolize anyone or anything. I think the religion of Jesus in its true genius offers me a promising way to work through the conflicts of a disordered world. I make a careful distinction between Christianity and the religion of Jesus. My judgment about slavery and racial prejudice relative to Christianity is far more devastating than yours could ever be. From my investigation and study, the religion of Jesus projected a creative solution to the pressing problem of survival for the minority of which He was a part in the Greco-Roman world. When Christianity became an imperial and world religion, it marched under banners other than that of the teacher and prophet of Galilee. Finally, the minority in my country that is concerned about and dedicated to experiencing that spirit that was in Jesus Christ is on the side of freedom, liberty, and justice for all people, black, white, red, yellow, saint, sinner, rich, or poor. They, too, are a fact to be reckoned with in my country."

Later, I had a most enlightening conversation with the warden of the Union Hostel for students. He was a Buddhist and was deeply troubled because of the influence of Christianity on Buddhist students. He opened the conversation by saying, "I look with alarm upon the number of Buddhist students who are attending Christian schools. Not because I fear that they will become

Christians. You see, I think that there is very little difference between the two religions. My concern is far different.

"I notice that the students who attend Christian schools abandon their own faith, yet show no interest in becoming Christians.

"If the Christian schools made them into Christians, I would have no quarrel with them. Instead, they make it easy for them to become spiritual drifters."

In reply, I stated what had been moving in and out of my horizon like a fleeting ghost through all the years, an elusive insight. I said, "It seems to me that Christian education has succeeded if it makes a man an authentic Christian, or it may make him a better and more completely devout Buddhist. For I believe that Jesus reveals to a man the meaning of what he is in root and essence already. When the prodigal son came to himself, he came to his father."

It must be remembered that this was our first experience as official guests—prestigious ones at that—in a foreign country. In addition we were the guests of the Indians in their homeland, in which they were not quite free to "be at home" at home. Everything was strange, new, different, and yet in our basic concerns we were very close and in the tradition of our faith we shared a common heritage.

On the whole, the experience in Colombo was instructive, in part because it was disturbing and depressing. The outstanding impression was what seemed to me to be an irreverent disregard for the personality of the peoples of the country. Servants were everywhere, and everywhere degraded. I recall how my soul was invaded with shock and anger when, during the meal in a teacher's home, he was making a crucial point to me and was frustrated because he had to pay attention to boning the fish on his plate. In disgust he put down his fork and fish knife and yelled, "Boy— come bone this fish!" Shades of the United States.

Another evening I recoiled as we sat at dinner to see that the overhead fan was attached to a pole, the pole to a pulley, and the pulley to a rope that disappeared on the porch, where a man was seated, the rope attached to his foot, which he moved back and forth to make a little breeze and keep the flies away.

The paradoxes of our mission now began to emerge. Our coming had been heralded by no less a voice than the world-renowned Dr. E. Stanley Jones, author of several books, including *Christ of the Indian Road*. The expectation, apparently, was that as Afro-American Christians on a pilgrimage of friendship we were to be singing, soul-saving evangelists, full of the grace of God as that grace manifested itself in what it had done for us as black people in American society. Yet, we were seekers of knowledge and sought to deepen the knowledge of *all* the people, including the Americans, concerning Afro-Americans. We determined to steer clear of fitting into an evangelical mode as defined for us by other Christians. Our purpose was to give the Indian people free access to our feeling about ourselves and our idiom. We wanted to be true to the spirit and the teaching of Jesus as we understood it, while at the same time steering clear of the seemingly obvious need of Christianity to be bolstered up by members of the darker races.

The experience in Ceylon served as a comprehensive introduction to India and the customs of its people. It is entirely possible that at times, emotionally, I overreacted because there was much in the Europeans' attitude toward the Indians that I recognized as a part of my own American experience. Yet, precisely what adjustment could be made to accommodate the ethic of a religion like Christianity to the political and economic demands of imperialism? What is the anatomy of the process by which the powerful and the powerless can draw their support and inspiration from the worship of the same God and the teachings from the identical source? As we moved more and more deeply into the heart of India these issues would become ever more clearly etched, climaxing in a conversation with Gandhi three months later.

Part of the answer to the persistent dilemma was disclosed in a conversation with a high court judge. I was surprised to learn that a man with an English-educated and sophisticated legal mind such as his was also a member of an evangelical, conservative, and extremely emotional Christian sect that reminded me of the Holy Rollers of my boyhood. I discussed this with him one evening at dinner. He said in essence, "I do not participate in all of the emotionalism. The excitement of the Holy Ghost and the physical expressions of faith do not affect me. I belong because they are the most articulate Christian group in the way they live. They cast their lot with the people, living among them, sharing their daily lives as one with them—such is their testimony to their faith. European though they may be, they live the life of the simplest Indians who make up the traffic and the poverty of this city."

On our first Sunday evening in south India, I preached in the Anglican cathedral in Madras. It was at vespers. When the service was over and I was taking off my robe, a young Indian man came up to me, tears flowing down his cheeks in a quiet flood. "You did my Master wrong tonight—it was a terrible thing." I looked at him in amazement, but before I could speak he continued, "You preached your entire sermon and not one time did you call my Savior by name—by name—not one time."

"Let me ask you," I replied, "did my words seem to you to be true to His teaching? Did you sense His spirit in our midst?"

"Yes, but this is not the point. You did not call Him by name. And it is important that His name be lifted up that He might draw all men unto Him."

I was most sympathetic with this young man's dilemma. Slowly, I was beginning to understand what it is like to be a convert from one religion to another. It is far more complex than a shift from one creed to another within the same religious tradition, because it means all categories of the new faith must be clearly defined. This becomes much more complicated when that new faith seeks to take root in a culture essentially different from its origins, particularly when the new faith is in competition with a well-established religion like Hinduism. In this instance, Christianity was struggling with a religion as well as a culture and a civilization. Christianity, therefore, had to be presented as a religion, a culture, and a civilization, else it would have no impact here.

In such a struggle, precise definitions, literal statements of faith, unambiguous codes of behavior become mandatory; one can be matched against the other. When a convert is defending his new faith in the old climate, he must have fine tools. When a man becomes a Christian in a "Christian" country, what is required of him is that he renounce his former, personal life, not the life of his culture and his heritage. This becomes a personal commitment indicating the change of his private heart, but the change is not of

117

necessity a judgment of his heritage and his culture. But in a country such as India, where the Christian religion is not part of the heritage and culture, it is required of the convert to renounce not only his private past, but also the past of his cultural and social identity.

As a culture, a civilization, and a religion, for instance, Hinduism defines the lines along which inheritance takes place. It determines diet and daily etiquette, and in other concrete ways defines the individual. The convert has to renounce the old to take on the new. This is most simply done by confining one's associations (and other aspects of a total life) to people who are of the new faith.

Within Christianity itself such cultural distinctions may occur within certain religious commitments of faith. For a long time dietary proscriptions obtained within Catholicism; they are active today among Seventh-Day Adventists and others. In Orthodox Judaism, dietary and strict marriage proscriptions obtain. Wherever such proscriptions are in evidence, religion and culture conjoin to define the behavior of one's total life.

It is clear, then, why many of the Indian students and others could not understand why Christianity did not influence social customs and cultural attitudes of discrimination and racial prejudice in America. I admitted faithfully that their observation was valid as far as our personal experience was concerned; I did not know of any religious institution that had successfully projected itself into our society in an environment that was not under control, one in which no lines were drawn as to race and color. This pertained to churches of all religious groups in the United States.

These reflections were in my mind all the time I was working in India. I knew that I would have to admit what they were saying to be true, even as I kept on affirming my own deeply felt religious faith. Challenged as I was in the vastness of Indian life, all the thinking and the working out of this problem that I had done over the years on the word of Jesus to the disinherited now came to the fore. It served as a useful tool in my hands.

At this point in the journey we were distressed when Phenola Carroll was taken ill with scarlet fever. Her husband and Sue and I were put under quarantine. We were given a bungalow tent on the grounds of a hospital. I was taken out of quarantine to do my lectures morning and evening but was not permitted to have tea or dinner away from our quarters. When people came to talk with me, we would talk on the tennis court. I would sit at one end, and the visitors would sit at the other. We had to talk loudly enough to be heard but never close enough for contamination.

It was under such circumstances that I visited with Stanley Jones. His years as a missionary in India made a contribution whose effects will perhaps last as long as the American missionary tradition in India. But even he, as a white American Christian in India, over and over and over felt the necessity to transcend the social contradiction that the fact of his Christianity created. In the face of that paradox he preached the gospel and proclaimed the universal Christ.

In the course of our conversation he asked, "Have you read my new book, *Christ the Alternative to Communism*?"

"Yes, a friend of yours in south India gave it to me to read," I replied.

"Well, what do you think of it?"

I told him that he had made a very good case for communism but, in the very nature of the case, he had to make a weak case for Christianity. Whenever he referred to one of the basic teachings of Marxism he found that the same principle was more clearly stated in Christian teaching. But when he sought to document the teaching by living example, the best he could do was to quote from the Bible.

"This seemed to me to be the weakness of your thesis," I said.

Our discussion changed to the question of church union between the northern and the southern Methodist Church; a timetable for this had been agreed upon. My fear was that the price to be exacted for the union of these two great historic divisions of Methodism would be the freezing of the black Methodist churches into a single segregated jurisdiction. Of course, this is precisely what obtained for many years after their coming together under one banner of Methodism. At that time, however, Dr. Jones felt that if the issue were to be made central at the general conference there would be no union. He was sure that eventually the spirit of the

Master would overcome. Time voted for him—many years after. In 1971, Edward G. Carroll, our companion in India, became the bishop of New England of the United Methodist Church.

My mind and spirit churned in a fermentation of doubt and hope. I was convinced there was no more crucial problem for the believer than this—that a way be found by which his religious faith could keep him related to the ground of his security as a person. Thus, to be Christian, a man would not be required to stretch himself out of shape to conform to the demands of his religious faith; rather, his faith should make it possible for him to come to himself whole, in an inclusive and integrated manner, one that would not be possible without this spiritual orientation.

Years ago I had made a tentative discovery when I preached for the first time in the Methodist Church in my hometown and, to my amazement, discovered that I had the same kind of religious experience there that I had had in my own Baptist Church. Now, in India, there was a redefining of that experience, only in a much more complex and subtle way. I had to seek a means by which I could get to the essence of the religious experience of Hinduism as I sat or stood or walked in a Hindu temple where everything was foreign and new: the smells, the altars, the flowers, the chanting—all of it was completely outside my universe of discourse. I had to find my way to the place where I could stand side by side with a Hindu, a Buddhist, a Moslem, and know that the authenticity of his experience was identical with the essence and authenticity of my own. There began to emerge a growing concept in my mind, which only in recent years I have been able to state categorically, namely, that the things that are true in any religious experience are to be found in that religious experience precisely because they are true; they are not true simply because they are found in that religious experience. It is not the context that determines validity. On any road, around any turning, a man may come upon the burning bush and hear a voice say, "Take off your shoes because the place where you are now standing is a holy place, even though you did not know it before." I think that is the heartbeat of religious authority. Little did I dream that the discovery that I began to make in the Methodist Church in Daytona, Florida, as a young Baptist preacher, would move in a straight line to the Temple of the Fish Eye in Madura.

This is not to say that all religions are one and the same, but it is to say that the essence of religious experience is unique, comprehensible, and not delimiting. Convention follows conviction; conviction is not validated by convention. As we moved through India, things began to sort themselves out, yet it was difficult to find the privacy to learn about the people or the economic, social, and political struggles. We were public figures. Always there were reporters and other representatives of the media seeking interviews and attending the public meetings. We were quoted in all the papers, and this in itself was a brand-new and threatening experience for our delegation. Naturally I found myself being extremely careful to choose terms because I knew that any statements of ours could easily be taken out of context.

In confidence, our friends advised us that our whole journey was under the watchful eyes of the British Criminal Investigation Department and that we should be aware of this at all times and make no public or private statements about the seething political situation. Nevertheless, I wanted information as to the real thought of the Indian people; how they looked at the British, how they looked at us, how they looked at the world, and, in their struggle, what they thought about their future. I felt that as long as I stuck to my interpretation of our own experience in America, referring to our struggle for civil rights and first-class citizenship, we would not offend the CID or the British powers in control. At the same time every Indian of any sensitivity could transpose what we were saying and apply it to his situation. Thus we would make some important contribution to them in their struggle and be permitted to journey through the several regions. But always we were fully and completely covered, as in an incident en route to Shantiniketan.

In Calcutta we took a train to Bhorpur to visit Rabindranath Tagore's university. There a man came up to say, "Where is your fourth member? Our information is that there are four of you in this party, but only three are getting off the train." Such was the constant surveillance! We suspected that our mail was opened and read. One night I was promised an opportunity to talk in free discussion with a group of Indian men from the various professions in the community. An Indian Anglican pastor had arranged it. He agreed to call a few people to meet in his study about ten o'clock in the evening. (He was embarrassed that the invitation could not include my wife, as by tradition no women were allowed.) That night we were sitting in his study talking informally before the serious discussion began. Suddenly he got up, walked out, and stood in the hallway so that he was visible to me but not to the others in the room. He beckoned, and I went out to him. He said, "I am sorry, I have failed you again. The man sitting to your left engaging you in conversation, even though he is an Indian, is CID. So, let us Indians say anything we want to say, we are at home, we know where we are. But you must not say anything critical of the government because, if you do, they will put you out at once."

The schedule was far more exacting than anyone had advised. It began shortly after daybreak with a quiet feminine voice announcing that it was time for Chota-tea and usually a hard roll. The humidity was so enervating that for me it took an act of will to get out of bed to prepare for the day. The hot tea was a miracle worker. On our first night in a small Indian town, a thoughtful friend had come by to welcome us and to give us advice. Do not eat any fresh, uncooked, or unpeeled fruit or vegetables, he said, and be careful of all drinking water. He also urged us to keep a flashlight under our pillows so that if we had to get out from under our mosquito netting and move around in our room we could first make a circle of light on the floor before putting our foot down, lest we disturb the nocturnal ramblings of some unsuspecting scorpion or cobra. The houses were all open, no window panes, with half-doors. For purposes of ventilation, the walls did not reach the bolsters supporting the roof. We slept in cots or beds without springs and on thin mattress pads for maximum circulation of air.

When our friend left, I sat for a long while in deep reflection. Sue urged me to come to bed, warning that the next day would be very full and exciting. I said, "Give me a few more minutes. I am conditioning my nervous system so that after tonight, until the end of the journey, it will be impossible for me inadvertently to step out of bed onto the floor without first making a circle of light to guide me."

In my public lectures, the basic theme, "The Faith of the American Negro," created the most uneasiness in the American colony. I spoke in terms of a faith in my own mind, my faith in the destiny of my people, and always, a faith in God. It was in response to my public lectures in Lahore that I received the following letter from H. W. Luce, father of Henry Luce, who founded *Time* and *Life*. We were both wrestling with the dilemma created by the paradoxes in the American situation.

Lahore
February 12, 1936

Dear Mr. Thurman:

I listened with a great deal of interest to your address last night at YMCA (as also in the one given by your colleague, yesterday morning, at Arya-somaj College). I shared also in the pleasure of the delightful group as your wife sang to them at the lovely home of Mr. and Mrs. Rallia Ram.

I have also been a missionary in China for thirty years, am an ardent internationalist and inter-racialist. From boyhood up I (and some millions of other whites in the United States also) have been interested in doing all I could to assist your group to attain the highest possible best.

That gives you my background and my family interest. Nevertheless, at the close of your address I had the feeling (shared by at least a few others) that, doubtless quite unintentionally, you had probably left a wrong impression on some of the thinking minds present.

The strong impression left upon me was that you felt the Negro race in America had suffered all it has suffered at the hand of the American whites—that they had not lifted a finger to help, and that your people, so far as they had gone, had attained all by their own inherent power. Not so much in what you said as in what you omitted was the impression given; and this could have been relieved by a very few sentences here and there.

Ever since I travelled as a Student Volunteer Secretary in 1895, covering southward the Mason and Dixon Line for the first time and going from Texas to Virginia I had some real interest and knowledge of your problems. I think of the millions of dollars and hundreds of lives which have been given in sacrificial service to your people and the many colleges and schools established.

I think of thousands of Negroes who have been helped to the highest education and opportunities; it might be that the very fact that you and your colleagues were personally capable of going on a mission to India (and having a journey which many of your supporters would gladly but will never be able to take) has been partly due to the interest of some of your white friends.

I think also of how few of those of your peoples who stayed in Africa have arisen as high as the majority of your people who came to America.

That night before you were, no doubt, Muslims; and you *could* have said, if it had been tactful, that it was largely Arab Muslims that brought the slaves to the coast.

I think of Livingstone and Stanley and many another man or woman who gave their lives to stopping the slave trade at its source.

While no doubt the idea of "non-secession" was a dominant motive for some in the war there were millions who fought and many died to free the slaves. Lincoln was animated by his belief that "no nation can exist half slave, half free."

I realize that one cannot put everything one thinks and feels into one address among several addresses. But it seemed to me there was many a place in your address where a sentence or two, or even a parenthetical phrase, might have led me to feel differently. As it was, I felt that your message, far from aiding peace might (as I said, quite unconsciously on your part) have the opposite effect. As I see it in the light of my understanding of your otherwise fine and able address, I would not be willing to contribute in the interest of good will and peace toward making such an address widely known in India or anywhere else.

I write in the kindest spirit and with all good will, solely to suggest as an older man to a younger, that your work, so far as I can see, would be more vital and creative if it touched upon the emphasis which I seem to miss.

Very sincerely yours,
H. W. Luce

At dinner one night, at a large university center, there was a discussion of colonialism and what it had brought by way of blessings to the country. A very beautiful young Indian woman, an instructor in a nearby college, whispered to me, "Dr. Thurman, do you know why the sun never sets on the British Empire?" "No," I replied. "I will tell you," she said. "God cannot trust the Englishman in the dark."

Everywhere we went, we were asked, "Why are you here, if you are not the tools of the Europeans, the white people?" Of course, there were many conspicuous exceptions to this, but the suspicion of the Indians was not easily turned aside. The central question was: Is Christianity powerless before the color bar? If it is powerless, then what do you have to tell us that has any meaning? And, of course, we were usually in the presence of our hosts, who were generally Americans, or British teachers, ministers, and physicians. I felt the heat in the question "If Christianity is not powerless, why is it not changing life in your country and the rest of the world? If it is powerless, why are you here representing it to us?" Hearing this, our party went from campus to campus, city to city, town to town, talking and lecturing and sharing. This question also presented a definite problem to the missionary, particularly the American missionary.

There was another complication that had direct bearing upon how our delegation was received. As we encountered Americans, it was our impression that they felt inferior to the British. This may have been because they were foreigners in British territory. My judgment is that it went deeper than that. It seems to me that Americans tend to defer to the English—or did so until recently—on the assumption that theirs is an old civilization and culture while ours is young and therefore uncertain and brash. My private thought is that our national uneasiness in the presence of the English is rooted in a lingering collective guilt for rebelling against the mother country. There is a deep need in the collective psyche of a people for a point of referral, a refuge, where identification is possible under a prescribed code of behavioral response. It is difficult for the voice of the people to be heard if it is not transmuted into a single symbol. Whatever may be the explanation, Americans tended to be defensive about our country and its culture.

There is still another element here. The English in India were not in England, to be sure, but they were in the empire presided over by the king-emperor and protected by the authority of the British flag. On the other hand, the Americans were not only foreigners as far as citizenship was concerned, but also functioned by leave of a government that could terminate that leave without accounting for it, or allowing appeals to it. This made for a riding sense of double jeopardy. The common tongue did not guarantee security. Always we were aware of the subtleties of arrogance when people expressed amazement that our English was well spoken. So pervasive was this general climate that night after night found Sue at the dinner table discussions mounting her soapbox in defense of the American dream and the grace we have given the English tongue. She rose to the occasion because, unlike the average American missionary, she was much more deeply sensitive to the contempt with which the colonials tended to regard the Americans. On sober reflection and much searching discussion with many of the missionaries, it became clear to us that they felt their stakes were different; certain basic commitments had been made to the government on their behalf by the organizations or institutions whose representatives they were. They had to be careful lest they might undo or counteract the tremendous good they felt they were doing in meeting the spiritual and human needs of thousands of Indians.

But for us there was investment in money, years, or even faith, reaching back over several generations. Once this awareness of difference was clear it had a curious effect on my mind; it at once freed me and bound me. It freed me to recognize immediately all that I felt and said in that land was the fruit of my own struggle toward a resolution of the problems created for me by the profession of the Christian religion. It bound me with a compassionate understanding of the nature of the dilemma for the most thoughtful American missionary and what must be the nature of his embarrassment by our presence, knowing what both of us knew about the limitations of the faith in changing and affecting the life of our own people. Out of this churning, a fresh, powerful sense of authority began to emerge, and it became the contagion that swept us along. We were prepared in context to deal with the vital issues that came to mind wherever we appeared.

At Christmas we were invited to spend the holidays with faculty friends, some Indian, some American, whom we had known in college or seminary back home. They chose to go up to Darjeeling for this vacation, and for us, after the rigors of south India, to spend these precious days seven thousand feet above sea level, within the sight of Mount Everest, was alluring. Some of the Americans had received gift packages from home, rare tins of coffee and other delectables for us to feast upon at the "top of the world."

Near the end of the Christmas feast came the *pièce de résistance*, a daring proposal for "valley dwellers" from the United States. We were invited to see the sun rise over Kinchinjunga. It would mean a two-mile climb up Tiger Hill, a circuitous route that made a gradual ascent. The schedule called for leaving at two o'clock in the morning. I accepted, but Sue and Eddie graciously declined.

The next day a few Indian students and I began the climb. It was the first exercise that I had had since leaving the ship. I was about twenty pounds overweight; it was obvious that the hospitality of every compound we visited was beginning to tell on me. I ate not only because I had come to enjoy the food, but for nourishment, energy, and strength to meet the schedule of every passing day. I had expected, therefore, that this excursion would be a little difficult—but it was terrible. I would walk about five hundred feet, spread my blanket out on the ground, and stretch out to rest. After much teasing and coaxing, I made it up to the top and was guided to a small pavilion.

It was completely dark. I could feel the presence of other people close at hand but could see no one. I knew that tourists from all over the world came here to witness the sunrise. Murmurs of conversations could be heard but not decoded. Then as dawn approached, everyone became silent. One could just hear now and then the sound of gentle breathing.

At first there was just a faint finger of pink in the sky, then suddenly the whole landscape burst into one burnished gold radiance: everything was clear. Beyond, the solitary glowing peak of Everest rose. The cameras were busy. We discovered that this view had not been visible for four weeks because of an overlay of heavy clouds. The glorious sight lasted no more than a minute; the clouds came together again and closed the view. I felt like Browning's "Paracelsus":

> I am a wanderer: I remember well
> One journey, how I feared the track was missed,
> So long the city I desired to reach
> Lay hid; when suddenly its spires afar
> Flashed through the circling clouds; you may conceive
> My transport . . .

127

But I had seen the city and one such glance
No darkness could obscure . . .

When I returned, I refused to tell Sue what had happened. I teased her smugly, saying, "If you hadn't chosen a cozy sleep, and remained down in the valley, you would have gone up the mountain with me."

More than forty years have passed since that morning. It remains for me a transcendent moment of sheer glory and beatitude, when time, space, and circumstance evaporated and when my naked spirit looked into the depths of what is forbidden for anyone to see. I would never, never be the same again.

Needless to say, my family has heard this story many times, and there have been good-natured and spirited debates as to which is the truer view, that from the mountain top or that from the valley floor. Some years later, Sue wrote in the April chapter of *Meditations for Women*, dedicated to the Poet of India, her experiences of that morning, in defense of the "valley dweller."

Two friends were spending some days in the region of Darjeeling. One of them had persuaded their companion-guide to go with him to the top of Tiger Hill, so that he might catch the vision of sunrise over the Himalayas. The plans were made; the hour set. They would start climbing at early morning in order to reach the summit for the one silver instant when Kinchinjunga would be flooded with rays of shimmering light.

The other friend remained in the valley. There were visits to make: A Buddhist priest in saffron robe would be sitting near a shop in a bazaar fingering his prayer wheel. Friendly street vendors would be peddling their wares of shining brass decorated with semi-precious turquoise. There would be salutations to the sunrise in a thousand different languages. "I shall not climb Tiger Hill. The valley is so pleasant. The object of my search is in the valley."

The mountain climber might return from his heights with an attitude of condescension toward the valley seeker, not perceiving that the preferences of their choosing indicated only the variation in their goals. Once the goal or quest of an individual is made clear, it is revealed that whether he searches mountain or valley, he finds his own "acre of diamonds" where he is.

As for going to Shantiniketan, Tagore's university, it was important for us to see Tagore because he was a poet of India who soared above the political and social patterns of exclusiveness dividing mankind. His tremendous spiritual insight created a mood unique among the voices of the world. He moved deep into the heart of his own spiritual idiom and came up inside all peoples, all cultures, and all faiths.

However, my chief concern was to have some time with Dr. Singh, who was the head of the division of Oriental studies in the university. One glorious morning we sat on the floor in searching conversation about the life of the spirit, Hinduism, Buddhism, and Christianity. When lunchtime came, I had to keep an appointment with some students. Getting up from the floor, massaging my usual charley horse, I looked at him.

He remarked, "I see you are chuckling."

I replied that he was doing the same. "Perhaps we are reacting to the same thing," I said.

"Suppose you tell me first," he remarked.

I said we had spent the entire morning sparring for position—"you from behind your Hindu breastwork, and I from behind my Christian embattlement. Now and then, we step out from that protection, draw a bead on each other, then retreat."

"You are right. When we come back this afternoon, let us be wiser than that."

That afternoon I had the most primary, naked fusing of total religious experience with another human being of which I have ever been capable. It was as if we had stepped out of social, political, cultural frames of reference, and allowed two human spirits to unite on a ground of reality that was unmarked by separateness and differences. This was a watershed of experience in my life. We had become a part of each other even as we remained essentially individual. I was able to stand secure in my place and enter into his place without diminishing myself or threatening him.

One of the other things that impressed me very much at Shantiniketan was that people from all over the world were teaching there. There was in the middle of the university a semibarbaric community of tribesmen; I don't remember what they were called. The idea was that the most basic, elemental idiom of the Indian people would be seen in the context of this international, intercultural, interracial setting. A common ground would some-how be established.

I had two encounters with Tagore while there. One was the lecture he gave to the students assembled under a banyan tree. It was an unforgettable experience. He bypassed my mind and opened up an intimate acquaintance with the anatomy of my own thoughts, feelings, and religious intimations. The next day Sue and I were invited to spend an hour with him in his little house on campus. We took seats in front of his chair. He sat looking at us, but also through and beyond us, and then he would make some statement, as he focused his mind, his eyes, on our faces; then he would take off again. I felt his mind was going through cycles as if we were not even present. Then he would swing back from that orbit, settle in, take us into account again, and sweep out. It was not necessary to have an exchange of questions. It was as if we were there and being initiated into the secret working of a great mind and a giant spirit. But there was no point at which I felt the kind of identity with him that I later felt in Gandhi's presence.

Sue stayed on at Shantiniketan a week longer, while the rest of us went on to Putna and Benares. She wanted to learn more about India's ancient musical instruments, one of which, the veena, a priceless possession, had been given her by our host, a famous engineer and architect, in Hyderabad. Later, three American Negro women students, Marian Martin Banfield, Betty McCree Price, and Margaret Bush Wilson, spent a semester at Shantiniketan, supported by funds from lectures on the beauties of Indian civilization which Sue delivered at many campuses and communities in the United States and Canada on her return home.

We were within a few weeks of the time to return to the United States, sailing from Colombo, the port of arrival. This meant coming from northwest India down almost the entire length of the country to south India and then getting a boat across to Colombo. And we had not seen Mahatma Gandhi! It was during the second day of my lectures at the University of Bombay that I said to Sue, "I think I will go down to the post office and send a telegram to Mahatma Gandhi at his ashram to see if we can see him. We can't go home without visiting him." The next morning I left for the post office to send the telegram. I passed an Indian in khadi cloth wearing a Gandhi cap. Our eyes met as we passed, though we said nothing. When I had gone about fifty feet something made me turn around to look back at him just as he turned around to look back at me. He smiled; I smiled. We turned and came toward each other and when we met he said, "Are you, you?" And I said, "Yes." He said, "Well, I have a letter for you from Gandhiji." I said, "That's wonderful because I am on my way to the post office now to send a telegram to him to see whether or not it is possible for us to see each other."

I read his letter; he said he knew our time was drawing to a close, yet we hadn't met. We must have a chance to talk. He was not at his ashram, but invited us to meet him at Bardoli, where he was resting for a few days, if our schedule would permit. The letter continued, "Bardoli is closer to Bombay than my ashram. But if you prefer, when your lectures are over, I will be back at the ashram and you can come there. If this is impossible I will come to see you." I quickly canceled everything scheduled. Sue, Eddie, and I got the train to a designated station where we were met by Mr. Gandhi's secretary at four o'clock in the morning. He took us to a mango grove in which there was a little bungalow tent, a place for Sue and Eddie to rest, while Gandhi's secretary and I sat in the grove talking about Gandhi and his movement until daybreak. When daybreak came, we were served hard rolls and tea and some fruit. Immediately after this, we started on our journey. Soon we came into a native state, an area which, for political reasons, the British allowed a large measure of self-rule, and there we met a man. He was well known to Gandhi's secretary and joined our party, even though he was not free to circulate outside the native state.

As the car drove up to an open field we saw a bungalow tent over which flew the flag of the Indian National Congress. Gandhi came out of the tent to greet us as the car came to a stop. His secretary turned to me and said, "This is the first time in all the years that we have been working together that I've ever seen him come out to greet a visitor so warmly." We were introduced and invited to sit on the floor of a rather large room in the center of the tent where there were two or three other Indians. Then, to my amazement, the first thing Gandhi did was to reach under his shawl and take out an old silver watch, saying, "I apologize, but we must talk by the watch, because we have much to talk about and you have only three hours before you have to leave to catch your train back to Bombay."

He had questions. Never in my life have I been a part of that kind of examination: persistent, pragmatic questions about American Negroes, about the course of slavery, and how we had survived it. One of the things that puzzled him was why the slaves did not become Moslems. "Because," said he, "the Moslem religion is the only religion in the world in which no lines are drawn from within the religious fellowship. Once you are in, you are all the way in. This is not true in Christianity, it isn't true in Buddhism or Hinduism. If you had become Moslem, then even though you were a slave, in the faith you would be equal to your master."

He wanted to know about voting rights, lynching, discrimination, public school education, the churches and how they functioned. His questions covered the entire sweep of our experience in American society.

Finally, he looked at his watch and with surprise said, "Our time is almost gone and I haven't given you the opportunity to ask me any questions at all."

Sue asked, with a tone of urgency, under what circumstances Gandhi would come to America as the guest of Afro-Americans.

"The only conditions under which I would come would be that I would be able to make some helpful contributions toward the solution of the racial trouble in your country. I don't feel that I would have the right to try to do that unless or until I have won our struggle in India. And out of that discovery and disclosure I may be able to have some suggestions about the problems involving race relations in your country and the rest of the world." Before we left he said that with a clear perception it could be through the Afro-American that the unadulterated message of nonviolence would be delivered to all men everywhere.

At that point we asked, "Why has your movement failed of its objectives, namely, to rid the country of the British?" His reply, as I reconstruct it over these years, is more pertinent to our concerns now than it was then. He said, in essence: "The effectiveness of a creative ethical ideal such as nonviolence, ahimsa, or no killing depends upon the degree to which the masses of the people are able to embrace such a notion and have it become a working part of their total experience. It cannot be the unique property or experience of the leaders; it has to be rooted in the mass assent and creative push. The result is that when we first began our movement, it failed, and it will continue to fail until it is embraced by the masses of the people. I felt that they could not sustain this ethical ideal long enough for it to be effective because they did not have enough vitality."

It struck me with a tremendous wallop that I had never associated ethics and morality with physical vitality. It was a new notion trying to penetrate my mind.

He continued, "The masses lacked vitality for two reasons. First, they were hungry. The thing I needed to do was to attack that problem. There was a time when the masses were not so poverty-stricken. They wove their own cotton cloth. This is fundamental, because the strategy of the colonial mentality is to forbid the colony to manufacture the finished product it raises. The Indian people are not permitted by the British to manufacture the cotton cloth. Instead, the raw material must be sent to textile mills in England, where it is made into cloth and shipped back to India. I wanted them to recapture what had been lost during the period of conquest; to revive the cottage industries, and the spinning wheel. Then every family could spin their own cloth to use as they needed. This was to be one plan of attack. The other was to raise their own food and live off the land.

"The second reason for the lack of vitality was the loss of self-respect." When he said that, I smiled somewhat smugly, as if I knew a secret. He said, "I see you are smiling." I said, "Yes, but it is not what you think." "I'll tell you," Gandhi said. "You are thinking that we have lost our self-respect because of the presence of the conqueror in our midst. That is not the reason. We have lost our self-respect because of the presence of untouchability in Hinduism." And then he gave us some rather startling statistics about the untouchables, their large percentage in the population, their completely subordinated position as far as the rest of India was concerned. "They are the scavengers, the worthless. If the shadow of an untouchable falls on the Hindu temple or, in some instances, on the street on which the Hindu temple is located, the temple is considered to be contaminated."

I said, "How on earth did you attack such a thing as that?" He was striking close to home with this. He said, "The first thing that I did as a caste Hindu was to adopt into my family an outcaste and make that person a member of my family, legally, and in all the other ways. This announced to the other caste Hindus, 'This is what I mean by what I am saying.' Then I changed the name from outcaste to 'Harijan,' a word that means 'Child of God.'"

His theory was that if he could make every caste Hindu, whenever he referred to an outcaste, call him a "Child of God," in that act he would create within himself an acute moral congestion that could not be resolved until his attitude was transformed.

"I became the spearhead of a movement for the building of a new self-respect, a fresh self-image for the untouchables in Indian society. I felt that the impact of this would be the release of energy needed to sustain a commitment to nonviolent direct action."

With this explanation, our time came to a close. But before we left, he asked, "Will you do me a favor? Will you sing one of your songs for me? Will you sing 'Were You There When They Crucified My Lord?'" He continued, "I feel that this song gets to the root of the experience of the entire human race under the spread of the healing wings of suffering."

"My wife is a musician," I said, "but the rest of us will join her." Under the tent in Bardoli in a strange land we three joined in music as one heartbeat. Gandhiji and his friends bowed their heads in prayer. When it was over there was a long silence and there may have been a few words that Gandhi used in prayer; then we got up to leave.

He gave Sue a basket of tropical fruit. At the door of the tent, I asked, "Would you give me something?" as I gazed at the spinning wheel beside him. "I would like a piece of cloth woven out of material that you yourself have spun from the flax." He asked his secretary to make a note of it. Within a year from that time I received in the mail a piece of cloth made from the thread that had been spun by Gandhi himself.

At the final leavetaking I said, "Will you now, ending, answer just one question? What do you think is the greatest handicap to

Jesus Christ in India?" It was apropos of something he had said to me about Jesus and the Sermon on the Mount. I wanted to know his real thought about the chief obstacle in his own country which prevented the spread of Christianity. He answered, "Christianity as it is practiced, as it has been identified with Western culture, with Western civilization and colonialism. This is the greatest enemy that Jesus Christ has in my country—not Hinduism, or Buddhism, or any of the indigenous religions—but Christianity itself."

And with that we bade each other good-bye.

Within a few weeks we had completed our assignment in north India and followed the way down the full length of the country to Colombo, where we would take ship for Europe and America. There were long stretches when each of us was engaged in a private world of rapidly shifting vignettes. Always I was overwhelmed by the sheer numbers of human beings ebbing and flowing like the tides of the sea. There were special scenes of distilled beauty such as the Taj Mahal by moonlight and again at dawn; the eerie melodies coming out of the night; the eagerness of little village boys pushing their way to our car, crying, "Hold! Hold! We want to see!"

There was the unforgettable face—second only to Tagore's, full of agony and yearning for India's independence, yet radiant with the aura of a vast compassion, transcending all barriers of time and space. It was the face of the young Madame Vijaya Lakshmi Pandit, daughter of the distinguished Nehru family, whom we met and talked with at the public meeting in Allahabad. We would see this face again and again in after years, in the quality of her fine performance, as the first woman president of the General Assembly of the United Nations and as India's High Commissioner to London and Moscow.

We would always remember the men students at Judson College in Burma, coming to our window one minute after midnight to wish us a "Happy New Year!" on January 1, 1936.

When we left India, our bags were filled with gifts from the colleges of India, Burma, and Ceylon to be shared with American faculties and students. A Russell's viper embalmed in a huge glass jar with smaller vials of assorted scorpion species not found in

135

our country had been given us by the medical faculty of St. John's College in Agra for the Medical School of Howard University. Then the precious collection of poetic works especially inscribed to our students by Sarojini Naidu, the warm personality well known at the time as India's greatest woman poet-politician. We had spent some hours with her at smaller intimate social gatherings following the public meetings in Hyderabad.

There were gifts for our children in Geneva, sent by Indian friends. Soon they would come with our sister to meet us in Paris, where we would take the train to Le Havre and sail for home.

Among the many gifts of the spirit I was bringing back with me was the "feel" of a moment of vision standing in Khyber Pass looking down into Afghanistan as the slow camel train ambled by en route to India—it was there that I knew a way must be found to answer the persistent query of the Indian students about Christianity and the color bar.

136

V

The Bold Adventure
—San Francisco

On October 15, 1943, I received the first of a series of letters from Dr. Alfred G. Fisk, a Presbyterian clergyman and professor of philosophy at San Francisco State College:

Dear Dr. Thurman:

You will probably remember speaking here at the Mills College Institute, and you may remember me as in charge of things. I am a good friend of your friend, Walter Homan.

A. J. Muste may have written you about the new interracial church we are organizing in San Francisco. The Presbyterian Church is giving us the building of the former Japanese congregation, and a budget of $200 per month. I have resigned the church I am now serving and expect to become co-pastor of the new enterprise. But we don't want it to be in any sense run by whites "for" Negroes. It should be *of* and *by* and *for* both groups. . . . We are committed to a real equality between the races in all aspects of church organization. The boards of the church, the choir, the Sunday School and its staff will all be of mixed character. The co-pastors will have absolutely equal status and will alternate Sundays in preaching and in taking other parts of the service.

Already, a very fine group of people are interested and have indicated that they will participate. . . . The director of the International Institute, the principal of a high school and others of like character say they will attend.

We want, then, a young man of as high caliber as possible. But with our limited budget we can only pay part-time salaries, at least to begin with. A student who would be finishing theological work (at the nearby Pacific School of Religion or Berkeley Baptist Divinity School) or a young man who would take a part-time position at the Negro center here (where they need recreation leadership) would fit in very nicely. We could pay up to $100 per month, and there are living accommodations in the church.

139

It seems to me that within a year the work should grow and be able to support a full-time man. I would probably continue part-time. . . .

Could you suggest to us the man? We are very anxious not to delay too long, lest we lose the enthusiasm we have now. It would mean, I am afraid, that someone would have to drop other things and come out as soon as possible.

Any help you can give us will be very much appreciated.

This letter was the first of a series of communications between Alfred Fisk and me. As for me, I felt a touch on my shoulder that was one with the creative encounter with the Khyber Pass dream of several years earlier. I considered the option of going to San Francisco myself. It meant a willingness to make the break with the twelve instructive and satisfying years in a broad university ministry. A motto used by the British War Resisters League flooded my mind: "It is madness to sail a sea that has never been sailed before; to look for a land, the existence of which is a question. If Columbus had reflected thus he never would have weighed anchor, but with this madness he discovered a new world."

As I weighed the cost for each of us, this is what seemed to me to be involved. For the family as a whole it would mean a basic change in life-style. We had never lived in a community as such, but had always been part of a university campus, with its built-in securities and curious uncertainties. We had never lived on a street where the environment was not controlled. Our living standard was not extravagant, but it was comfortably middle-class and secure. Although our daughters attended public schools, at home they were surrounded by college students. Their peers, for the most part, were children whose parents were employed by the university. In addition, they were constantly exposed to a steady flow of different nationalities, cultures, and races that were a part of the goings and comings in our home.

For Sue, it would mean separating herself from the world of her interests on the campus and in the East. As founder-editor of the *Aframerican Woman's Journal* and chairman of the archives and museum department of the National Council of Negro Women, she would find the move to the West Coast to be a handicap. And she would be a continent removed from her mother, with whom she maintained the most intimate contact and communion, despite the distance between the District of Columbia and Dermott, Arkansas.

As for me, it meant giving up the security of a tenured full professorship and my position as dean of chapel at Howard University. More important, I would be denying myself the ever-increasing opportunity to develop my career beyond the campus, at a time when my creative powers were beginning to peak. The move also required a drastic reduction in income for our young family, with its growing needs. Yet, given the challenge of the opportunity, none of these obstacles seemed formidable.

When I applied for a leave of absence from the university, the president reminded me that I was not eligible for a sabbatical and would have to take the leave without salary. He asked me about my plans for supporting my family during the period; he raised the question more as a personal friend than as the chief official of the university. I gave a pious answer, but one that I believed utterly. "God will take care of me." I believed it then, and it remains to this day an affirmation of my total self. The leave was granted under the conditions set forth by President Johnson in his recommendation. I was fortunate to secure the services of our friend Dr. Melvin Watson to take over as dean of the chapel and live in our residence on campus.

The leave secured, the whole family was caught up in enthusiasm. We would be pioneers in California a century after the gold rush of 1849. To our joy and surprise, there was a contagion of this spirit among many of our friends on and off campus. The Council of Churches in Washington hosted a farewell testimonial dinner on the eve of our departure. The dinner committee was chaired by our close friend Coleman Jennings, a lay reader of the Episcopal Church. The major address was given by Mrs. Eleanor Roosevelt, who, as it turned out, was one of the first national associate members of the church. She and many others signed their commitment cards in time to be included at the formal inauguration ceremony of the church, October 8, 1944.

It was a cold, foggy day in July when Sue and I shivered into San Francisco, but the city loomed before us as the loveliest sight we had ever seen. Crossing over on the ferry from Oakland, drinking coffee, as we would do many times in the years to come, we shared a sudden awareness that destiny rode with us right into the city. Here would be the meeting and blending of the concerns of two men, one black, one white, moving against a background of similarities in education and religious training and yet, in important ways, coming together from opposite ends of the earth.

In spirit we met at two critical points: we were sensitive to the immorality and amorality of the Christian church in its ineffectiveness in the face of racial discrimination in its own body, as well as in the general society; in the second instance, we were convinced that a way could be found to create a religious fellowship worthy of transcending racial, cultural, and social distinctions.

Alfred Fisk had written me with almost daily anguish and distress. It was his conviction that in the immediate war years, the city of San Francisco could forge new answers in religion to the torturous questions raised by migrations of unfamiliar ethnic groups, the social cacophony of its great port of debarkation during the war years, and by the bleeding wound caused by the ruthless deportation of the Japanese to "safe" camps in the center of the country. In response, he gathered around him a small group of people with similar concerns and dedication, and they became the nucleus of the new church-to-be.

In the days that followed our arrival, we planned an inaugural service, which, in the authentic tradition of Thomas Starr King, was held at the First Unitarian Church of San Francisco, and our little group experienced a sense of inspired purpose that would remain and grow with us as we moved from our first meeting place at 1500 Post Street to two tentative locations and finally became permanently established in our present home setting, at 2041 Larkin Street.

And who were the individuals who brought their personal dreams to be interpreted and implemented by this commitment? Some were third- and fourth-generation Californians. A larger group came from all parts of the United States to work in defense industries. Many were in military service en route to and returning from the Asian and South Pacific war zones. There was the Sakai group, who took their name from the Japanese home where they lived, the owners having been sent to a relocation camp.

To me, each member was like Heywood Broun's "first robin,"

who ventured ahead of the flock, flying from dead winter straight into uncertain spring. None was more intriguing than Alfred Fisk. He was a doctor of philosophy from an Ivy League university, a voting socialist, a confirmed pacifist, an ordained Presbyterian clergyman, a devoted follower of Jesus Christ, a social activist; the Great War was the catalyst that precipitated his emergence in a leadership role at that particular moment in American history. His wife, Eleanor, had a background as interesting as his. Born of educator-missionary parents in China, she had an amazing gift of grace, which gave warm assurance to the venture from the start. Dr. Fisk continued to serve the congregation on a part-time basis for two years after the church was established, while maintaining his position at San Francisco State College.

Most of the major denominations were represented in the membership with persons of other faiths sharing worship with us and joining in all intercultural and international activities. There were humanists and others with the widest range of political concerns and orientations. The one thing we had in common was a vast hunger for a better way of living together than we had ever known and a deeper spiritual hunger that only the God of life could satisfy. Within this broad context each of us had his or her own dream and dedication out of which came the statement of sacred commitment hammered into words that early summer and finally established as the basis of membership in the Church for the Fellowship of All Peoples:

I affirm my need for a growing understanding of all men as sons of God, and I seek after a vital experience of God as revealed in Jesus of Nazareth and other great religious spirits whose fellowship with God was the foundation of their fellowship with man.

I desire to share in the spiritual growth and ethical awareness of men and women of varied national, cultural, racial, and creedal heritage united in a religious fellowship.

I desire the strength of corporate worship through membership in The Church for the Fellowship of All Peoples, with the imperative of personal dedication to the working out of God's purpose here and in all places.

Once an official roster of the voting members was sustained, it was thought wise to discontinue any organic relationship with the Presbyterian Church, or any other religious denomination in the future, in order to give our new congregation freedom to open wide its doors to all denominations, nationalities, races, and cultures who desired to live their daily lives by the tenets of such a demanding commitment.

Here at last I could put to the test once more the major concern of my life: Is the worship of God the central and most significant act of the human spirit? Is it really true that in the presence of God there is neither male nor female, child nor adult, rich nor poor, nor any classification by which mankind defines itself in categories, however meaningful? Is it only in the religious experience that the individual discovers what, ultimately, he amounts to?

The experience of worship became the keystone of the entire structure. My basic concern was the deepening of the spiritual life of the gathered people. It was during this period that I became truly aware of the discovery I had made in India—what is true in any religion is in the religion because it is true; it is not true because it is in the religion.

Our worship became increasingly a celebration before God of life lived during the week; the daily life and the period of worship were one systolic and diastolic rhythm. Increasing numbers of people who were engaged in the common life of the city of San Francisco found in the church restoration, inspiration, and courage for their work on behalf of social change in the community. The worship experience became a watering hole for this widely diverse and often disparate group of members and visitors from many walks of life.

As this began to happen locally, all kinds of visitors to the city found their way to the Sunday morning worship service to have their dreams confirmed. The list is long; among them, Josephine Baker, the American-born Parisian dancer, who was in the midst of the major project of her life, which was to adopt a group of children of varying cultures and thus to create her own interracial family; Judge and Mrs. Waites Waring, he a scion of an old Charleston family, who as a federal judge had ruled against the lily-white Democratic primary in the state of South Carolina and had seen lifelong friends turn against him and treat him as an outcast; Alan Paton, the South African novelist, whose book *Cry the Beloved Country* was completed in San Francisco and given to a member of the congregation to type and see it through the critical stages of publication after Mr. Paton's return to his homeland.

There was also interest in the church on the part of local political social radicals. During the war years the San Francisco Labor School was at its peak. This school was an active training ground for developing leaders among the longshoremen and laborers in the huge shipbuilding industry. Many attempts were made directly and indirectly to involve the church in its program. But even the most radical of our congregation were eager to safeguard the centrality of the religious commitment that held the concerns of the spirit and the worship of God at the center. However, radiating from this center were our deepest personal and corporate concerns for the total community; and we worked faithfully to implement this imperative of our commitment. We were citizens in the classical Greek sense, concerned with all aspects of the welfare of the state, responsible but penetrating critics aiding in every effort to make the good life possible for all people. As often as possible I made myself available to serve the wider community of San Francisco, even on various secular occasions.

One year I was invited to give the prayer at the opening session of the constitutional convention of the Cooks and Stewards Union International. The president declared the convention open and invited the membership to stand in silence as a tribute to all their comrades who had lost their lives at sea during the war. Then when the lights were lowered, a fan was turned on the American flag, stirring it gently in the breeze, and taps sounded from the balcony. At the conclusion he announced, "Dr. Thurman has a statement to make." I moved to the podium and said, "Let us pray." Then I prayed as if each of us was alone in the large auditorium. When I finished and turned to go to my seat, the president met me and shook my hand. "Hell, that was good!" he said. It occurred to me then that prayers are always good in this most charming but secular of cities.

It was not long before I realized that what I had learned and experienced as to the meaning of love had to be communicated as a witness to the God in me and in our personal conduct as a witnessing congregation.

What had I learned about love? One of the central things was that the experience of being understood by another was of primary importance. Somewhere deep within was a "place" beyond all faults and virtues that had to be confirmed before I could run the risk of opening my life up to another. To find ultimate security in an ultimate vulnerability, this is to be loved. Yet, I had questions. Could this be cultivated in a primary exposure to another human being? Could a climate be established in which it is reasonable and possible for one person to trust another to that extent? Was it possible for such experiences to be programmed? I did not know the answers, but Fellowship Church would be a testing ground. And though at times we might expect to contravene our own guidelines, we remained to a large extent courageously optimistic.

I began with the concept that goodwill which did not have as its center a hard core of fact and understanding was futile and mere sentimentality. True, we had within our congregation an exciting cross section of ethnic and cultural backgrounds. Under the fervor of many exposures we were growing accustomed to one another's presence as individuals, but at first little more. How to "thicken" the relations and give content to their character was the issue. The content of understanding was provided in several ways. Every Sunday after services small groups of us would have lunch together in Chinatown, at Fisherman's Wharf, or in some other international section of the city. Every primary exposure provided opportunity for additional facts to be shared about other persons and groups. A series of monthly intercultural fellowship dinners was held, in which the decor, the program, and the menu were authentically planned by one of the national groups in our membership. After such exposures, "our love began to grow more and more rich in knowledge and in all manner of insight." A church library was developed in which all kinds of intercultural materials were circulated. The first collection was purchased with the royalties from my first book. At the Sunday coffee hours there were exchanges at many levels, which measured our depth of understanding from week to week.

A series of intercultural workshops was held for children, giving

My special oak tree

Grandma Nancy

Mamma Alice

Revisiting Miss Julia Green, my first teacher

My senior class at Morehouse College, 1923

Ushers at Rankin Chapel, Howard University

Sue and I in the early days at Howard

On a Pilgrimage of Friendship to India   *With the Reverend Edward Carroll in Bomba*

*Gandhi bids
good-bye to Sue*

Fellowship Church delegation to UNESCO in Paris

Above, at the pulpit of Fellowship Church; right, with Eleanor Roosevelt and Coleman Jennings at testimonial dinner

Above left, with Rabbi Alvin Fine at the Tenth Anniversary Dinner of Fellowship Church; right, at Vassar College Commencement with Sarah Blanding, president of Vassar, and Adlai Stevenson; below, liturgical dancers and choir of Marsh Chapel, Boston University

Right, Dr. Harold Case, president of Boston University, and Mrs. Case greet us

Left, celebration in honor of Phillis Wheatley at Boston University; below, dedication of the Howard Thurman Listening Room at the Cathedral Church of St. John the Divine, New York City

Above left, on our thirty-fifth wedding anniversary; right, our grand-children; below left, my sister, Madaline; right, our daughters, Anne and Olive.

to them a feel for and knowledge of children of cultures different from their own. Wherever possible, local persons from the cultures under study were invited to share memories of their childhood, often bringing their own children with them. One summer, Hopi Indian children from Arizona were invited to visit us as guests of the children's intercultural workshop. It was very illuminating for these children to discover that they recognized many of the games and exercises the other ethnic groups shared in common. Included in such orientations was an introduction to the great religions as well. One small boy who had made a great discovery told his mother when he went home, "I knew Jesus was a Baptist, but I had no idea that he was a Jew!"

In the relationship between black and white Americans, understanding was more complicated. The general assumption was that information in this particular was "taking coals to Newcastle," that mere familiarity of presence meant knowledge of fact. But we soon discovered that in many instances, even in neighborhoods that were mixed and tension-free, there were frequent contacts without any fellowship. As one member remarked, "It had never occurred to me to visit on any basis of friendship in my neighbor's home. Now that I think about it, it is incredible. We have greeted each other and we often chat together in the market down the street. But . . . . I can't believe we've never gone any further than that." The philosophy that emerged can be schematized, I think, quite simply. Contact without fellowship tends to be unsympathetic, cold, and impersonal, expressing itself often in sick or limited forms of ill will; ill will easily becomes the ground for suspicion and hatred. The reverse is also true. Contact with fellowship is apt to be sympathetic; sympathetic understanding often leads to the exercise of goodwill. It must be remembered that at this time the war with Japan and Germany was peaking. In San Francisco, anti-Japanese feeling had surfaced as open propaganda. Scattered everywhere were billboards showing the familiar caricature of the Japanese— large horn-rim glasses, protruding buck teeth, the legend managing in every instance to use the word "Jap" rather than Japanese. The war industry had brought an invasion of black and white people from the South and the Southwest, with a professional group to serve them, bringing into the region still-fermenting germs of ancient prejudices inherited from the bitterness, agony, and frustration of centuries of human bondage and the long struggle for freedom that followed. There was a large Filipino male population in the city, far removed from the warmth of their own firesides where relations between men and women would have made for normal patterns of caring and security. These were stirring times for us, as violent storms of change swept the American West Coast and extended to the farthest outposts of the Pacific.

In the midst of this, Fellowship Church was a unique idea, fresh, untried. There were no precedents and no traditions to aid in structuring the present or gauging the future. Yet Sue and I knew that all our accumulated experiences of the past had given us two crucial gifts for this undertaking: a profound conviction that meaningful and creative experiences between peoples can be more compelling than all the ideas, concepts, faiths, fears, ideologies, and prejudices that divide them; and absolute faith that if such experiences can be multiplied and sustained over a time interval of sufficient duration *any* barrier that separates one person from another can be undermined and eliminated. We were sure that the ground of such meaningful experiences could be provided by the widest possible associations around common interest and common concerns. Moving out from this center of spiritual discovery many fresh avenues of involvement emerged. Art forms provided a natural expression: the development of the liturgical dance, both as an art form and as an expression of worship, culminating in a dance choir; the formation of an English handbell choir, taking its message of unique music to shut-ins and to hospitals, as well as giving an occasional heightened dimension to the music in the Sunday worship service; frequent art exhibits of the creative expressions of individual members. And around all of these and other activities, one basic discovery was constantly surfacing—meaningful experiences of unity among peoples were more compelling than all that divided and separated. The sense of Presence was being manifest which in time would bring one to his or her own altar stairs leading each in his own way like Jacob's ladder from earth to heaven.

As the program of the church evolved, the church building became a place around which contacts could be multiplied. Increasing numbers came from the general population, thus occasionally providing a kind of "instant" fellowship during the week. It seemed crucial to me to find means for multiplying the occasions that brought people together in the same environment. Perhaps a sense of the fellowship could be maintained, if this were done. But the coming together had to have a point, serving mutual ends. A useful vehicle was developed in organized study groups, the contents of which would give to each of us a sense of fact with reference particularly to people different from ourselves. The range was wide. There was the study of religious experience, using such books as Rufus Jones's *Mystical Religion*, William Adams Brown's *Meaning of Prayer in an Age of Science*, George Buttrick's *Parables of Jesus*, Hugh Black's *Dilemmas of Jesus*, and Louis Finkelstein's *The Pharisees*. We had a special series on the family, led by a psychiatrist recommended by the Mental Health Committee of San Francisco, a new approach in the 1940s.

The expanding program, the rapidly increasing membership, and public attendance made it necessary to find a permanent meeting place at once. Even in this process we were involved in intercultural relationships. The first small chapel in which the church was organized was owned by the Japanese-American Presbyterians before they were sent out to relocation camps; our second building belonged to the Methodist Filipinos; the third was the Art Colony on Washington Street; and, at last, the church on Larkin.

This, too, had a significant history. It was purchased from the St. John's Evangelical and Reformed Church, a congregation organized in the late nineteenth century by the Reverend Gustav Niebuhr, father of the distinguished theologians Richard and Reinhold Niebuhr. Reverend Niebuhr had come to San Francisco from his native Germany to minister, through the Evangelical Synod, to German immigrants whom he wanted to bring into closer relationship with other national and racial groups of the city. His daughter, Hulda, visited us in this church one day and told of her father's deep commitment, that were he alive he would be pleased that the building was now the home of Fellowship Church. It was important to us, too, that the cost of it was met by people all over the country, the many national associates, who believed in what became the Fellowship dream. It was felt that the local membership should be left only with the responsibility of supporting the ambitious program that would have been a challenge to a much larger congregation.

In a few years we had established a broad base for a worship program that would vitally affect every man, woman, and child in the membership—a sermon, vesper, and intercultural workshop series. A sample of the invitations sent out in one year alone illustrates the scope of activities with which we were concerned.

Individual members witnessed to the Fellowship dream as little by little there emerged an informed community of Fellowship Church carrying its own contagion. As such contagion began to invade the wider community many new problems in human relations arose. One member who lived in an apartment on Nob Hill was advised by the management that it would be impossible for her to have minority group members of the church visit her, the whole matter rising to a crisis when she had an informal supper party for a committee of the board of the church, of which she was chairman. Later she moved to another apartment where she was free to entertain her friends. Another member who had a rental cottage on her property decided to lease it to a non-Caucasian person. The surrounding neighbors took umbrage, but she held her ground and went on with her plans. A family from the church enlarged their residence by making an apartment on the third floor and wanted to offer it to a minority person. The woman invited her neighbors in for tea to let them know that such was her intent. There was much heated discussion, which ended in some understanding and acceptance. But a few days after that, in the shipyard where her husband and many of the neighbors worked together, he narrowly escaped being crushed to death by a beam one of his neighbors let fall "accidentally" over the very spot from which he had just moved away. As the community experience of the church spread there was a stirring far beyond the boundaries of the Fellowship itself.

What was happening within the membership was highlighted and dramatized by my own experiences as I began functioning as pastor beyond our own immediate perimeters. Because of the wide diversity of peoples who attended services and meetings at the church, the demands for counseling were far greater than the needs of the immediate membership. After the first year, this aspect of my ministry increased to a point that for several hours each day

YOU ARE INVITED TO
FELLOWSHIP CHURCH

For a Sermon Series on

October 8   RELIGION AND LIFE
>> *Dr. Howard Thurman, Minister*
>> *Fellowship Church*

October 15   RELIGION AND EDUCATION
>> *Dr. J. Paul Leonard, President*
>> *San Francisco State College*

October 22   RELIGION AND SOCIAL ADJUSTMENT
>> *Mr. Joe Grant Masaoka, Reg. Dir.*
>> *Japanese American Citizen's League*

October 29   RELIGION AND PRIMARY RELATIONSHIPS
>> *Dr. Anna Rose Hawks, Dean of Women*
>> *Mills College*

November 5   RELIGION AND SELF-GOVERNMENT
>> *Mr. Frank A. Clarvoe, Editor*
>> *San Francisco News*

November 12   THE RELIGION OF THE PROPHETS AND SOCIAL CHANGE
>> *Rabbi Saul White*
>> *Temple Beth-Sholom*

November 19   THE RELIGION OF JESUS AND SOCIAL CHANGE
>> *Dr. Howard Thurman, Minister*
>> *Fellowship Church*

FELLOWSHIP CHURCH

VESPERS

Monthly throughout the year

October 1   WORLD COMMUNION SERVICE *with Meditation*
                Dr. Howard Thurman

November 19   MUSIC AND LITURGY OF THE SYNAGOGUE
                Cantor Rinder of Temple Emanu-El
                The Fellowship Choir

December 24   LIVING MADONNAS
                Christmas Music
                Fine Art and Worship

January 28   ARC OF THE DAY
                A Liturgical Dance Service
                The Fellowship Dance Choir

February 25   UNTO THE HILLS AND THE SEA
                A Color Motion Picture Service

March 23   GOOD FRIDAY
                A Drama Service

April 22   MOTION TOWARD WORSHIP
                A Dance Service
                The Fellowship Dance Choir

May 27   EVENSONG
                A Music Service
                The Fellowship Choir

Sunday evenings at 7:30 o'clock

FELLOWSHIP CHURCH
INTERCULTURAL WORKSHOP

The Second Sunday of the Month

September 10   JAPANESE GUESTS
> *An International Dinner and Program*
> *Honoring Japanese University Students*
> *and Toshio Mori, Author*
> *6:30 o'clock—Reservations*

October 8   THE POETRY OF WOODFORMS
> *An Exhibit by Cornelia Chase, Choir Soloist*
> *Poetic Interpretations by Dr. Thurman*
> *4 o'clock—Tea*

November 12   INTERNATIONAL COMMUNITY CHORUS CONCERT
> *First Performance*
> *Corrinne Barrow Williams, Director*
> *8 o'clock*

December 10   AN EXHIBIT OF PAINTINGS
> *Peggy Strong, Artist*
> *4 o'clock—Tea*

January 14   INTERNATIONAL NEW YEARS
> *An International Dinner with*
> *Foods Around the World—Program*
> *6:30 o'clock—Reservations*

February 11   NEGRO WOMEN IN AMERICAN LIFE
> *A Lecture-Exhibit*
> *Intercultural Workshop*
> *Sue Bailey Thurman, Chairman*
> *4 o'clock—Tea*

except Sunday, I counseled those needing to be listened to. A cardinal rule was that any person who came to see me more than once had to agree to attend the religious services on Sunday morning. It was not important that such persons join the church but just that they had to be willing to expose themselves to the spiritual climate in which I functioned. I accepted no fees but invited persons who raised the question to make a contribution to the life and work of the church.

The most immediate extension of the climate of the Fellowship was in connection with the sick, the dying, and the burial of the dead. In the first place all the major hospitals were closed to black physicians. All the staffs, including orderlies and janitors, were seldom open to minority personnel. There was no climate either of acceptance or of tolerance for the phenomenon which I represented as a clergyman administering to the diverse needs of a "mixed" parish.

When one of our members was hospitalized at Stanford University Hospital, I went to visit her. The desk nurse was nonplussed when I asked for Miss L.'s room. "Who are you? What do you want?" I explained that I was her minister. "Are you sure? How do you spell her name?"

I replied by saying, "Before I answer your question, I must explain to you why you are reacting to my presence as you are. There is nothing in the total experience of your young years that would prepare you for such an occasion as this. Miss L. is a member of the Church for the Fellowship of All Peoples—an integrated church in the San Francisco community. I am her minister and have the minister's privilege of visiting her." While I was speaking, I heard someone call my name. It was Miss L.'s private nurse, saying her patient was waiting for me and asking that I follow her. I visited her daily. In the process, a totally new experience involved the entire staff. The patient became the focus of much attention, providing yet another opportunity for spreading the message of Fellowship Church.

On another occasion, I was called to the telephone to speak with a nurse at the University of California Medical Center. One of the terminally ill patients, a Mrs. Brown, had urged her to ask me to come to the hospital as soon as possible despite the lateness of the hour.

As I got off the elevator, I observed, at the far end of the wide corridor, a nurse sitting behind a desk. She did not look up until I spoke, standing directly in front of her. Again there was the same reaction that I had become accustomed to in San Francisco hospitals.

"What are you doing here? What do you want up here?" Now her panic was obvious as her hand reached for the telephone.

"Are you the young lady who called a minister for Mrs. Brown?"

"Oh," she stuttered, "come with me."

We walked in silence all the way to the end of the hall. There she opened a door, and speaking rather softly said, "Mrs. Brown, the minister is here. Is this the one?"

When Mrs. Brown saw me, she reached out her hand and with great effort thanked the nurse, then said quietly to me, "Thank you for coming. Because of the medication, my sleep each night is very troubled and restless. It occurred to me that if you could read to me or just talk with me quietly, your voice would be soothing and I might drift into deep natural sleep again."

I began with certain of the Psalms and other things that were source materials for my own spirit. After a while I heard the gentle breathing of one sinking into untroubled sleep. Releasing her hand, I drew the covers close around her shoulders, turned off the light, looked down at her for a long moment, and walked out. I discovered then that the same nurse had been standing at the door watching the entire procedure. As we walked *together* now down the hall, she inquired about my church. "May anyone attend? It was a wonderful thing that just happened to poor Mrs. Brown." Afterward it was my privilege to greet her several times at worship.

As my own mother's end approached, it became necessary for us to move her to California to live with us. Sue went to Florida to close our home there and bring her to San Francisco. At that time accommodations were difficult for Negroes, but she was able to get a drawing room for Mamma, who was practically bedridden. Her last days were spent with us in the environs of Fellowship Church, though she was never able to walk well enough to attend the services. In any event, the interracial church was outside the experience of her seventy-six years. She did not understand what I was doing, but she trusted me. There were people of all races and life-styles coming and going in our house. This, too, she could not credit in her own emotions, but she accepted it all with quiet grace.

During the late forties and early fifties, there were few black physicians in San Francisco. Dr. Carlton Goodlett was one of the pioneers. He had completed undergraduate work at Howard University, and like Dr. Leroy Weekes of Los Angeles had been a member of my first board of ushers at Rankin Chapel. When we moved to San Francisco, it was a great comfort to find him engaged in the practice of medicine in the city. At once he became our family physician. When Mamma became gravely ill, Dr. Goodlett got her admitted to Stanford Hospital to attend her there. She was comfortable, and the care was good, but she seemed increasingly apprehensive. Finally, one day she said, "Howard, you've got to take me home."

I said, "Mamma, you need to be here."

"No, if I've got to die, I want to die at home. Everybody here at the hospital is a 'Buckra' "—a term she used to denote white people. "The first chance they get, you don't know what they will do to you. I'm scared to go to sleep at night, and you just have to take me out of this place." That afternoon I moved her back to our house on California Street. Soon afterward she died—at home.

As the Fellowship Church congregation further penetrated the wider community, its ministry confronted another stronghold of prejudice in the city's mortuaries. At this time, in the mid-forties, there were very few mortuaries servicing the needs of the black community. My first service for a white person from the church had all the elements of raw drama. This was an elderly member who had had a heart attack riding a streetcar and died in the arms of a Negro conductor. She had moved to California from Oklahoma. How long she had lived here before the organizing of the church is not a matter of record, but I learned a little about her life before she came to San Francisco. Under what circumstances it was I do not now remember, but it was alleged that her father had been killed by a black man long ago in the South.

The service for her was held at one of the oldest mortuaries in the city. The management was quite perturbed when they found that I would conduct the ceremony. They telephoned to ask if I knew a white minister who could share the service with me. The person speaking was friendly but quite frank. "You see, if Negro members of your church attend her service and see you officiating, they may decide that when they die, they too could be buried from our parlors. And that would never do."

In spite of this, the ceremony proceeded as planned while several of the staff sat in the rear to see this phenomenon all the way through. After this, there were other services held in this place, and at various other white mortuaries throughout the city.

Such memories flooded my awareness upon my return to San Francisco after the Boston years, when I sat alone for one hour in one of these mortuaries with the body of one of my dearest and closest friends, an early member of Fellowship Church. She did not want a service of any sort. She wanted only that she and I have the last hour before cremation. I sat alone with her body and my memories of what her life meant to me and to many others during her more than ninety years of living the Fellowship commitment.

The spirit of the Fellowship extended far beyond the limitations of professional services. Sue and I made many friends, sharing the widest range of experiences and contacts over the years. In addition to these were associations in community-wide organizations. At one and the same time, one or the other of us served on the boards of the YWCA, the Conference of Christians and Jews, the Urban League, the NAACP, the International Institute, the Mental Health Council, and the Council for Civic Unity. Our services were in fullest demand as speakers to interpret our concept of community in various spheres of living. I spoke before the Commonwealth Club for their famous Friday luncheon at the Palace Hotel. I was the narrator in Honegger's *King David Oratorio* with the San Francisco Symphony Orchestra and the San Francisco Choral Society, under the baton of Dimitri Mitropoulos, the guest conductor from the Minneapolis Symphony Orchestra, and later with Artur Rodzinski.

Beyond these were the invitations growing out of strictly religious concerns. I served as minister of the day for Commencement at the

University of California at Berkeley and was the guest preacher in Jewish temples throughout the area.

While Sue was the editor of the *Aframerican Woman's Journal*, dissemination of factual history concerning black people, through the archives-library-museum department, had been stressed in every issue. This emphasis soon became an established part of the program of Fellowship Church, under the auspices of the intercultural workshop. With the upcoming centennial celebration of the California gold rush of 1849 eagerly anticipated throughout the state, Sue prepared a series of articles on "Pioneers of Negro origin in California," which was published weekly in a local newspaper and later in book form. This was given wide distribution in the city, especially among the many newcomers. Old settlers of the community learned from it as well, so they were ready to join heartily in the centennial celebration with full knowledge of their own involvement in the heritage and traditions of the West. The church yearly observed National Negro History Week and was cited by Dr. Carter G. Woodson, founder of the Association for the Study of Afro-American Life and History, as a "pilot church" because of the miniature stage sets of events, heroes, and heroines of black history, past and present, that were created by church members and featured during the annual celebration.

The choice of Corrinne Williams as director of the choir marked a new development in the unfolding of music as a concept of worship, and in its power to move out into the community in ever-widening circles. A spiritually sensitive human being, superbly gifted as teacher and performer, she was the embodiment of the Fellowship Church idea long before it became a literal fact.

With the first funds contributed toward her services by Todd Duncan, the great baritone and a former colleague at Howard University, Mrs. Williams formed an interracial, intercultural group of serious music students, which included the Fellowship Quartet, composed of a Caucasian, a Chinese, a Chicano, and an Afro-Amercian. This remarkable quartet formed the nucleus of the Fellowship Church delegation to the Fourth Plenary Session of UNESCO in Paris, traveling under the auspices of the intercultural workshop. As chairperson of the intercultural workshop, Sue and Lynn Buchanan, our able executive secretary, were directors of the tour. There was much interest and excitement aboard ship when the quartet gave concerts on the *Queen Mary*, going over, and the *Queen Elizabeth*, returning home. They had similar experiences in Paris, where they sang in the concert series at the University of Paris and at the historic American Church. The quartet, with its director, gave its services free of charge or for a minimal fee, considering themselves ambassadors, giving rare and exquisite voice to the Fellowship dream.

The communal growth and development of Fellowship Church marked also my own personal pilgrimage. The unfolding of the pattern here was the scenario by which I was working out the meaning of my own life. In the validation of the idea, I would find validation for myself. All programs, projects, and such were as windows through which my spiritual landscape could be seen and sensed. This qualitative experience I sought for all who shared in the Fellowship community—a search for the *moment* when God appeared in the head, heart, and soul of the worshipper. This was the moment above all moments, intimate, personal, private, yet shared, miraculously, with the whole human family in celebration. Often there was the need for quiet, for silence, to deepen the collective, corporate sense of worship, and many times during this period in the Sunday services there came "breaths" of waiting. Expanding the use of creative quiet made possible the communication with sick and shut-in members and national associate members in distant cities who were brought into these moments of silence and waiting together.

This experience became very real to me during the semester I was visiting professor at the University of Iowa. The mother of one of our members was suffering the last stages of a terminal illness. I had called to see her often and, on the last visit before leaving the city, proposed a way that we could keep our "times together." I would meet her in the silence, at exactly the same time twice each week, and we would be together in the presence of God. Each time I came home for a brief visit, we would share our experiences. Again and again we discovered that distance became more and more irrelevant. At last it seemed as if there was no distance separating us at all.

When I returned to the church at the end of my leave, I proposed to a meeting of the congregation that as many as cared to should join me in a service of quiet and meditation from ten thirty to eleven o'clock each Sunday morning in the sanctuary. On the first Sunday the sanctuary was nearly full. At the end of the period, I arose to make a simple statement of two sentences that had surfaced in me; that was all. In the morning service immediately following, I urged all who had attended out of curiosity to stay home. But in time, the thirty-minute period and the formal worship service became one essential continuity. There emerged a mystical unity between the meditation and the Sunday service of worship, making one creative synthesis. Perhaps the most amazing disclosure was the fact that, again and again, individuals who had scheduled appointments for counseling canceled, because in the total worship experience their needs had been met.

The Sunday morning service focused on the spiritual vitality of the sermon, where all the elements came together—instruction, guidance, inspiration, conviction, dedication, and challenge—in an enveloping all-embracing Presence. It was here that guidelines were projected by which love could "grow more and more rich in knowledge and in all manner of insight." I found that projecting a sermon series was the most useful procedure. The core of my preaching has always concerned itself with the development of the inner resources needed for the creation of a friendly world of friendly men. I felt that the church program itself and the problems inherent in the effort to extend the Fellowship community into the larger environment would provide the testing of the practical efficacy of the religious experience. The result of this attitude exposed us to much criticism because we did not fit the limited definition of an "activist" group. It was my conviction and determination that the church would be a resource for activists—a mission fundamentally perceived. To me it was important that individuals who were in the thick of the struggle for social change would be able to find renewal and fresh courage in the spiritual resources of the church. There must be provided a place, a moment, when a person could declare, "I choose!"

A minor incident illustrates this point. One evening I walked past one of the most elegant department stores in the city. There was a window display of a black woman and several children, the stereotypical "Black Mammy and Pickaninnies." I was shocked and angered. The following Sunday morning, I invited my entire congregation to go by this store to see the "interesting" window display and react to it in their own way. I was careful not to say what it was, nor why I wanted them to see it. By noon on Monday, the whole display had been removed. There are times when guidance as to techniques and strategy is urgent, when counsel, support, and collective direct action are mandatory. But there can never be a substitute for taking *personal responsibility* for social change. The word "personal" applies both to the individual and the organization—in this instance, the church. The true genius of the church was revealed by what it symbolized as a beachhead in our society in terms of community, and as an inspiration to the solitary individual to put his weight on the side of a society in which no man need be afraid. It was not merely a building, a novel undertaking in structure and formal commitment, it was not propaganda or a new teaching—no, it was a spirit which it did not create itself, but off which it dared to become an embodiment and living witness. By special grace, it emerged at a historic moment in world crisis created by the struggle between totalitarianism and democracy.

There remains one other comment about my preaching ministry. I believe that above all else the preacher's life experiences, with his successes and failures, hopes and aspirations, make up the only authentic laboratory in which all his fundamental commitments can be tested. I know my own life better than I can ever know any other. Inasmuch as my life is lived as a black man in a predominantly white society, my personal adventures are profoundly influenced by this fact. The result is that in the most unlikely moment, there may spring into my mind an incident or experience that is mine because of my racial fact. Often, in a flash, a direct insight about human relations may be revealed to me in a manner not at all possible if I were undertaking to teach the ethic of human relations. It is in this sense that again and again the entire congregation would suddenly be faced with the challenge of injustice or racial bigotry, leading to direct queries or comments and opening wide the door for teaching, for suggested reading, and for action. It was my discovery that more than campaigns or propaganda, however efficacious in creating the climate for social change, my gifts moved in the direction of the motivation of the individual and what could be done by the individual in his world, in his home, in his life, on his street.

There are unforgettable moments that illustrate this. The day the bomb fell on Hiroshima, my young Japanese secretary sat in my office as the news came over the air. She had family there. We were both devastated by the announcement. She used my large hand-kerchief to absorb her tears. No words were said. There was only the sound of the broadcast, with its lurid description of the carnage. We could establish no psychological distance between ourselves and the horror of the moment. The experience flowed together as a single moment in time. This was Fellowship Church, not in action but in *being*.

Through it all, abiding personal friendships were created out of qualities of being that have made them last through all the years. It is in the realm of these friendships that the significance of the spread of the Fellowship Church community made its most abiding impact. It is a kind of freemasonry, spreading all over the world. There has not been a single day since the beginning of the church that I have not been moved by its spirit. It was not the unique essence of any particular creed or faith; it was timeless and time-bound, the idiom of all creeds and totally contained in none, the authentic accent of every gospel but limited to none, the grow-ing edge that marks the boundaries of all that destroys and plunders and lays waste. For a breathless moment in time, a little group of diverse peoples was caught up in a dream as old as life and as new as a hope that just emerges on the horizon of becoming man.

VI

*The Weaving of
a Single Tapestry*

1. Boston: One

When I became the full-time minister to the Church for the Fellowship of All Peoples, I was sure that I had made my last vocational move. During the nine years at San Francisco I had several invitations to change positions, one to serve as a professor at Oregon State University, in Corvallis, commuting once a week at least for a semester. I decided against this, but I did accept an invitation to teach for a semester at the University of Iowa School of Religion. My commitment, however, was to remain at Fellowship Church to build a new kind of religious institution in American society.

I had exciting ideas about a new building to house the church. We were in a favorable position, for our present building was debt-free. We had paid off the mortgage in three years and were buying the house next door, looking to our expansion. Friends in the city had offered twenty thousand dollars toward building a new structure whenever we decided to relocate. My dream was to build a structure consisting of a sanctuary, a studio theater equipped both for electronic audiovisual presentations and for drama, a dining room, parlors, and classrooms—and an inner court. This setting would contribute to a year-round program, integrating religion, art, and various cultures. The centerpiece of the building would be the sanctuary, and in it would be graphic designs in stone and wood, depicting the natural evolution of man's worship of God. Thus, a worshipper in this inclusive atmosphere would have a sense of being a part of all of the strivings and the deepest yearnings of the human spirit to come to itself in its Creator.

In the midst of this I felt myself growing! My mind was expanding, and my spirit was enveloping things beyond my furthest aspirations. Sue and I were totally involved in our work, our community; we were comfortably settled, for life.

Then, in 1953, I accepted an invitation from Dr. Harold Case, President of Boston University, to come to Los Angeles to meet with him and his wife, Phyllis, to talk about a plan he had for Boston University.

The year before, when I had been invited by my friend Walter Muelder, then dean of the Graduate School of Theology at Boston University, to become a member of the faculty there, I had declined. But I sensed that the proposal that Harold Case would make would be very different.

I had known the Cases for many years; in fact, it was because of an experience that we had shared years earlier that I decided to go to Los Angeles to talk with them. I had been invited to speak at the Methodist national student conference in St. Louis. When my train arrived, I was met by a delegation from the conference. We went to the Jefferson Hotel for breakfast, after which they took me to the auditorium for my morning's address. At noon, the same committee and I came back to the hotel for lunch. As soon as we sat down, the waitress filled our glasses with water and went away. Presently, the chairman was called away from the table by the manager of the hotel, who said to him, "You brought this man in here for breakfast this morning and I said nothing about it. He had been overnight on the train and he was your guest speaker. But his presence in the dining room violated the agreement that your organization made with this hotel, that you would not require us to feed or house any Negro delegates to this conference."

There was a heated argument and finally the manager said, "You may take him up to your room and be served there, but we can't serve him in the dining room." The chairman returned to announce, very awkwardly, that the hotel had given its ultimatum. I could not accept their hospitality under those circumstances. I called one of my student friends, who was interning at the Homer Phillips Hospital, and we had lunch together.

At the lecture that evening, I told the students what had happened, and what their church had committed them to. "The time will come," I said, "when you are in the same position as the men who made this commitment on your behalf. When that time comes I want you to remember this experience."

When the lecture was over, I went to the train station. As I walked into the station, I was paged, and was paged intermittently for about a half-hour. I did not answer. When I got to my railroad car the Cases were standing there waiting for me. They expressed their regret about what had happened, and Harold Case said, "Our main purpose for meeting you here is to say that if the time ever comes when we can take some firm, even dramatic action to show that the incident that happened here is not our desire or in keeping with the true genius of the Methodist Church, I want you to know that you can depend upon us to do it."

This incident was in my thoughts as I walked into the Statler Hotel in Los Angeles to meet the Cases. Harold Case's proposal was indeed different from any others I had received. He said, "I am inviting you to become a part of the faculty and the administration of Boston University. I am prepared to offer you the deanship of the university chapel and a professorship in the School of Theology, where you will be designated Professor of Spiritual Disciplines and Resources. My dream is that you may be able to develop in the chapel at Boston University the kind of inclusive religious experience that you have developed at the Church for the Fellowship of All Peoples at San Francisco. I think your opportunity at Boston University can be more far-reaching and significant than you now realize because Boston is an academic center that attracts students and religionists from all over the world. You will have an absolutely free hand to build the kind of worship structure and organism that you wish."

I said, "Well, I need time to think about it, to talk with Sue and examine many things. When do you think this should begin?"

"In the fall," he said.

This took me by complete surprise. I had so little time. For many people, our leaving would betray the ideals they had reposed in us; they had built hopes on what we had projected. It was more than my mind could handle at the time. We talked most of the day about the possibilities.

When I returned to San Francisco, Sue and I talked about it, and our family discussed it. Then I took the chairman of the board of the church into my confidence. I prayed for guidance even as I weighed alternatives. Still I could not get a feeling for what I should do.

I was scheduled to give the Religion and Life Lectures at Wellesley that spring. Before I left, I embodied in a memorandum to the board of the church the basic implications of the invitation. It concluded with the following paragraphs:

To develop a congregation somewhat like this in a university community is to touch at every step of the way hundreds of young people who themselves will be going to the ends of the earth to take up their responsibilities as members of communities. Conceivably, this means the widest possible dissemination of the ideas in which I believe.

The fact that one of America's great universities takes the completely unprecedented step in American education to invite a Negro to become one of its administrative deans, on behalf of a development in religious meaning and experience, in itself makes a limitless contribution to intergroup relations at this fateful moment in the history of America and the world.

At the moment, and I emphasize the words "at the moment," it seems to be in line with the vision which first sent me forth from Howard University to live and work in the church here.

I am fifty-two years old, which means that according to the classical American timetable, I have thirteen years of active work. This gives me no sense of urgency but it does point up the fact that if my life is to be spent to the fullest advantage on behalf of what seems to me to be the great hope for mankind, it is important to work on its behalf where there is the maximum possibility of contagion.

I would like it clearly understood that I have made no decision nor have I made any commitment of any kind with reference to this matter. I present it to you primarily for your information.

While I was at Wellesley, I visited Boston University, saw the campus, and had another chance to talk with President Case and others. I spent an afternoon at President Case's residence, where I met his administrative assistant, and then a little later, the dean of the Graduate School of Theology. At length they took me on the campus and into the chapel. I walked around, taking in everything. Finally, after we reviewed the potentialities inherent in such a venture, Dr. Case turned to me and said, "You haven't said a word. We don't know what you are thinking. You haven't asked any questions, you haven't indicated at all where you stand in this whole matter."

I said, "There isn't anything for me to say. I can't make a move until in my heart I get the word and that word has not come through. But I will tell you one thing, that if I come, I think all of you will have a brand-new experience; you will have to learn to work in tandem with a black man. If I come, there will be times when this will cause you discomfort. Such an eye-level encounter will be foreign to your experience." I dealt with this subject at length because I had had repeated experiences at Fellowship Church in which substantive issues were debated not on their own merits, but on the basis of a deep-seated and, for the most part, unconscious racism, including my own. I knew that I would experience the same phenomenon at Boston University if I were to accept the position.

Coming back on the train, I wrestled with my spirit. Would I do violence to my dream and my commitment by resigning from Fellowship Church? I wanted to have a clear mind, so that when I got home and Sue and I talked, I could match my thinking and my judgment with hers. Together, we could arrive at a conclusion that would involve a committed action, a true decision.

One element in my thinking was the unique vocational dilemma that I faced. I could not think only of my own self-fulfillment; I had to consider the implication of my choice. If I accepted this invitation, I would be the first black man to occupy such a position in the history of the country. The potentialities for positive social change were enormous. But to do so, I would have to give up the church, which had already had a significant racial and religious impact, not only in San Francisco but nationwide. The church guaranteed my sharing in the future religious life of American society. Boston University was a large, impersonal institution. The credit of standing in my own clean place, professionally, laying claim to my own contribution, would perhaps be lost.

What of my family? How could I even think of subjecting them to yet another pioneering move? I had suffered very unpleasant racial experiences in Boston during an earlier period, and I did not want to expose them to a climate I myself did not trust. Would they be subjected to insults and discrimination as I had been? For all our sakes, I did not look forward to returning to the controlled academic environment we had left in Washington. Further, Boston

University was Methodist in origin and history. The School of Religion was a Methodist seminary and I was not at all sure, despite the assurances of President Case, that he had the power to allow me the freedom I would need to develop the chapel in my own way. I knew that the pressures on him would be great, not only because of my background and race, but because my theology might be seen to be in conflict with the Methodist Church of America.

All these issues were further complicated by the fact that the chapel itself was nearly moribund. Dr. Case had said that the religious services had not attracted thriving support either from within the university or from outside it. Sometimes, he said, there were more people in the choir than in the congregation. It was his anticipation that the uniqueness of my coming would in itself attract a full chapel. It would be up to me to maintain that attendance. If I failed, one more door might be closed against black Americans. It would be said that it took a great deal of courage on the part of the administration to put a Negro in this place, and he failed. No one would remember that the situation was in bad shape when I got there, and so much drama would attend my coming that people who had never heard of Marsh Chapel would now know about it, and point to its failure if it occurred under my administration.

When I returned to San Francisco, the family and I decided to accept the challenge and move to Boston. Later, the matter was presented to the congregation. I felt that it was very important to work out a plan so that the church could view my departure as a step in its growth rather than a retreat from its ideals and dreams. We organized a self-study group; we went into the whole question of what kind of church we wanted to become in the future. At length, the members decided that the church should not change in character, but should continue on course under new leadership. I would remain as long as possible to help in the transition period, and also remain in touch with the church throughout the year.

I arrived in Boston in September, about a week before the university opened. The word spread across the campus. I knew that the first Sunday or two, even standing room would be at a premium because people would be curious to know what this man would do and how he would be accepted. The move from San Francisco had created a great deal of national coverage. The *Atlantic Monthly* had just published a profile of my life. Shortly thereafter, *Life* published its list of twelve ministers in the United States who, on the basis of a national poll of the clergy, were at the top of their profession. I was one. *Yankee* ran a feature article that focused attention on the chapel and the beginning of my ministry at the university.

On the Monday morning after my first Sunday service, the *Boston Globe* sent a reporter to interview me. She was a perceptive woman who had been around Boston for years and knew the university well. We talked a long time and as she was getting up to leave she said, "Thank you very much. I wouldn't miss staying in Boston to see what is going to happen to you and to this chapel."

I had about ten days in which to prepare for the first service. I decided that I would try to create an atmosphere of worship in which any seeker could find his place at the altar. This was a bold and radical step in that setting. There was an established order of service that had been observed for two years, but it was not one with which I felt at home.

During the first three years it was possible to develop a well-integrated chapel staff. Beth Ballard, the permanent secretary, scheduled counseling hours, gatherings, and meetings. In her relations with the university community, she became a symbol of the caring spirit of the chapel's services. The choir director, Professor Allan Lannam, and Dr. Max Miller, the university organist, formed the musical core of what became a chapel team. Together we were able to create patterns of worship expressive of the most sensitive religious ideas and spiritual concerns. The entire program was rounded out by the imaginative dedication of the women's committee and a group of parents who shared in the planning of a special program for the children whose parents attended the regular Sunday services.

The following statement appeared in the Sunday morning bulletin on the first Sunday and throughout my ministry at the university:

The Sunday morning worship service is so designed as to address itself to the deepest needs and aspirations of the human spirit. In so doing, it does not seek to undermine whatever may be the religious context which

WITH HEAD AND HEART

gives meaning and richness to your particular life, but rather to deepen the authentic lines along which your quest for spiritual reality has led you. It is our hope that you will come to regard the Chapel not only as a place of stimulation, challenge, and dedication, but also as a symbol of the intent of the university to recognize religion as fundamental to the human enterprise.

In about three weeks the basic structure of the service had taken shape. A unique addition was a change in the structure of the period of meditation and prayer. It opened with the choir singing the first stanza of the prayer hymn, a cappella. Then followed the time of meditation, at the conclusion of which the congregation sang the remaining stanzas. The time of meditation was the heart of the total experience of worship. In it I sensed the inner quality of the mood of the people, the mood of the times, the vibrations of feeling flowing from the predicaments and needs of the individuals in the worship service. It communicated in vital currents the smell of life in the aura of the worshippers. I would sniff this, somehow, and react to it. I tried to lay it all before God in prayer. I was never able to pinpoint precisely when I would move from the verbalizing of this need and the description of the present predicaments of individuals as I felt them, or particular conditions in the world, to the act of prayer itself. They blended as one moment of experience in the presence of God.

Sometimes the whole experience would be a prayer. At other times I would move from the depths of my reflection, and the next thing I knew I would hear myself talking to God. They were not two separate experiences; there was no boundary. It was one accent, one synthesis. I felt the hearts and minds of the worshippers were receptive to whatever insight my mind and my heart could share with them. This form obtained in the worship Sunday after Sunday. I also decided that I would preach most of the time, though I had inherited a list of guest speakers who had been engaged to come to the university. I thought it necessary that the congregation and I have our baptism of fire over a protracted period, the entire academic year. I wrote to everyone who was scheduled to preach that year, explaining to them my intent. The sole exception was an invitation to President Case to preach. In subsequent years, a few members of the various faculties and an occasional visitor shared the pulpit. But I regarded my primary responsibility as being both preacher and minister to the university.

The chapel congregation was an unusual mixture. There were students from the university, although during my first year fewer than two thousand students lived within walking distance of the campus. It was a commuter's university. By the time my tenure ended as dean of the chapel, more than a decade later, nearly six thousand students lived on or near the campus. In those early days, however, many came from some distance away, but they came in numbers. There were also students from neighboring colleges: Wellesley, Northeastern, Harvard, Simmons, Tufts, and others. Professors and staff personnel from the larger university community also returned to the campus for Sunday services. In addition to the academic population, the larger community was well represented.

One of my favorites was a lady from Roxbury. She was simple in manner and unsophisticated. She reminded me very much of my mother. One Sunday after the service she stopped to greet me. She expressed her appreciation for the service and said, "I think I'll come over here every Sunday except the first Sunday, when they have communion in my church." Not only did she come, but she volunteered to help. She became the "mother" of the choir. Every Sunday she would get to the chapel early enough to see that the girls, particularly, wore their robes neatly and looked well. If something needed pinning or sewing, she would do it on the spot. Then she stood by the door and inspected each choir member. Once she said to me, "I cannot give much money in the offering, but once or twice a month I will put a little piece of money in your hands so you can put it in the basket for me."

From time to time certain "old-timers" in the university, such as professors in retirement, would attend chapel. One Sunday morning a greatly revered retired administrator of the university came to the service and was deeply moved by it. At the coffee hour he took me aside to say, "I want you to know that few times in my life have I had this kind of profound religious experience. But it is important for me to tell you that when Harold Case announced that he had invited you here as dean of the chapel, I did everything I could to oppose your coming. I tell you this with sorrow. Now I feel that bringing you here may be regarded in the future as one of the most significant contributions of his administration." I would later learn that there had been much opposition to my appointment and ministry both on racial and theological grounds. It is to his everlasting credit that Harold Case never revealed to me even a hint of the pressure to which he was subjected.

The Sunday chapel service was broadcast simultaneously over WBUR, the university's radio station, and rebroadcast in the evening. One Sunday after the evening broadcast we discovered that the tape had been accidentally erased. It was our only file copy, so the following Sunday the announcer asked if anyone in the radio audience had made a tape of the sermon. To our amazement, we received eight tapes and many phone calls, not only from the Boston area but also from other New England states.

One of the local television stations sponsored, as a public service, a daily series of religious talks, called "We Believe." I was invited to participate. I hesitated to take this assignment at first, because I communicate best before a live audience. I proceeded through the first broadcast with some anxiety because it was a brand-new experience. I had conducted a radio service in San Francisco for three years, but there I had a sense that members of my own congregation were listening. But a television camera makes all the difference in the world: it is indifferent. As soon as I began, I found myself talking to the cameramen and the other people who moved around the set, and they began to listen. They became my audience, and the interplay between our minds made it possible for me to concentrate and ignore the camera. I worked out my own format, and it became, for me, a satisfying experience. Letters from listeners began coming, asking for personal conferences and copies of the talks. Since each broadcast was taped, I arranged with the station to make transcriptions available. Soon we had a large mailing list. I announced on the air that while it would not be possible for me to have personal conferences with any of my listeners, I would be glad to answer any correspondence to the extent my time and energy allowed.

Before leaving for an eight-month stay in the Far East, I pre-recorded programs covering the period of my absence; during the month of August, I did some thirty-two tapes. It was ninety-eight degrees in Boston when I did the Christmas tape. One of the pranksters in the studio painted a large sign reading "Merry Christmas" and stood in my view as I talked and wiped the perspiration from my dripping face.

The television program became a very important aspect of my ministry. Some heartwarming friendships were made during that period, although most of these people I have never seen, and will never see. Our friendships thrive to this day through letters and mementos.

Many people who came to chapel every Sunday listened in on Friday morning as well; others who first learned of Marsh Chapel services by listening, began coming to chapel on Sunday morning. I had not realized the extent to which this was happening until, one Sunday morning at the coffee hour, a family came by with their little boy. He always waited until everybody was through shaking hands and then he would get his hug and his pat; we were good buddies. But on this particular Sunday morning he said, "Dean Thurman, I am not going to hug you anymore, I am not going to let you hug me anymore. I am not going to say anything to you anymore because last Friday I was sick and I couldn't go to school and my Mamma let me see you on television and I kept saying, 'Hi, Dean Thurman,' and waved, and you wouldn't wave back!"

When I came to the university, I was also appointed Professor of Spiritual Disciplines and Resources in the Graduate School of Theology, with the understanding that I would have a semester to get my bearings as dean of the chapel and teach the second semester. Such was not the case. Two days before classes were to begin, I was informed by the acting dean that in addition to my course in spiritual disciplines, I would also be a part of a team teaching homiletics, the art of preaching. When I was presented with this proposition, I threw up my hands. I said, "In the first place, I don't think homiletics can be taught, and certainly not by the team approach. I am trying to get adjusted as dean of the chapel. I simply can't do it."

Then it occurred to me that there was something that I would like to try from which I would learn much myself. I asked the acting dean if he would give me five students from the regular class in homiletics and let me work with them in my own way. I decided we would spend half the semester reading the Bible. The men took turns reading the Bible aloud in the chapel. I would sit in various places to listen; then I would make any suggestion that occurred to me. The other students were free to do the same thing. My observation had been that so many ministers, even those who were good speakers, did not have any feeling for reading the Bible aloud so that meaning can be communicated and moods shared. This is what I wanted them to learn. The men worked three hours a week reading the Bible over and over again until, as one man said to me, "Dean, this stuff is coming out of my ears."

In the second half of the semester I scheduled my class periods for late afternoon, when the other classes were over. I brought a record player and played music for twenty minutes. I wasn't concerned that the music be familiar to the students, only that it create a mood for them. When it was over, I would open the Bible to a preselected place and say to one of the men, "Will you preach a short sermon on this passage?" This demanded extemporaneous expression. In a split second everything the student had ever heard about the passage or any experience he had ever had relating to it had to come together in a homiletically useful and significant manner. At the end of the sermon, the other students would give their reactions.

One day, I opened the Bible to the story of the Good Samaritan and handed it to a student. He read the story aloud, closed the Bible, and said, "I will give you a modern version of that story. Two days ago, just as it was getting dark, a man was walking by the School of Theology, when another man jumped from behind the hedges and attacked him. He was assaulted and robbed, then pulled off the sidewalk. In a few minutes, the dean of the School of Theology came out of the building and passed where the man lay. He was on his way to a meeting of the Ecumenical Council downtown and his mind was full of agenda items. He did not see the man at all; he did not even hear his groans. The next person to come by was the dean of the chapel. He had just finished a discussion on Meister Eckhardt. His mind was trying to work out the difference between God and the Godhead in Eckhardt's interpretation. He did not see the man at all; he did not even hear his groans. The next man to come along was Bob Ward, the custodian at the chapel. Bob saw this man and said, 'My God! What the hell happened to you?' He called to a security guard and said, 'Call the hospital and get an ambulance over here right away. I'll try to make him comfortable until the ambulance comes.' When it came, Bob said, 'Take care of this man. I am due at the hospital for my own treatment tomorrow and I'll drop in the emergency room and take care of the bill.' "

As the student sat down, there was a twinkle in his eye. This was homiletic discourse at its amusing best.

The second course—Spiritual Disciplines and Resources—was new to the curriculum of the School of Theology. I had no idea how to teach such a course because, to my way of thinking, the life of the spirit and the meaning of religious experience are intensely personal. It communicated itself in certain worship settings, which had been my way of expressing the pulse of spiritual experience, but it was not the sort of thing that one talked about. One spoke out of it, and one undertook to live out of it, and to react out of it, but to make it literal and regularly accessible to students would be difficult indeed. As a child, the boundaries of my life spilled over into the mystery of the ocean and the wonder of the dark nights and the wooing of the wind until the breath of nature and my own breath seemed to be one—it was resonant to the tonality of God. This was a part of my cosmic religious experience as I grew up. To teach this was another matter.

Now within two days I had to begin to teach. To my amazement, some seventy-five or eighty students had signed up for the course. As the course developed, I tried various meditative techniques before beginning the lectures. Sometimes we would settle in and be quiet. For many of these men, that in itself was a radical departure from the familiar classroom pattern. For several sessions, at a certain point of "centering down," I would say, "I am going to pronounce a word that is loaded with connotations and variant meaning. When I write the word on the board, I want you to write whatever comes into your mind. Don't reflect, just write three or four sentences and pass your paper in." Sometimes I would write a sentence on the board having to do with an aspect of spiritual life as I viewed it. I would give them a few minutes in quietness, then ask them to write whatever came to them as a result.

The fundamental aim of the course, as I saw it, was to help men and women who were going into the ministry to acquaint themselves with their own inner life. I felt that the idea could be caught, but I did not think it could be taught.

2. Boston: Two

Perhaps the most satisfying aspect of my total experience at Boston University was my function as a pastor. There were many people who came to worship every Sunday and became fully involved in the process of my ministry at all levels. Even when the university was closed for holidays, the chapel held services as usual, and the attendance remained constant. There was continuity and a growing sense of community in what we were about.

There was a large choir made up of students and a small group of community persons. Professor Lannam and Dr. Miller and I met once a week to talk and chart the dimensions of worship for which we were responsible. Each of us was open to the inspirations and suggestions of the others. Occasionally the organist would compose an original musical response, and the choir director, who was quite poetic in his literary expression, would write the words to complement the music. The three of us were of one mind and one fundamental purpose. I chose the hymns and had them ready for the weekly rehearsal. Certain hymns I chose over and over again—"Breathe on Me Breath of God," "Oh, Master, Let Me Walk with Thee," "Spirit of God Descend upon My Heart," to name a few—hymns that I loved, hymns that spoke to me. The choir began to call them "Dean Thurman's hymns" and brought a special dimension to them whenever they were sung. The Sunday morning service was a time of synthesis, not only of our dedication, but of our talents. Our gifts were blended to make the service speak with one voice, which we hoped was the voice of the experienced spirit of God.

The Sunday morning service and the other aspects of the chapel ministry became the nucleus of a new organism that had begun to emerge. Without a name, without a label, without any struc-

179

ture other than the Sunday morning service and its unique spiritual expressions, the chapel service became the meeting of a church congregation. In that sense it functioned not so much as a university chapel, but as a church without a name and without sectarian bias. The organism was in the hearts of the people. Gradually, pressure developed to objectify this amorphous spirit and to give it formal structure. The congregants wanted to feel they could *join* the chapel. As a result of this mood, the president of the university gave his permission for a group of congregants from the community and the university to form an ad hoc committee to develop a proposal for the organization of Marsh Chapel. The committee members represented the spectrum of people who considered the chapel their church. The university was represented by the dean of the chapel, the dean of the School of Theology, a vice-president, and several students—a doctor on the staff of the Peter Bent Brigham Hospital, the executive secretary of the YWCA, and several other Bostonians represented the wider community. We met for an entire semester, and from our efforts there emerged a well-considered plan for creating the kind of structure which would provide for membership in the chapel. Just prior to my going on sabbatical from the university for a year, the report was completed and presented to the president and through him to the trustees.

While I was away I received a cable from the chairman of the committee, who was also a vice-president of the university, saying that the trustees were unwilling to grant permission for the kind of organization we were projecting. The issue turned on one very interesting point. It was the consensus of the committee that the organization of the chapel should be autonomous. They sensed the conflict in a relationship that was open to the freedom and the guidance of the spirit and also subject to the authority of the university. They felt that the authority for the structure was inherent in the structure itself and in its commitment. The university trustees could not permit any such autonomous organization to exist within the overall framework of the university because they were solely and totally responsible for the activities of any organization that might emerge within the university family or within its several schools and colleges. They argued that if they permitted the chapel to have autonomy this action would set a precedent that would become, in time, unmanageable, and would do violence to the spirit and letter of the university charter. As a result, the chapel organization never got off the ground.

Here again I learned an old lesson, with new implications: how difficult it is to trust the genius of an idea or a movement to grow and to perpetuate itself without finally feeling the necessity to formalize itself in some way. Inevitably, the price paid for the structure is apt to be a corresponding loss of freedom. It was not long after this that my term of tenure at the university closed and I resigned the position as dean of the chapel and became university minister-at-large. As I look back on the effort to reorganize the structure of Marsh Chapel I think I was the greatest stumbling block to the organization. There is an intrinsic contradiction between the freedom of the spirit and the organization through which that freedom manifests itself. This contradiction, this paradox, is inherent in the nature of man's personal experience of freedom itself. The sense of freedom exists within the framework of our structured and articulated obligations. If it is to compete with these obligations, then its free-flowing nature must be harnessed so as to compete on an equal footing. It too must be structured and contained within a mold. The only function of the mold is to give substance to the spirit, that we might relate to it as we do to other competing obligations when the pressures build within us to make a choice. But when, inevitably, the mold begins to choke the spirit, the mold is broken and the spirit breaks out anew, only to encrust itself in another mold, and so the process continues. This has been the historical pattern of religion and indeed all of society's creative expressions.

The chapel provided glorious opportunities for the communal celebration of life and death and for the widest range of the human experience. Set in the midst of a Methodist university which was moving more and more away from its church-relatedness, the chapel stood as an ecumenical consortium at the center of campus life. The School of Theology, white Methodist in orientation, was broad, open, and, in some ways, universal in its appeal. Yet it remained rooted in the Methodist Church. If a member of the university community or the chapel congregation wanted to be

181

married, and desired the Methodist marriage ceremony, I would put him in touch with the faculty of the School of Theology; the formal denominational marriage ceremony was always available to them. If they wanted to be married by the dean of the chapel in the sanctuary or elsewhere, I used the ceremony I had developed through the years, a ceremony created as an expression of the sacrament of marriage itself. It was my purpose to express something that had personal meaning for each couple. I was impelled to use the words and prayers that represented the finest, the most sensitive demands of my own heart and my own life. This meant, of course, that many marriages that I performed during that period were marriages of people who were part of the chapel congregation, including university personnel and many from the greater Boston community.

Another significant aspect of my ministry as a pastor had to do with funerals within the university community. In these situations I was faced with a delicate problem in human relations, for when people are suffering the loss of a loved one, they withdraw into the privacy of their pain. It is a time when people and close friends rally around the grieving family. It is not the moment for the unfamiliar. The bereaved should not have to make any sort of adjustment to the strangeness of a new personality or an unfamiliar order of service. Such things can be privately devastating to the human spirit at times of such vulnerability. Occasionally, this put me in an awkward position in my function as dean of Marsh Chapel. The question I faced at such times was how to define and carry out my ministry as dean of the university chapel without intruding upon the privacy of the bereaved. Should I offer my services and the use of the university chapel or should I wait to be asked? It was a dilemma. If I knew the family, it was relatively simple. Often, however, I found myself waiting for the initiative to be taken by the family or someone representing them.

But now and then there were occasions that created a vacuum. At such times I took the initiative and moved directly into it, especially for persons who had no religious constituency in the Boston area, except the university chapel. The chapel then became the ceremonial solace of religion to see them through personal tragedy, the resource upon which they could draw. A young Thai

woman, who had graduated from the School of Business Administration, was killed in an automobile accident. Because it was a
most unusual accident, the car and the body were impounded. Her
only relatives in America were a brother and a sister, both students
in the Boston area. The university administration wished to respond in an official capacity in this case and I was called upon to
conduct her funeral service in Marsh Chapel.

All the Thai students in the New England area attended the
service, as well as an official representative of her government, who
came from Washington to share a special ceremonial as part of the
funeral ceremony. The young victim was a Buddhist. I could not
have a Buddhist ceremony, as such, but I used all the elements of
music and the spoken word at my disposal in a service that sought
to transcend the differences in our cultures. The service, including
the formal statement by the Thai minister, was taped. The body
was cremated and the ashes sent to her native Thailand. American
students joined with others from many lands to honor the leavetaking of this beautiful girl. I also sent the tape of the service, with
a personal note, to her family.

Several years later my oldest friend, Dr. Frank T. Wilson, secretary of education for the Board of Foreign Missions of the Presbyterian Church, U.S.A., arranged a lecture tour for us. We flew
from Manila to Bangkok to take the day-long train ride through the
Malayan jungle.

The next morning, when Sue and I met, she said, "The most
amazing thing happened. The two women in my compartment
were from Bangkok. When they found that I was from America,
from Boston, and from Boston University, one said, 'One of my
closest friends had a very great tragedy connected with that university. Her daughter was killed in an accident in Boston and the
ashes sent back with an accompanying tape recording. It seems as
if some official at Boston University had a very fine funeral service
for her and was thoughtful enough to send my friend the tape of
the service.'" And Sue said, "Well, I am the wife of that man. I
was present at that service and the man, my husband, is up in the
car ahead."

The other incident had far-reaching implications. A Japanese
girl, employed as a night nurse at Peter Bent Brigham Hospital,

while completing graduate study work at the university, committed suicide. She came home to her lonely room near campus after attending a World War II movie that depicted the Japanese people as less than human. She left a note saying, "Even here I have no friends." Her body was discovered and turned over to the coroner. She was not generally known in the university and no one knew of any immediate family to be notified of her death. Friends of mine at the hospital asked that I arrange a service for her since all of her associations were at the Brigham. I arranged for the funeral. The newspaper announcement of her death stated that she had no family and was alone. But the afternoon before the service her sisters appeared in my office. They said they had not known where she was because she had been estranged from her family since becoming an American citizen. They had read about her death in an Associated Press dispatch and had come from Seattle to claim the body.

When we came to the end of our conference and were standing at the door, I spoke again of the service and offered any further help I could give. One sister said they had already made arrangements to take the body back home with them. When she finished I said very softly, "I will see you tomorrow." It was one of the most desolate moments that I ever experienced in all my ministry because I felt we had failed both the dead girl and now her two sisters, who were in Boston among strangers, a continent away from home. The service was held in the sanctuary of the chapel. It was attended by two or three doctors still in their white coats, and a group of nurses who had come over from the Brigham. When the service concluded, the casket was opened and the participants came down to view the body. The two sisters were left sitting alone on the front pew. I came down to escort them to the casket. We stood together looking down at their sister. The one who had been the most unyielding in her bitterness toward her sister for the long years of silence reached over and gently stroked the dead woman's face. Then she began to speak to her in Japanese, at first quietly, and then in louder and louder tones until she screamed and the tears came. She fell over her sister's face, kissing her lips and moaning—a pitiful, unearthly sound. At last the scene

184

was over. I walked with the two women out of the chapel and led the casket across the plaza to the hearse.

I did not notice that workmen in the area and custodians from adjoining buildings had stopped to watch our little procession. Later I learned that word had spread about the suicide of the young Japanese woman with no family; they were drawn to the scene to see how the chapel would handle her service since she had committed suicide. The next day I was told, "The men are all buzzing about what you did for the Japanese girl." One man said to me, "Even the Catholic fellows were impressed that you would do this for a Jap, and a suicide. Even though she had no connection with the chapel you showed so much compassion that it just turned them upside down."

After that, these men would go out of their way to wave at me as I passed. I began to see them or their families occasionally in chapel on Sunday. There was a subtle change in their attitude toward me and in the attitude of the entire university as to the meaning and mission of Marsh Chapel.

A very important aspect of my total ministry in Boston, as at Howard University, was the genius and vision of Sue as the wife of the dean of the chapel. It was she who insisted that once a month, after chapel service on Sunday, the entire sixty-five-voice choir should be invited to our home for dinner. On these Sundays these students and their friends would pour into our house on Bay State Road. They would sit in chairs, on the floor, on the stairs, spreading out, relaxing, reading the *Boston Globe* and the *New York Times* before the meal. There was a kitchen crew made up of our daughter Anne and a group of young people who were a part of our extended family. All afternoon the students would eat, visit, sing, and revel in their own company. This ritual constantly reinforced the relationship between our family and the larger group of students who shared in the chapel ministry.

There were also smaller groups that came in for meals or for tea or simply to visit. Sue has a rare gift for doing things that seem impromptu because of the ease with which they are done, but which come out of a well-integrated, well-disciplined sense of responsibility and caring for the many students we have served.

Another aspect of the ministry in which Sue played a critical part was in the development of an organization of women within the chapel community. Various faculties of the university were called together to join with women from the chapel to form the Women's Guild. The coffee hours for which they assumed responsibility and the fellowship following the Sunday service were an extension of the mood and the quality of their gathering for worship. Hostesses for all occasions selected from this group were an essential part of the chapel's community program. At length the guild developed into a well-organized unit, providing a gentle aesthetic touch to the total program of Marsh Chapel.

The death of the Japanese student inspired Sue to work out a plan of action based on her observation, made almost immediately upon our arrival, that although there were hundreds of foreign students, there was no structure within the university family that administered directly to their social and personal needs. One of her lifelong commitments has been to attend to the stranger, and particularly the cultural stranger, so that he or she returns home not only with an American education but also with some feeling of the pulse beat of American life as it is expressed in personal acquaintances and contacts. In this instance, she organized a committee consisting of faculty and administrative wives, which was called the Internationl Student Hostess Committee. All the resources of the chapel were at the disposal of this group, whose primary function was to bring foreign students together with American faculty and students in lasting bonds of friendship. Out of their work came the first student reception rooms for foreign students and eventually a building dedicated entirely to their needs. Faculty families "adopted" students so that they spent their holidays in American homes. Monthly birthday parties brought together representatives from the forty or more countries included in the student body. The committee also published an international cookbook, consisting of recipes from the international students and faculty wives from all departments of the university and, with the proceeds from its sale, established a permanent loan fund for the students. Sue's work and caring heart were deeply appreciated. At the tenth anniversary of the university's international program she was guest of honor and was presented with a plaque, which read:

The International Student Hostess Committee of the Boston University Women's Guild presents this Citation to its Founder, Sue Bailey Thurman, in recognition of her concern and sensitivity to the needs of international students, dedication to the enrichment of spiritual and aesthetic values, promotion of the cause of freedom and justice for all peoples, devotion to an inclusive world fellowship, and her imaginative and creative endeavors toward the realization of these high ideals.

Presented on the occasion of the Tenth Anniversary Dinner of the International Student Program of Boston University, April 8, 1964

Because of the profound emotional upheaval that I had experienced in separating myself from the Church for the Fellowship of All Peoples and moving to Boston, I was determined not to put myself through such an experience again. I felt at that time that I left behind some wounded spirits, not to speak of the deep anguish in my own heart. Notwithstanding that, I *had* to be obedient to another urging which, I felt, was an extension of the earlier one that had sent me from Washington to San Francisco.

I was scheduled for retirement from Boston University July 1, 1965. But as happened to me twice before when changing positions, I did not want to go through the psychic pains of withdrawal both for myself and those who felt dependent upon my ministry. Therefore, I arranged for a leave of absence from my chapel duties but remained at the university as minister-at-large, with the freedom of movement as challenges emerged. The first two years I was technically "dean on leave" from the university and the final year my official title became minister-at-large engaged in the wider ministry.

Two San Francisco friends, who wished to remain anonymous but who shared our common commitment, made a gift to Boston University, sufficient to underwrite my salary for three years, to equip a new office and provide a secretary. They wanted me to be free to respond to any need that fell within the context of my commitment. It was their purpose, further, to give to the university a

187

period of three years before my retirement to find the right successor who could carry forward the ministry of Marsh Chapel. It was a rare gift. The university accepted it with the understanding that the full intent of the donors would be faithfully executed. However, my successor was appointed early in the next academic year.

This three-year period brought several changes in our life-style. We moved out of the dean's residence on campus to live in downtown Boston at 80 Beacon Street, on Beacon Hill. For the first time we felt ourselves a part of the city itself and particularly its past, in which our own history as a people was involved. In one of the chapel programs the previous year we had commemorated the 175th anniversary of the death of Phillis Wheatley, first recognized black poet of America, who came to Boston on a slave ship in 1761. Our honored guests on this occasion were Roland Hayes, the tenor; Georgia Douglas Johnson, the poet; Meta Warrick Fuller, the sculptor. On another occasion a life-size mosaic of Harriet Tubman by David Holloman was unveiled at Marsh Chapel and presented to the Harriet Tubman House in the city of Boston.

From our apartment directly across from Boston Gardens, we took many early morning walks along the Freedom Trail. We were surrounded by many reminders of the past, the monuments to Robert Gould Shaw, and the 54th Infantry, the African Meeting House built by black masons in 1806, and the statue of Crispus Attucks.

Free from university responsibilities as wife of the dean of chapel, Sue could pursue her abiding interest in Afro-American history. It was during this period that she founded the Museum of Afro-American History. Before our retirement from the university, it was incorporated, with Dr. Nathan Huggins, the American historian, serving as its president while he was on the faculty of the University of Massachusetts. From these early days the museum developed under new leadership which honored Sue by giving her the title of honorary president.

As part of my wider ministry it was our privilege to make two trips around the world. The first leg of that journey was spent in Nigeria (see "Africa"). Later we spent two weeks in Israel. For a long time I had looked forward to a visit to Israel. Through many of my friends I had heard much; I had shared in many long discussions about the meaning of a homeland to a people who had for so long a time been wanderers over the earth. It was in these discussions that I caught rare glimpses of the way in which the "living traditions" had served as a surrogate homeland for the sons and daughters of Israel; it mattered not how completely at home they were in the land of their particular birth and upbringing. The scent of the homeland of their forefathers, the soil in which the very embodiment of the idiom of the people was cradled at that far-off time when the covenanted group first became aware of a strange and awesome destiny—all of these came together in a daring paradox when the modern state of Israel was born.

Our visit to Israel had two specific elements in it. It was important to me to experience firsthand the flavor of a people who had been the object of persecution, a qualitative ostracism and isolation all over the world for hundreds of years, but who had kept before them, in varying degrees, the dream of returning to the land of their fathers. I was puzzled by something else that seemed to stand over against the sense of homecoming—I refer to the overriding notion that the dream of coming back to the land of the fathers was a political and nationalistic fulfillment rather than merely a spiritual returning or homecoming to a soil made sacred by divine encounter. Always one has to keep in mind that Judaism is a culture, a civilization, *and* a religion. In this Judaism is not unique. The same is characteristic of Islam, Christianity, and Buddhism. Therefore, it is crucial to understand in what sense the individual is relating to his historic faith. The individual devotee may be a believer in the religion, the culture, or the social phenomena of which his religion is the embodiment. My approach to the faith was primarily historic and yet, as a religion, Judaism was of primary significance. Needless to say, in my mind all these currents moved over my total landscape, giving to my anticipation a blurred outline rather than a sharp focus. I did not know what to expect.

At first I observed everything through the eyes of my own religious background. This is the land made sacred because it was the place where Jesus was born, lived, and died. Because of a lifelong association with the great figures of the Old Testament, the names of places, rivers, mountains, were chiseled in my spirit. They were the familiar heroes of my own faith from my childhood. All of this gave to my anticipation a sheen of unreality taking on the characteristic of a waking dream. I did not know what to expect; yet I knew *what* I was expecting and tried in devious ways to protect myself from disillusionment. Everything I saw and experienced had to be interpreted against a background, an apperceptive mass that my own life story had given me through all the years of my living. Yet there was nothing in my experience that had or could have prepared me for the adventure that awaited us.

We were not prepared for Jerusalem. There was nothing in evidence to remind me of what through the years I had come to think of as the city of Jerusalem. This of course was due in large part to the bias of my own background and the fact that this was not the Jerusalem about which I had read and studied. It was not the Jerusalem of the Bible, as I knew it—that Jerusalem was part of a lore and tradition of another age; it was the Jerusalem of the Prophets, of Jesus, and of Paul.

I was in quest of a spirit that seemed to evade me on every hand. What I needed and wanted to do was to tarry in Jerusalem. I needed time to get still enough to wait until the heartbeat of the city of David could surface to break the stillness surrounding my waiting spirit. If only I could have sat on one of the high places surrounding the city during a long night of silence! Here, as I watched the procession of the stars and constellations as they marched across the heavens, muted sounds of genuine comment from the rocks, ancient trees, and wise old hills would whisper to me through the long night watch what they have seen and experienced through the slow march of the centuries. If this could have happened I would have been able to glimpse the soul of Jerusalem which was obscured from my view and my sensitivity. Not only were my own limitations responsible but also the Jerusalem of my present experience was in profound conflict with what the Jerusalem of my imagination had taught me through the intimacy of my religious tradition and teaching. I felt the great gulf that separated me from the present place and the symbolism of what that place meant in the history of my own life and tradition. I do not desire to see it again. It is important that I wanted to get back to the long-time security of *my* Jerusalem, which does not exist in any place or any time but which is a part of the fluid area of my own living experience. For Jerusalem represented to me a city through which many currents were flowing, a city of violence, a city of great spiritual discovery. It was a city I had associated more dramatically with Jesus than any other. To me it was a more radical expanse of the heart of the spiritual idiom resident in Him than in any other place. In accordance with my religious tradition, however distorted and colored may have been His experiences in that city, it was here that Jesus, the Palestinian Jew, moves into a dimension of meaning and significance for untold millions who are touched by His spirit and healed by faith in His experience of His Father, the God of Abraham, Isaac, and Jacob.

In a subsequent journey we met students and faculty in parts of Japan, the Philippines, Egypt, Hong Kong, and Hawaii. As the time for retirement approached, it was suggested that in keeping with the custom of the university, we would be honored with a special dinner at which time there would be the usual testimonial and appropriate gift. I countered with the idea of a public meeting in honor of a type of ministry rather than a person. President Case accepted the suggestion and the meeting was set up for its execution. A complete mailing list was made, including former students, friends, associates, radio and television mailings, and so on. All these were invited to attend.

It was a beautiful setting in the Student Union. Many people came from many places. The major address was given by Ambassador Joseph Palmer, who at the time was director general of the Foreign Service in the State Department. The program was shared by a former student who had come from Iowa for the event, my succesor as dean of chapel at Howard University, a long-time friend, a professor of surgery at Columbia University; a childhood schoolmate from days in Daytona.

The chairman of the gift committee was Dean George Makechnie, one of my closest associates and friends at the university. On this occasion he presented me with a check for ten thousand dollars—which became the first solid foundation for the recently established

Howard Thurman Educational Trust, incorporated under the laws of the state of California.

This marked the end of my formal extended academic career and marked the beginning of a new challenge for my life as chairman of the educational trust that bears my name. With the change of residence from Boston to San Francisco at sixty-five I began a new career.

3. Africa

We had been sailing for two or three days along the west coast of Africa, but the coast had not been visible. It was so overcast that moonlight could not penetrate. All I knew was that the ship's officers had said Africa was nearby. I went down to my cabin. I prepared for bed and pulled back the curtain of the porthole, and, as I looked out, the clouds broke, the mist disintegrated. There in the moonlight, for the first time in my life, I beheld the west coast of Africa. I wept, or rather, I shed tears without weeping. I sat immediately on the side of the bed, and wrote these words in my journal:

From my cabin window I look out on the full moon and the ghosts of my forefathers rise and fall with the undulating waves. Across these same waters, how many years ago they came. What were the inchoate mutterings locked tight within the circle of their hearts? In the deep, heavy darkness of the foul-smelling hole of the ship, where they could not see the sky nor hear the night noises nor feel the warm compassion of the tribe, they held their breath against the agony.

How does the human spirit accommodate itself to desolation? How did they? What tools of the spirit were in their hands with which to cut a path through the wilderness of their despair? If only death of the body could come to deliver the soul from dying. If some sacred taboo had been defiled and this extended terror was the consequence—there would be no panic in the paying. If some creature of the vast and pulsing jungle had snatched the life away—this would even in its wildest fear be floated by the familiarity of the daily hazard. If death had come, being ushered into life by a terrible paroxysm of pain, all the assurance of the Way of the Tribe would have carried the spirit home on the wings of precious ceremony and holy ritual. But this! Nothing anywhere in all the myths, in all the stories, in all the ancient memory of the race, had given hint of this torturous convulsion. There were no gods to hear, no magic spell of witch doctor to summon, even one's companion in chains muttered his quivering misery in a tongue unknown and a sound unfamiliar.

O my fathers, what was it like to be stripped of all supports of life save the beating of the heart and the ebb and flow of fetid air in the lungs? In a strange moment when you suddenly caught your breath, did some intimation from the future give to your spirit a wink of promise? In the darkness, did you hear the silent feet of your children beating a melody of freedom to words which you would never know, in a land in which your bones would be warmed again in the depths of the cold earth in which you would sleep, unknown, unrealized and alone?

My earliest knowledge of Africa came from Christian missionaries who occasionally visited the churches in Daytona Beach. Although they were themselves Afro-American, they spoke as missionaries and had little feeling of identification or kinship with the African people.

In high school I had an African classmate, Henry Nemle Sia, who came from Sierra Leone. He was a robust and vital man whom I remember well because when he tried out for football he refused to encumber himself with even the meager protective equipment used in those days. He was stronger, more muscular than the rest of us. He talked with us many times about his cultural life as a boy growing up in Sierra Leone. But it was a far-off land. At Morehouse College there was a visitor from the Gold Coast, an older man, a minister educated in part in this country, who came to talk about life in Africa. But his point of view was essentially that of the missionaries whom I had heard as a child.

My grandmother had been a slave, and although she spoke very little of her early life, I associated Africa with slavery—the slavery of my forebears, the slavery of my grandmother. This association must have created in me an unarticulated identification with the African people because I felt immune to the propaganda of the missionaries about the African "savages." I remember with a kind of desperation and anger an experience with the Daily Vacation Bible School that I conducted as a divinity student in Virginia when I worked there as a summer assistant in 1924. At the end of my first year I wrote a pageant of all nations; in it all the peoples of the earth were represented by the children, who brought their offerings to the altar—a very typical, unoriginal production even at that time. It really outraged me that none of the youngsters wanted to be Africans, so negative was their attitude toward Africans and so thorough their conditioning. I remember that I called the whole thing off because I felt so absolutely helpless about the way in which we had been propagandized, even in the Christian church.

During that same summer I came in to the young people's meeting one Sunday afternoon and saw a tall, striking black man addressing the group. I had never before seen him and wondered who had brought him. He was talking to the young people saying, "I'm from Africa. I am a Moslem. I came into your town this morning and I decided that since this is the Christian Sabbath I would like to attend a church. So, I walked down the opposite end of this street, and came to a church with a sign, First Baptist Church. I started in to worship and was told at the entrance, 'This is not the First Baptist Church you are looking for. You are looking for the First Baptist Church for your people,' and they directed me here. So I came here and this is what I find. In the Moslem religion there would be no such distinction made." I shall remember as long as I live how he ended his talk to these young people on that Sunday afternoon. "Allah laughs aloud in his Mohammedan heaven when he sees the Christian spectacle: the First Baptist Church White, and the First Baptist Church Colored."

These images of Africa moved in and out of my mind through the years; and the propaganda that victimized my children in Roanoke persisted in American culture for decades. It said, "You are all trapped, bound together as inferior people, black men over the world: this is your common heritage." There was no inspiration to recognize a common fatherland. But the testimony of my grandmother was just the opposite. Even though she herself was one or two generations removed from Africa, she always had a sense of dignity and strength that I instinctively recognized to be rooted in her African past.

Even in our churches, where missions were early established to operate schools and hospitals, the appeal to the congregation was to "help" the African native, with no indication or appreciation of the culture and the civilization we shared, or the tremendous background of history to which the black people of that great continent could lay claim. It was not until I was a college student that I became even casually acquainted with the idea of ancient African kingdoms, so great was the care taken to guarantee that black Americans would have no identity with their ancient past.

I remember reading in the opening section of Book I of *The Iliad* a passage in which one of the lesser gods went to visit the kingdom of Zeus and was told that Zeus and his retinue had gone to visit "the far-famed Ethiopians." The teacher carefully made a distinction between the Ethiopians and the Africans, and maintained that while the Ethiopians were black, they were not classified as Negroid. He found it necessary to make this distinction so that we would not identify our African heritage with the Ethiopians, who struck the whites as more imperious and fundamentally a more worthwhile race of human beings.

As the years unfolded I knew that at some time I must visit Africa; it was a vague longing. I also knew that I could not go until I was ready for the journey. I had some reservations, some hesitation about walking on African soil, for fear I might destroy the African mystery which in some way had become part of my adult being. Preparation for the trip began in earnest when I joined the faculty of Howard University and met Professor Leo Hansberry. His gift was to stir an entire campus to think historically about the African peoples. Hansberry had spent a lifetime in research, going back to discover and share information about ancient black African kingdoms. He lectured on this subject until his death and left an unpublished manuscript on which he had been working as his life's contribution to this particular cause. This knowledge Hansberry made available to me and to all faculty groups and classes at Howard. It seemed at first a fine but isolated scholarly work that had no flesh and blood, no continuity that reached into the present. But when you talked with him face to face, his conviction was such that he stirred an old racial memory somewhere in your own past. I loved Hansberry and on the slightest provocation would create extra opportunities for him to talk to students, or to faculty or community groups in our home.

Gradually, Africa emerged from the fogs of memory. I moved to San Francisco. The United Nations was formed. African nations slowly gained their freedom from colonialism. There began to appear in news items and on radio and television statements from African representatives to the United Nations sent by rulers who themselves were black Africans.

But it was not until 1963 that both the opportunity and the means came for me to visit Africa. My wider ministry from Boston University had already been arranged. Among the people to receive honorary degrees from the university that year was Dr. Kenneth O. Dike, vice-chancellor of the University of Ibadan. I told him that I would like to visit Nigeria in the fall. Shortly after he returned home I received an invitation to come to Ibadan as a visiting lecturer in the department of philosophy and religion. Dr. Dike and I agreed that the university would be our home base, but that my lecturing schedule would allow time to travel out of the city, away from the urban and academic life. I longed to discover the sources of indigenous African religions, to explore the underground spiritual springs that ran deep long before the coming of Islam or early Christianity. I hoped to find a common ground between Christian religious experience and the religious experience in the background and in the heart of the African people. If such a common ground could be located and defined, it seemed to me that the finest insights of Christianity could be energized by the cumulative, boundless energy of hundreds of years of the brooding spirit of God as it expressed itself in many forms in the life of a great people.

I accepted Dr. Dike's invitation with great enthusiasm. I applied for a visa immediately and booked passage by ship from New York. Sue made plans to fly over several weeks after my arrival. But as the time to sail approached, my visa had not yet come. In New York, I spent hours at the Nigerian consulate trying to get clearance, but to no avail. Finally, I decided to sail to England to talk directly with the university representative at the University of London; the University of Ibadan, in keeping with colonial practice, was part of the University of London system.

The representative in London expressed much interest in my going to Nigeria and talked again with the officer in charge of visas, assuring him that my work was very important to the university. Even so, I did not get the visa before setting sail for Lagos.

The understanding was that when I arrived at this port city, the visa would be there waiting for me. The steamship company was willing for me to go on board, if I could guarantee round-trip passage in the event I could not enter the country. That much was settled.

While waiting for the ship in London, I met an American black man from Cambridge, Massachusetts, Mahmud Mohammed, who had become a Moslem. He had read in the *Boston Globe* about my visit to Nigeria. He was working in the library school and in Arabian studies at Ibadan. At once he gave me his friendship and his help. He and his wife had lived in Ibadan the previous year and had enjoyed the life there. We talked for many hours as we walked about London. On the night before sailing, he invited me to go with him out beyond the Wimbledon district to visit with the head of the Moslem mission in London.

The head of the mission, a Pakistani, was thrilled when he found that I had been to his country, to India, before there was a Pakistan as such. For more than an hour he subjected me to a tirade against Christianity, and a paean to the Moslem faith. He leveled two basic criticisms against Christianity: the trinitarian doctrine, which he considered irrational, and the futility of turning the other cheek. As I listened to him, I became detached and then more and more irritated because his diatribe consisted of thin and worn clichés, but I was impressed with a deep and fundamental spiritual quality that underlay his narrow sectarianism. When he abandoned argument, a spiritual vitality flowed from him in a gentle stream.

I was interested in what he had to say about Jesus. According to the Koran, he said, Jesus would appear from time to time when a great urgency demanded it. Jesus was crucified, but did not die on the cross, because God would not suffer His prophet to die an accursed death. During a storm, he said, with the help of Pilate, Jesus was taken down from the cross and Joseph of Arimathea treated him with herbs and ancient medicines. When Jesus was revived, He came back to be with His disciples and then disappeared to the East, where He continued to teach and to live.

The day came when the ship sailed from Southampton. I was overwhelmed by the friendliness of the Africans whom I met on board. A face would seem quite immobile and taciturn, the eyes steady and unmoving; then suddenly, it would open with radiance and a vibrant smile. Nevertheless, when I began to meet and talk with Africans on board ship, I became aware of my own emotional insecurity in their presence. As I thought about this, the most obvious reason seemed to relate to my inability to speak any language other than English. Most of the Africans, on the other hand, were fluent in French, German, and English, as well as their regional dialects. In my schooling as a student of theology, the language requirements were geared to train us to read the various interpretations of biblical texts and the literature of religion. The emphasis, necessarily, was on Latin, Greek, and Hebrew.

The deeper reason for my sense of insecurity was, however, the resurgence of the old dilemma I had experienced in India: the paradox of being a black Christian minister who was representing and, by implication, defending a religion associated in the minds of many of these nonwhite peoples with racism and colonialism. The Africans traveling with me were Moslem. Nigeria itself had a large Moslem population. This fact created a gulf that would be difficult for me to span, primarily because I would have to find a way to establish a sense of communication with members of this great religious tradition that would negate the proselytizing tendencies of both religions. I had been trying all my life to do this through my preaching. In my mind, religion had become so identified with sectarianism, and its essence so distorted by it, that I felt the need to bring to bear all the resources of mind and spirit on the oneness of the human quest.

I was also aware that there would be those at the university who were totally indifferent to religion, especially Christianity. My presence as an Afro-American—my blackness—would be our common meeting ground. As I thought about this group, I began to come to grips with my own motivation for going to Africa. I had been listening to three young Nigerians discussing the political and social problems of their country. Two were lawyers; one had trained at Oxford and was returning to teach school. They spent many hours every day exchanging ideas about Nigeria's future. They constantly referred to the dynamics of revolution. They spoke of the necessity for a strong leader to heal the internal divisions created by colonialism. They talked about graft, unemployment, and political self-interest. Above all, they regretted that the intellectual leadership in the country was badly fragmented and determinedly individualistic. As I listened to these young men I realized that I had heard—and used—all these arguments over and over again among friends at home in discussions about our own country. It was so familiar. It had nothing to do with race, culture, language, or place, but everything to do with the human situation, the human predicament, the human plight. Yet, for me, the African experience that awaited would be unlike any other. For I would learn at last what the impact of Africa would be on me as an Afro-American returning to the starting place. I would meet the motherland.

At last we arrived at Lagos. Now, I felt, I will know my fate. Would I be allowed to enter the country? I had no visa, but the night before a government minister had assured me that he would see me through. At Immigration I was told to step aside. A short time later an old friend from Boston, Asa Davis, appeared. I had not seen him for more than five years. He had been sent by Dr. Dike to deliver me to Ibadan. After a telephone call I was let through, though my passport was held.

We drove to Ibadan, leaving Lagos behind quickly. Our driver was swift and reckless. Along the way I saw some overturned automobiles; a section of the road we traveled had been under water, but had been shored up to make traffic possible. Suddenly the road began to curve, and I was conscious that we were climbing very gradually. I was impressed by the masses of rooftops turning brown with rust, and the throngs of people. And the children! There were children everywhere. The babies rode on their mothers' backs, seeing what their mothers saw, sharing their mothers' world. As we passed through the tiny villages along the way I saw clusters of people dressed in colors more beautiful than I had ever seen. Everyone, it seemed, was busy. There was a barber shaving a man's head with a razor, a goldsmith, and a peanut vendor, selling from a container just outside his door.

Finally we arrived at the university, where I was to meet the director of religious studies, Dr. Bolaji Idowu. The resident professor of the philosophy of religion had been unexpectedly recalled to Scotland, and Dr. Idowu asked that I cover his classes, as well as deliver the weekly public lectures as previously arranged. I agreed reluctantly. Although I looked forward to this additional contact with the students, I was afraid that the extra responsibility would necessarily confine me to campus and make it hard for me to pursue my interest in indigenous African religions.

I decided that in my lectures in the department I would focus on the general problems of the philosophy of religion, rather than on Christianity and its particular meaning. In this way I hoped to find a common ground on which to meet the minds of Moslems, southern Baptists, Methodists, missionaries, and nonreligionists at the university.

As I began to know Dr. Idowu better, I discovered that he seemed to live in two separate worlds. The first embraced the idiom of African culture that was his heritage, including the myths and spiritual climate that had nurtured him and his people since their beginnings. The second world consisted of a Christology and a theological system inherited from the West. He was a Methodist and had been educated in England. He was a good churchman, not unlike many white orthodox Christian ministers and teachers I knew in Europe and America. Yet he was also the son of a chief. The religion of his forefathers was an inescapable part of him. He described to me often the etiquette and ritual of tribal life. And Christian though he surely was, he honored them.

As I listened to Idowu talk about his religious heritage, I was deeply moved. It seemed to me that here in Africa were still preserved perhaps the oldest religious memories of mankind. I have always been convinced that each region of the world has its own memories—in rocks and in the trees, in sunsets and in the animals, in the wind, in streams. And in the people. They record the movement of time and they are alive.

When a new religion, such as Christianity, comes in, it must be nourished by the memory of the region if it is to survive. If this fails to happen, the new "learning" must be artificially fed, artificially financed, and artificially nourished. If, on the other hand, a way can be found by which the new religion and the ancient memory of the region can have free, easy access to each other, the genius of the past and the genius of the present can embrace.

When I discussed the possibility of the synthesis of African culture and Western Christianity with Dr. Idowu, he told me of the development of the African church, as distinguished from the Anglican, Methodist, and Baptist churches. The African church had broken away and established its own leadership in reaction against the missionary influence of traditional Western Christianity. In their order of service they adhere somewhat to familiar forms, including the Book of Common Prayer, in the case of the Anglicans. But they have also made certain significant changes. They have developed their own hymnody and introduced indigenous dances and drums into religious worship.

Idowu was eager for me to attend such a service. He recognized the need of some of his countrymen to find expression for their Christian religion in ways that honored their cultural heritage. But as a traditional Western Christian, he did not feel such a need and did not believe the future of Christianity in Africa lay in that direction. The cultural conflict, as I saw it, between the idiom of his background and Western orthodoxy had been psychologically resolved by separating the two in thought and practice without denying either one its prerogatives. His attitude was not unique; on the contrary, it was shared by every orthodox African Christian with whom I spoke, including my students.

Through Asa Davis I met many Afro-Americans living in Ibadan, as well as Nigerians from a variety of backgrounds. I remember in particular a dinner party given by a young Afro-American couple, to which I was invited as guest of honor. It was my first encounter with Nigerian and American black intellectuals who were in no way involved with either church or religion. Among the guests were the Nigerian poet and playwright Wole Soyinka and his wife. We hit it off at once. I found him thoughtful and sensitive. I liked his keen sense of humor. There was also an atomic physicist in the group who taught at the university. He spoke of the absence of laboratory equipment in the high schools, and of how few men and women were ready to do university work in his branch of science. There was quiet courage and faith in his eyes, but his soul seemed exhausted. A young graduate student in economics from Manchester was trying very hard to get a fellowship to Harvard. It was stimulating to share their interplay. There was a light touch, a breezy sophistication. It was the sort of gathering that could be found in any cosmopolitan American city.

More and more we were conscious of the compelling voices of women in these groups. Adun Ogunbameru's voice was one of these. She would later study in America on a Howard Thurman Educational Trust scholarship, which permitted her to take an A.B. from Spelman College and a Master's degree in library science from Pratt Institute. She would return to Nigeria to serve as librarian first at the University of Ife and presently at the University of Lagos. There were other faculty women and students actively participating in all facets of university life.

I was invited to give a lecture before the Press Club in Ibadan. It was presided over by the deputy premier of the western region of Nigeria, Fahni Kayode, a man of charm and ability, a brilliant lawyer who had trained at Cambridge University. He was a fighter and a politician. When he heard the news of the bombing death of the children in Birmingham, Alabama, during those terrible days of the sixties, he personally sent a gift of two hundred pounds to the families of the dead children through the American consul in Ibadan. He had a striking personality, stubby beard, clear, penetrating eyes, and a wide and contagious smile. He was the sort of man whose bearing said, "I'm living my life intentionally, by God!"

My lecture that night was on the Negro revolution in America. It had been well advertised and the room was full to capacity. There were many Americans present, both black and white. They were there to hear what I would say, how I would say it, how accurately I would state the facts. Presenting objective material, using notes, is not one of my gifts. I had therefore made a very careful outline of the history of Negroes in America from the arrival of the first cargo of slaves in 1619 to the rise of the renewed impetus of the civil rights movement after 1954. It was a review of the social struggle as it affected Afro-Americans and as it contributed to the evolution of American society itself. When I had finished, there were several questions. I had inadvertently omitted references to the impact on Afro-Americans of the Black Muslim movement at home and on the emerging African nations on that continent. I was challenged on both points and frankly admitted my error; otherwise, my remarks were well received.

As a result of that lecture, Deputy Premier Kayode invited me to call on him at his office. I asked him about the relations between

Nigerians and American blacks. "The American Negroes who come to Nigeria fall into several groups," he said. "First, there are those who are pleased to be on a friendly basis with white Americans. They are flattered to be on a first-name basis with them, with the back-slapping and all that goes with that. They oscillate between the white and Nigerian groups. Then, there are those black Americans who are critical of Nigerians because we have not taken revenge on the white man since we gained independence by kicking him out of the country. They are impatient with us because we do not treat Europeans here as white Americans have historically treated blacks. They do not understand that we are in extremely short supply of trained Nigerian technocrats and administrators to run the country. We see the arrogance and bigotry of many white people, but we need their knowledge and their skill. So we look the other way and wait. We wait while we learn. When we learn all that we need to know, we will react to their subtle abuses, and they will leave. Some black Americans do not understand this strategy.

"A third group of black Americans has come with scientific and technical skills to help us develop our country. They have no pretensions, and we flow together and discover deep ties of heritage of which we were scarcely aware before."

"What about the future of the country? What do you see, or foresee?" I asked.

He looked at me for a moment. "I'm no good at prophecy. But the gulf between the educated and the powerful and the masses of the poor grows wider every day. There is hunger. It will get worse. Unemployment is everywhere, but the extended family system and the abundance of nature tend to make existence possible. Labor organizations are weak and uncertain. And there is regionalism, which divides the people. But one day the regions will unite, and the masses will speak with one voice. When that day comes, there will be bloodshed and God help us all. I see no other way to purge the country of the evils that are destroying it." He referred to the immediacy of the internecine struggle soon to plunge his country into civil war.

Sue and I received an invitation to spend a weekend as guests of the Ilowu, the hereditary chief of the Kingdom of Ofu, two hundred miles north of Ibadan. As we drove along, the landscape began to change and, because we were climbing to a higher elevation, the weather became cooler and less humid. We arrived almost at sunset. The palace was a large rambling structure which sat back from the main street. The entrance was rundown, but still showed traces of past elegance. To the rear of the palace was a series of smaller dwellings, all connected to each other and to the palace itself. These housed the Ilowu's several wives and many children.

We were greeted by a servant who led us up winding stairs to a waiting room with easy chairs against the wall. The carpet was worn, and the fabric covering the chairs needed repair. Overhead was an electric fan. On the walls were many pictures of the Ilowu and members of his family, particularly his father, grandfather, and great-grandfather, some taken with British royalty. Also on the wall was a citation signifying the knighthood that England had conferred upon the Ilowu.

Presently, his senior wife, whom we had met in Ibadan, came in and greeted us. She said that His Highness would join us shortly. Meanwhile, we were offered refreshments. The Ilowu swept in, greeted us enthusiastically, and sat down on a stool-like throne. He rested his feet on a leather ottoman and expressed regret that we had not arrived in time for lunch, or to see his House of Chiefs with whom he meets daily to conduct the business of the region. We had also missed the drummers and the dancers, but when I expressed a particular interest in the talking drums, he agreed to summon these drummers to the palace the following morning. He said that we were to be the overnight guests of an Englishwoman (married to a Nigerian sculptor) who was head of the English department in the Ilowu's college. At length, our hostess arrived. When she entered the room she dropped to both knees before the Ilowu. Then she rose and was greeted by the Ilowu, who introduced her to us.

As promised, three talking drummers came to the palace the next morning. The drums were about two and one-half feet in length and they were covered on both ends with tight skin. The sides were laced with what appeared to be strips of cane held together by woven cloth; they expanded like bellows. The Ilowu asked me what I wanted the drums to do. I had noticed at a distance of about a hundred feet an old tin can lying on the ground near an open door. I said, "Tell the drummer to have one of the men pick up that can, bring it to me for inspection, and then return it to its original place." The Ilowu gave the instructions. The other two drummers stood about twenty feet away as the chief drummer began to "speak" the directions with his drum. As soon as the first sounds were made, one of the drummers became very alert. He seemed to be listening carefully. He hesitated a moment and then walked in the direction of the tin can, rather uncertainly at first. The drummer kept up the rhythm on the drum, and then the man walked straight to the can, picked it up, and brought it to me. I took it, looked at it as if to examine it, then gave it back to him, whereupon he threw it on the ground nearby, turned, and walked away. The drummer immediately began a spirited rhythm. The man froze in his tracks, listened, then turned around, walked back to the discarded tin can, picked it up, and carried it back to where it had been originally. When this happened, the crowd outside the door of the palace burst into applause.

Then the Ilowu said, "Tell him to go over to the building across the street where the policeman is standing and tell him to come to me at once." The policeman had his back to us. When the drum sounded the command the same man walked hurriedly over to the policeman and spoke to him. The policeman looked in our direction, then ran toward us. He stopped in front of the Ilowu, saluted, and spoke to him in Yoruba. Again, there was general and spontaneous applause. The drummer also said with his drum, "Happy birthday, man from beyond the seas," when he was told that I had recently had a birthday.

The Ilowu seemed to be aware that he was functioning in the last phase of a dying system. All around were indications of subtle decay. The number of audience rooms and the intricate pattern of stairways and dining and sitting spaces bespoke of a long-lost grandeur. The whole thing was dramatized when he took us on a walk through his gardens. As we moved into the area behind the palace he said, "During my father's time all this space was covered with buildings, offices, and other structures essential to the maintenance of the kingdom. And over there, where the market is, were more buildings, and far beyond, for nearly five square miles, the palace grounds stretched. In the time of my grandfather, this area extended for miles in every direction, but now this is all that is left, and I am having a difficult time keeping this up. The Parliament makes a grant that is completely inadequate to meet my responsibilities to all the people in my area, some two hundred thousand of them."

We were driven out to his farm where, for the first time, we saw coffee, cocoa, and rubber growing. It was a fine farm, and the Ilowu said he would like to devote all of his time to agriculture. He felt that if he had a sufficient grant from Parliament with which to make his agricultural experiments, the results would be profitable to the total economy of the region.

The weekend at Ofu gave me a firsthand view of the indigenous culture which I had so longed to see. It was also at Ofu that I learned of the assassination of John F. Kennedy. Word had come by phone the night we arrived from Ibadan. The first call said that the President, Vice-President, and the governor of Texas had all been murdered. Later, we learned the true story. Joseph Palmer, the American ambassador, whom I had met, asked me to come to Lagos to conduct the memorial service to be held on the grounds of the embassy on Sunday afternoon. He asked me to plan the service and deliver the eulogy. The service would be attended by international emissaries to Nigeria, cabinet members, and other officials of the Nigerian government, as well as private citizens, black and white, American and Nigerian.

The next day we returned to Ibadan, where we were met by a government car and driven to Lagos. We went directly to the American embassy and were ushered in to Ambassador Palmer's large second-floor office. There he and I and members of his staff planned the program, which was to begin at five o'clock. By the time we had finished it was nearly three o'clock; I had two hours to write the eulogy.

As I sat in the library of the ambassador's residence, staring at the yellow pad on which I would write, seeking to create out of my own spirit an acceptable eulogy, I pondered. Acceptable to whom? The ambassador? The American community of Lagos, black Americans, white Americans? The legations? The Nigerians themselves, many of whom were so incensed by the irrationality of the tragedy that momentarily they hated all things American? Or should I write the eulogy for those who would read it at a later time far removed from this moment of crisis? Presently, I dismissed these questions. My mind became clear and free, and I wrote words that expressed my personal thoughts and feelings. I did not have to make a single correction in the text as the words flowed from my pen.

And then there was the prayer. As I wrote this, I realized that I had not been mindful of the tortured spirit of the assassin himself. Rumors concerning his identity—and plots and conspiracy—were wild and rampant, and I was aware that mention of the killer, even in words to God in public prayer, could inflame the highly charged emotional atmosphere of the moment. I chose to omit any reference to the assassin, and to this day my spirit is troubled by this fact.

The service was very simple. It opened with the ascription:

God of our Spirits, in whom there is life and wisdom and love, we seek Thy blessings upon us as we gather to memorialize the sudden passing of President John F. Kennedy.

> Drop Thy still dews of quietness,
> Till all our strivings cease.
> Take from our souls the strain and stress,
> And let our ordered lives confess
> The beauty of Thy peace.

The Twenty-third Psalm was read by Ambassador Palmer, after which I gave the following eulogy:

The time and place of a man's life on earth are the time and place of his body, but the meaning and significance of his life are as vast and far-reaching as his gifts, his times, and the passionate commitment of all his powers can make it.

President John F. Kennedy is dead.

It is given but rarely to an individual the privilege of capturing the imagination of his age and thereby becoming a symbol of the hopes, aspirations, and dreams of his fellows, so that often in their enthusiasm and relief they are apt to forget that he was the symbol—that he stood for them, and his strength was their strength, and their strength was his strength, and his courage was the courage he drew in large part from his faith in them and their faith in him.

This, by the grace of God, was John F. Kennedy's privilege.

When he became President of the United States, the youth of the land and the young in spirit were caught up in the sweep of his confidence, his sense of purpose, and his direction. There was an aura of destiny in his assurance. When he said, in essence, "Do not ask what can my country do for me, but rather what can I do for my country," the winds of God blew across the land. When the Peace Corps was announced and it was clear that he was calling upon young and old alike to become apostles of sensitiveness, placing their lives and talents at the disposal of human need anywhere without benefit of anything other than the opportunity to give, "the morning stars sang together and the sons of God shouted for joy." They felt that, for yet a little while, life and time were on their side because the future belonged to them.

Again, by the grace of God, it was John F. Kennedy's privilege to become the first Roman Catholic to be elected President of the United States. This marked a turning point in the history of the nation. It was a recognition of one of the basic elements in the genius of the democratic dogma—that a man must be free to worship God after the manner of his own spirit and in accordance with the private promptings of his personal conscience as expressed in a free choice of the faith to which he will give his devotion and his life. As a Protestant clergyman, I rejoice to say that people as a whole found spiritual strength in his authentic devotion to his own faith. By some instinctual wisdom they sensed that a man must be at home *somewhere* in order to *feel* at home anywhere.

Again, by the grace of God, it was John F. Kennedy's privilege to become the voice of the American conscience in the matter of the civil rights of its citizens, particularly of the twenty million American Negroes and other so-called minorities in the land. Whatever may have been the impatience as to the speed with which his leadership affirmed itself, there was never any doubt that he was acting out of the center of an informed heart and a conviction as to the true spirit and meaning of democracy and the American dream. It was his insistence that the North, the South, the East, the West were held together by a spirit that transcended all sectionalism and that after the laws had spoken and the formal intent of the nation had declared itself in a language all could understand, the ultimate place of refuge for any man was in another man's heart.

What he felt to be true of his own country he dared to project as the creative possibility of all the nations of the earth. The unfinished work, the outlines of which he has vouchsafed to us in his living, may we carry on and may what we leave undone be the sacred work of those who in their turn shall follow us.

The time and place of a man's life on earth are the time and place of his body, but the meaning and significance of his life are as vast and far-reaching as his gifts, his times, and the passionate commitment of all his powers can make it.

Let us pray:

Close present Father, to whom Life and Death are expressions of Thy Wisdom and Thy Love, wilt Thou accept our stricken hearts and unabated grief as but an expression of our frailty and the depth of our dependence upon Thy Grace.

When we are most ourselves we know that there is in Thee strength sufficient for our needs, whatever they may be. May this assurance hold us in the Way lest our feet stray from the places, our God, where we met Thee.

Brood over us with Thy Spirit as we stumble along the Path of our Remembrance:

We remember President Kennedy and say our muted Amens to his spirit as he spreads his life before Thee in his sudden homecoming. And we rest in what he reports to Thee concerning us, his people, whom he loved with such abiding affection.

We remember his family, particularly she who called him husband, those who called him father, brother, son, and who cradled him in all the love and tenderness that are within the power of mortal man to share with mortal man. Out of all that Thou has garnered from all the generations of the suffering of Thy children, share with them the full measure of Thy Grace in all the levels of their pain.

We remember him upon whom falls the vast responsibility of office at this fateful moment in the history of our world. Be strength to his weakness, steadiness to his faltering steps, courage to his heart, vitality to his body, vigor to his mind, and keep before his eyes the vision without which we shall all stumble in the darkness. Tutor us in all ways needful to companion him with confidence and help.

We remember all the nations and peoples of the world who hoped with us that together a way may be found to lift the burden of war and the threat of war from the heart, to move the great weight of poverty from the backs of the poor, to bring in a time of tranquillity when everywhere, at home and abroad, the barriers that separate shall be no more and men will love and trust each other and nations will dwell together as friendly peoples underneath a friendly sky.

Our words are ended and the rest is silence.

> Let the words of our mouths
> and the meditation of hearts
> be acceptable in Thy Sight,
> O Lord, our strength and our Redeemer.

When the service was over, the ambassador and I stood on the lawn to greet the people. I was impressed by the genuine grief of the hundreds of people who filed by, many with tears in their eyes. The Russian ambassador took my hand, held it, looked deep into my eyes, said not a word, and moved on.

VII

The Written Word

During my tenure at Howard University, I agreed to participate in a lecture series for the American Friends' Service Committee. On tour one evening, I encountered a young woman who was deeply committed to the concept of pacifism. This involvement had led her to a study of the thirteenth chapter of I Corinthians, and in turn, as she was an artist, to reproduce the thirteen verses in the Corinthians chapter in artistic lettering, with a pastel drawing suggesting an interpretation of the mood each verse inspired in her.

The following fall, I received a letter from her asking me to write a prose poem relating to the ideas contained in these verses. I was reluctant to accept the challenge. I had never considered myself to be a writer. However, my secretary knew of this request and with Sue conspired to commit me to the project. Although I balked at first, I trusted Sue's instincts and decided to write a prose poem each week relating to one of the verses, and to have the poem printed on the back of the weekly bulletin of the Sunday service for Rankin Chapel. It had long been my custom to select some significant poem or prose passage to be printed in the bulletin. My undertaking to write the poems on the Corinthians passages marked the beginning of my experience as an author.

Shortly after moving to San Francisco, I met Rosalyn Keep, a remarkable woman who was owner, editor, designer, and printer of the Eucalyptus Press of Mills College. A true artist of rare sensibility, she taught courses in bibliography and printing. For several years, the Eucalyptus Press designed and printed an annual Christmas card which I wrote to express the spirit of Fellowship Church. In time these cards were sold worldwide and provided an important source of income for the church.

On seeing the text of the poems of I Corinthians, Miss Keep convinced me to let Eucalyptus Press publish them. The hand-set, beautifully designed book was entitled *The Greatest of These*. It was my first venture in book publishing. It circulated at the church and many were sold throughout the country, requiring a second printing. While teaching at Spelman College, I gave a series of chapel talks devoted to the Negro spiritual. They appeared in the alumnae magazine under the title *Deep River*. Later, Miss Keep published them in San Francisco under the Eucalyptus imprint.

All through the early years I used my writing to communicate the concept and ideal of Fellowship Church. It was useful to the central mission of my life at that time, nothing more. But it became more.

Each winter I was invited to preach at several eastern colleges and universities. During my annual visit to Harvard in 1946, Dean Sperry invited me to give the 1947 Ingersol Lecture on Immortality presented each year by the Divinity School. He was dean of the Divinity School, a man for whom I held a particular friendship.

I felt challenged by the possibility of discovering the grounds of my own thought on immortality; and I was well aware that Negroes were rarely invited to give endowed lectures. I accepted his invitation. I wrote him saying I was choosing the Negro spiritual as the focus of my thesis. It was important to me that he knew why I had chosen this particular approach because I was sensitive to the pervasive notion that black scholars were incapable of reflective creativity on any matters other than those that bore directly on their own struggle for survival in American society. In my view, this attitude had an inhibiting effect on otherwise creative, thoughtful minds, and I deeply resented it. I chose to examine Negro spirituals in spite of this prevailing opinion and not because of it. My instincts told me to mine the Negro spirituals again, this time for what they could tell me about life and death. To augment my own collection, I borrowed the text of spirituals from the libraries of Fisk University and Hampton Institute. As I studied the material, I became increasingly excited by the depth of insight the songs revealed.

The genius of the slave songs is their unyielding affirmation of life defying the judgment of the denigrating environment which spawned them. The indigenous insights inherent in the Negro spirituals bear significantly on the timeless search for the meaning of life and death in human experience. I sought to establish a beachhead of thought about the slave's religious creativity in the presence of those gathered in assembly in perhaps the most prestigious academic institution in our society, with the hope that the ideas generated would open the eyes of the blind and deliver those in another kind of bondage into a new freedom. Thus, however briefly, they and the slave would stand side by side together as children of life.

Much of the preparation for the lecture was done under extreme pressure. During the early years at Fellowship Church, the congregation met in a small building with no room for an office. Our family lived in a crowded, congested apartment. I had no place to work, to write, or to think. I was offered the use of the facilities of Temple Emanu-El, which included a library, a quiet lounge, and the assistance of a secretary. I completed almost all of the research and writing of *The Negro Spiritual Speaks of Life and Death* in the library and lounge of the temple.

The event at Harvard was attended by considerable curiosity. I was the first black man to be invited to give the Ingersol Lecture. I was not associated with any denomination, and I was from California, a state viewed by the majority of the eastern theological establishment as a hotbed of free-wheeling, not to say bizarre, unorthodoxy.

The cornerstone of my presentation was the slaves' unique view of life and death as testimony to the immortality of life itself. It is the wisdom of the spirituals that the unfulfilled and undeveloped can only have a future; those who are fulfilled, rounded out, finished, can only have a past. In the spirituals the human spirit participates in both past and future through the *present*, but it is independent of both.

His [the slave's] tragedy would be that nothing beyond the moment could happen to him and all of his life could be encompassed within the boundary of a time-space fragment. For these slave singers such a view was completely unsatisfactory and it was therefore thoroughly and decisively rejected. And this is the miracle of their achievement, causing

217

them to take their place alongside the great creative religious thinkers of the human race. They made a worthless life, the life of chattel property, a mere thing, a body, *worth living!* They yielded with abiding enthusiasm to a view of life which included all the events of their experiences without exhausting themselves in those experiences. To them this quality of life was insistent fact because of that which deep within them, they discovered of God, and His far-flung purposes. God was not through with them and He was not, nor could He be, exhausted by any single experience or any series of experiences. To know Him was to live a life worthy of the loftiest meaning of life. Men in all ages and climes, slave or free, trained or untutored, who have sensed the same values, are their fellow-pilgrims who journey together with them in increasing self-realization in the quest for the city that hath foundations whose Builder and Maker is God.

Even though the terms of the Ingersoll endowment made it necessary that the lecture be published, during the year following its delivery, in the Harvard Divinity School *Quarterly*, I was free to have it published elsewhere as well. I signed a contract with Harper and Brothers in New York to publish the lecture under its original title. Some ten years earlier, while I was still at Howard University, I had received a letter from Eugene Exman, religious editor of Harper's, asking that we meet to explore the possibility of my writing for publication. After we spent several hours together in my office, there began a friendship that lasted to the end of his life.

My next book was also identified with a lecture, which predated it by fourteen years. In 1935 I gave the Annual Convocation Lecture on Preaching at Boston University. I had been wrestling with ideas concerning the significance of the religion of Jesus to the powerless and disadvantaged for some years. I structured some of these ideas for the lecture. Under the title "Good News for the Disinherited," the lecture was published as an article in *Religion in Life* the following summer. In January 1944 the same theme was further developed in a prose-poem, "The Great Incarnate Words," which appeared in *Motive*, a publication for Methodist youth. During the intervening years, I had continued to struggle with the central issue, which was the apparent inability, the demonstrable failure of Christianity to deal effectively with a system of social and economic injustice with which it existed side by side throughout the Western world. Was the impotency owing to a betrayal of the genius of the religion, or did it result from a basic weakness in the religion itself? My quest for an answer reminded me again and again of my need to preserve, at all costs, the inspirations and the strength I drew from my commitment to the religion of Jesus.

Four years later, the opportunity came to express my thoughts fully in writing for the first time. A young acquaintance of mine, a brilliant black Methodist-Episcopal minister, Carl Downs, had become the president of Sam Houston College in Austin, Texas. Shortly thereafter, Dr. Roy L. Smith, a retired Methodist minister, became the publisher of Abingdon-Cokesbury Press. He was concerned that black ministers received so few opportunities to publish, presumably because of their limited readership. He expressed this concern to his friend Carl Downs and shortly thereafter established, at Sam Houston College, the Mary S. Smith Memorial Lectures, with the specific condition that the lectures be written and delivered from manuscript. When the lectures had been given, the manuscripts were to be submitted to Abingdon-Cokesbury, one of the most influential religious publishing houses in the country, thus opening the way for black churchmen to publish their ideas.

I was asked to inaugurate the Smith Memorial Lectures and chose as my theme "Jesus and the Disinherited." This comprehensive study was, in fact, the development and completion of my original thesis begun in 1935. My experience with the editor at Cokesbury was my introduction to the world of commercial book publishing. The earlier work with the Ingersol Lecture had been simple. That lecture was the equivalent of a single chapter in a book, and the text had already appeared in the journal of the Harvard Divinity School. By contrast, problems surrounding the publishing of *Jesus and the Disinherited* were many and various. The editor had returned the manuscript, the pages covered with red ink—suggestions, criticisms, rephrasings. I was unaccustomed to this. Every comment, question, or criticism I took as a personal affront. My conference with the editor in New York was even more disconcerting. Ever critical, this man seemed nevertheless detached and indifferent. He was positive about nothing save the fact that the book could not be published without the suggested changes. At the end of our conference he returned the manuscript to me for revision and expressed his interest in its publication only after the changes were made. Eventually, we worked through our differences by compromise and capitulation, and I was gratified when a book club chose *Jesus and the Disinherited* as one of its selections.

At Fellowship Church, I continued to write a weekly meditation for the Sunday bulletin, as I had done at Howard University. In addition, each week I wrote a special piece to be used by those who attended the thirty-minute period of meditation preceding the Sunday morning service. The response was so enthusiastic that I was persuaded by my friend John Chambers, at Harper's, to prepare them for publication as a book of meditations.

When preparation of the manuscript was complete, I met with the publishers in New York to select a title. During the course of the meeting, John mentioned that he had arranged for a friend a series of lectures on the meaning of religion. To his amazement, the majority of those attending were psychiatrists, whereupon I remarked, "That shows how deep is the hunger."

"That's the title we are looking for," he said. "Let's call the book *Deep Is the Hunger*."

And so it was. This was the first of the three books of meditations I would write. *Deep Is the Hunger* was followed by *Meditations of the Heart* and *The Inward Journey*. From the beginning, the meditations were a channel through which I was able to place my own resources at the disposal of those who shared experientially in my pilgrimage. But there was more! The meditations were an expression of my own hunger and hope. Through them I joined the spiritual quest of those to whom I ministered.

In 1969 I was asked to publish a volume of prayers. I felt some conflict about this because in prayer the full range of vulnerability of the human spirit is laid bare before the Creator of life and all existence. Nevertheless, it seemed important to publish *The Centering Moment*. As I edited the prayers, there emerged gradually a sense of sharing that neither violated my need for privacy nor inhibited my spirit, for it took place within the heart of the divine encounter.

Shortly after I moved to Boston, I began to record the background and history of my beloved Church for the Fellowship of All Peoples. I knew it to be a unique expression of organized religion in our society whose development should be documented and preserved as witness to the challenge it represented. The manuscript was completed in 1959 and submitted to Harper and Brothers. My editors were not enthusiastic. They were convinced that the history of an institution, and particularly a church, would not attract a wide enough readership to justify publication. I could not argue the point of marketing. But I believed in the manuscript and the story that it told. At length we reached a compromise. I accepted a reduction in the amount of my royalties through the first printing, thus sharing the risk and cost of publication. The first printing sold out within ninety days.

Sue gave me the title, *Footprints of a Dream*. The question facing our small group in those early days was whether a religious fellowship could function nonexclusively in an environment with strong patterns of segregation. The book is a comprehensive log of the events, confrontations, and discoveries we shared as we sought for an answer. In 1975 the letters exchanged between Dr. Alfred Fisk and me during the planning stages of the new church were published. The volume, appropriately entitled *The First Footprints*, documents the stirring of our dream. *Temptations of Jesus*, published during the Boston years, was given recognition in the thirty-fourth anniversary celebration of Fellowship Church. Selected lines from this text had been set to music by the well-known minister-musician Marvin Chandler and presented on this occasion. Later it was recorded and sung by the Glee Club of Morehouse College.

The Luminous Darkness was written at the request of my editor at Harper's, who felt that it would be an important contribution to the total literature of the civil rights struggle of the sixties if I made available my reflections on the meaning of segregation in American life. I had rejected all forms of segregation and was acutely aware of how it damaged the soul of a people—black or white. Its climate was all-pervasive and one had to exercise great care never to give to it the nerve center of one's consent through despair or self-deception. I had reflected long and often on the issue and had sought in many ways to express my concern within the context of my dedication. The writing of *The Luminous Darkness* bore witness to my concern for a world free of racial hatred and strife. The entire book was written in two sittings. The final paragraph is a summary of my concern and the ceiling of my hope:

There is a spirit abroad in life of which the Judeo-Christian ethic is but one expression. It is a spirit that makes for wholeness and for community; it finds its way into the quiet solitude of a Supreme Court Justice when he ponders the constitutionality of an act of Congress which guarantees civil rights to all its citizens; it settles in the pools of light in the face of a little girl as with her frailty she challenges the hard, frightened heart of a police chief; it walks along the lonely road with the solitary protest marcher and settles over him with a benediction as he falls by the assassin's bullet fired from ambush; it kindles the fires of unity in the heart of Jewish Rabbi, Catholic Priest, and Protestant Minister as they join arms together giving witness to their God on behalf of a brotherhood that transcends creed, race, sex, and religion; it makes a path to Walden Pond and ignites the flames of nonviolence in the mind of a Thoreau and burns through his liquid words from the Atlantic to the Pacific; it broods over the demonstrators for justice and brings comfort to the desolate and forgotten who have no memory of what it is to feel the rhythm of belonging to the race of men; it knows no country and its allies are to be found wherever the heart is kind and the collective will and the private endeavor seek to make justice where injustice abounds, to make peace where chaos is rampant, and to make the voice heard on behalf of the helpless and the weak. It is the voice of God and the voice of man; it is the meaning of all the striving of the whole human race toward a world of friendly men underneath a friendly sky.

In the early evening of the day of Martin Luther King, Jr.'s, death, radio station KPFK in Los Angeles called me in San Francisco to ask me to prepare a statement about Martin's death that could be played at frequent intervals during the entire night. They gave me two hours to write it, at the end of which time the call came and the following is the statement I read by telephone for the broadcast:

Martin Luther King, Jr.
1929–1968

Martin Luther King, Jr., is dead. This is the simple and utter fact. A few brief hours ago his voice could be heard in the land. From the ends of the earth, from the heart of our cities, from the firesides of the humble and the mighty, from the cells of a thousand prisons, from the deep central place in the soul of America the cry of anguish can be heard.

There are no words with which to eulogize this man. Martin Luther King was the living epitome of a way of life that rejected physical violence as the life-style of a morally responsible people. His assassination reveals the cleft deep in the psyche of the American people, the profound ambivalence and ambiguity of our way of life. Something deep within us rejects nonviolent direct action as a dependable procedure for effecting social change. And yet, against this rejection something always struggles, pushing, pushing, always pushing with another imperative, another demand. It was King's fact that gave to this rejection flesh and blood, courage and vision, hope and enthusiasm. For indeed, in him the informed conscience of the country became articulate. And tonight what many of us are feeling is that we all of us must be that conscience wherever we are living, functioning, and behaving.

Perhaps his greatest contribution to our times and to the creative process of American society is not to be found in his amazing charismatic power over masses of people, nor is it to be found in his peculiar and challenging courage with its power to transform the fear-ridden black men and women with a strange new valor, nor is it to be found in the gauntlet which he threw down to challenge the inequities and brutalities of a not quite human people—but rather in something else. Always he spoke from within the context of his religious experience, giving voice to an ethical insight which sprang out of his profound brooding over the meaning of his Judeo-Christian heritage. And this indeed is his great contribution to our times. He was able to put at the center of his own personal religious experience a searching ethical awareness. Thus organized religion as we know it in our society found itself with its back against the wall. To condemn him, to reject him, was to reject the ethical insight of the faith it proclaimed. And this was new. Racial prejudice, segregation, discrimination were not regarded by him as merely un-American, undemocratic, but as mortal sin against God. For those who are religious it awakens guilt; for those who are merely superstitious it inspires fear. And it was this fear that pulled the trigger of the assassin's gun that took his life.

Tonight there is a vast temptation to strike out in pain, horror, and anger; riding just under the surface are all the pent-up furies, the accumulation of generations of cruelty and brutality. A way must be found to honor our feelings without dishonoring him whose sudden and meaningless end has called them forth. May we harness the energy of our bitterness and make it available to the unfinished work which Martin has left behind. It may be, it just may be that what he was unable to bring to pass in his life can be achieved by the act of his dying. For this there is eloquent precedence in human history. He was killed in one sense because mankind is not quite human yet. May he live because all of us in America are closer to becoming human than we ever were before.

I express my deep compassion for his wife, his children, his mother, father, sister, and brother. May we all remember that the time and the place of a man's life on the earth are the time and the place of his body, but the meaning of his life is as vast, as creative, and as redemptive as his gifts, his times, and the passionate commitment of all his powers can make it.

Our words are ended—and for a long, waiting moment, the rest is silence.

April 4, 1968

Disciplines of the Spirit is the distillation of my Smith-Wilson lectures given at Southwestern College in 1960 and the Wilson lectures at Nebraska Wesleyan University in 1961. They are a discussion of spiritual dimensions found at the very core of human experience—growth, suffering, prayer, reconciliation.

The Search for Common Ground, published in 1971, is a radical departure from the rest of my writing. There I sought to examine the paradox of conscious life which, on the one hand, declares unequivocally the uniqueness of the private life, the sense of being an isolate and alone, the urgency to savor one's personal flavor, but, on the other hand, asserts the necessity to feel oneself as a primary part of all of life, sharing at every level of awareness a dependence upon the same elements in nature, caught up in the ceaseless rhythm of living and dying, with no final immunity against a common fate that finds and holds all living things.

What is the common ground that sustains the private adventure of the individual or solitary life? Is it merely conceptual? A great idea, the hunger of the heart rationalized into a God-idea, a notion? Or are these but the scent of the eternal in all living things, perhaps reaching its apotheosis in man, in the religious man most clearly? My quest led me to examine theories dealing with the beginning of life as found in creation myths, to study the testimony of living structures, to take a critical look at the dreams of prophets and seers, to go beyond that to the common consciousness binding all of life and, finally, to come full circle to the paradox of identity.

My conclusions are not definitive, but they point the direction in which others must go in search of the idiom of community in a strange and bewildering society in which the integrity of the individual life seems to be put under siege by the vast impersonal processes of life. It may be that the only clue to the eternal available to us is found in the tight circle of time and space by which our little lives are grounded and defined.

A Track to the Water's Edge represents a belated expression of gratitude for a particular gift of grace from Olive Schreiner, whose existence was unknown to me until long after her death. In 1925 at a student retreat in Pauling, New York, I was introduced to Olive Schreiner's *Dreams*. As I listened to the reading of "Dream of the Hunter," I knew that through its portals I was being led into a wonderland of the spirit and the imagination. Since that time, I have secured a copy of any of her writings I could find in bookstores or libraries in this country, in England, and in her homeland of South Africa.

My book, subtitled *The Olive Schreiner Reader*, is a paean to the light that her genius shed on many dark areas of my own path. The fact that she was an Englishwoman, born and bred in South Africa, might have created a dilemma for me as a black man, but it did not, for it is at a level transcending the issues of nationality, race, or even culture that her significance for me is defined.

. . . She possessed what comes through to me as an innate, instinctual sense of the unity of all life. It was this emphasis in her writing that was the first external confirmation of what had always been an active ingredient in my own awareness of life. As a boy in Florida, I walked along the beach of the Atlantic in the quiet stillness that can only be completely felt when the murmur of the ocean is stilled, and the tides move stealthily along the shore. I held my breath against the night and watched the stars etch their brightness on the face of the darkened canopy of the heavens. I had the sense that all things, the sand, the sea, the stars, the night, and I were one lung through which all of life breathed. Not only was I aware of a vast rhythm enveloping all, but I was a part of it and it was a part of me. It was not until I read Olive Schreiner that I was able to establish sufficient psychological distance between me and the totality of such experiences to make the experience itself an object of thought. Thus, it became possible for me to move from primary experience, to conceptualizing that experience, to a vision inclusive of all of life. The resulting creative synthesis was to me religious rather than metaphysical, as seems to have been true in Olive Schreiner's case.

As I look back on my writing years, it is clear to me that it was, for the most part, the demanding requirements of lectureships that forced me to set down in systematic fashion the seminal concepts that have nourished both my mind and my spirit over many years.

The Creative Encounter develops certain ideas for which the Merrick Lectureship at Ohio Wesleyan University provided the catalyst. In it I treat with the recurrent challenge of my life: how to honor my feelings without vitiating my power of reflective thought, how to escape the aura of sentimentality typical of the religious quest, as well as the prejudgment of emotionality with which black people are associated, while giving full rein to that which I feel. It is a misreading of the role of feelings to separate them from the function of mind at work! No matter how clear and penetrating and detached may be the vast reaches of creative thoughts at their best, they are but lifeless forms until they are energized by the continuum of emotion that is always present and antedates the emergence of mind. After all, it may be true that what is called "thought" is a function of feeling, reduced to slow motion. This book interprets the meaning of religious experience as it involves the individual totally, inclusive of feelings and emotions. It examines, in a limited way, the effect of the sense of Presence upon the total life of the individual, both as a private person and as a member of society. The religious experience is defined as a dynamic encounter between man and God through the experience of prayer and human suffering. All of this has to do with the inwardness of religion.

The outwardness of religion is examined in terms of the impact of the religious experience itself on the individual nervous system, thus altering ingrained behavior patterns as the new life takes hold and spreads its influence through all of living.

The book necessarily discusses the meaning of love variously and successively from the ordinary human need for love we feel in infancy to the grand fulfillment of the personality in the experience of the love of God. It is the testimony of a personal quest: it shows many indications of seeking, perhaps little evidence of finding. No claim is made other than that, despite fumblings, errors, and grave shortcomings, one senses that as Browning's "Paracelsus" puts it:

> . . . to KNOW
> Rather consists in opening out a way
> Whence the imprisoned splendor may escape,
> Than in effecting entry for a light
> Supposed to be without.

Though I have published these and other books, my craft remains the spoken word. Even when I am writing, I hear the sound of the word as it goes on the page. If the sound does not please me, I am reluctant to write the word. Nevertheless, it may be true: *scripta littera manet.*

VIII

Mind-Grazing

Madison, Florida

My mother's oldest sister, Mary, lived with her husband, Pizeah, in the town of Madison in the northern part of the state. They owned a farm and raised cotton as the money crop. Their garden provided an abundance of vegetables. It was here that I had my first experience in feeding pigs, driving a mule-drawn wagon, and picking cotton. The first time I tasted coffee was at Aunt Mary's— a mixture of coffee, milk, and sugar was thought to make castor oil palatable. To this day I can smell the cornbread and the cakes cooking in the big wood stove that dominated Aunt Mary's kitchen, a large room that also served as the dining room. On Saturday night we took turns bathing in a large tin tub with water heated in buckets on the stove.

The food was, for us, somewhat unusual, but it was very good. There were freshwater fish like none we had eaten before. Our family rarely ate fish from the freshwater lakes near Daytona, because fish from the ocean and the Halifax River were abundant and easily available. One of my favorite dishes was gopher stew. The gophers lived underground, and entrances to their dens were scattered through the cotton field. They were of the tortoise family, their bodies protected by a shell. To kill one was a skillful but cruel undertaking. By rapping on the front of the shell, one would tempt the gopher to stick his head out to investigate. Before he knew what was happening, his neck would be pinned down and severed. Then the shell was split open, the meat removed, cleaned, and prepared for cooking. I was too young and otherwise preoccupied to know or care about how the meat was cooked. All I do know is that the gopher provided a stew unlike anything I had tasted in Daytona.

Occasionally Uncle Pizeah would go coon and possum hunting. Of coon, I remember only that the meat was lean and the flavor wild and gamy, but possum was my favorite. Aunt Mary would dress the animal and bake it intact. Then she would put it in a large pan surrounded with sweet potatoes. The skin was crisp and flaky, and the flavor of the meat was delicious beyond description! It was years later that I discovered that the possum was a notorious scavenger; but it remains a part of the magical tastes and smells of my youth. On the farm in Madison I first saw a smokehouse, a small wooden structure, windowless, with a chimney in the center of the roof. There were rafters extending from wall to wall. And there was the smell of it—a subtle mixture of hickory smoke and ashes, and the pungent odor of fresh meat succumbing to the gentle, relentless heat.

Mamma never made these late summer trips to Madison with us. Nor did Aunt Mary ever visit us in Daytona. It was Grandma's pilgrimage. The slave plantation where she grew up was in this area. She never spoke of it; she did not point out landmarks. Her thoughts were locked behind a wall of fierce privacy and she granted to no one the rights of passage across her own remembered footsteps.

Trips to Jacksonville

My first train ride was on a weekend excursion to Jacksonville, Florida—110 miles away. Grandma took me with her to visit her son, my Uncle Gilbert. He lived in a large two-story house with a big yard and a picket fence. The furniture, the rugs, the dishes were the kind that I associated with white people; I avoided sitting on the chairs for fear they might break. Aunt Maggie did not appear until "long after sunup." I had never seen such pretty clothes in all my life.

In those days Uncle Gilbert had his own bakery. I can still smell the freshly baked bread and see the piles of cookies and other goodies. I could eat all I wanted and could not understand my sudden loss of appetite. I saw my first penny ice-cream cone during this visit. I took five cents of my little treasure, bought five penny cones of several flavors, took them into my room, and put them carefully away in the bottom of my suitcase so that I could take them back to my sister, Henrietta. She would be as excited as I! Imagine our looking together, two and a half days later when I returned to Daytona, at the soggy mess at the bottom of my little suitcase. I wept.

On Sunday we went to church. It was a grand building, finer than most of the white churches in Daytona. It was curious that I have no memory of the service, only the vestigial remnants of confusion. I was a little boy suddenly plunged into a strange world in which people looked like him but seemed apart. They were not white; they were not black. I was anxious to get back home to Daytona, where I could feel me and be me.

Bearimore

Since the early traumatic experience when a dog tore a piece of flesh out of my leg, I lived with an organic fright, but it was far outweighed by my natural love for dogs. Ever present was the overwhelming impulse to rub their ears, scratch their backs, and nuzzle the underside of their necks.

In my adult life there have been two dogs in my family. The first was Bearimore, who came to us during the early years at Howard University. As both our girls were very small, my excuse for taking him in was that he provided security for them. This was only partially true. I needed the dog myself because I loved him on sight. He was a mixture of Samoyed and collie, with beautiful black and white markings. The girls named him Bearimore; he looked like a little teddy bear. As he grew larger, they said, he would look like a bear "even more."

Almost at once he became the campus mascot. At all football games he marched with the band, because his favorite person outside the family was Sergeant Brice, the bandmaster of the ROTC. Bearimore belonged to the campus and he knew it. For several years he attended a class in education which met three hours a week. How he knew where and at what hour to appear is anyone's guess. But he did. The professor, when he called the roll, always included "Bearimore Thurman."

Late at night when I was working at my desk he would stretch out in a corner for a quiet sleep. Somehow he seemed to sense when I stopped reading. He would rouse himself and walk over to me for a scratch and a visit. When I picked up my book again, he would return to his corner for another nap.

His favorite food was lamb breast, which we could buy at a neighborhood market, three pounds for twenty-five cents. Most often he ate it raw. Once in a great while I would cook it in a special way that he seemed to enjoy.

Each afternoon, Bearimore would lie in wait for the paper boy, who cycled down the long walk in the center of the campus, then turned on the sidewalk alongside our yard. Bearimore would meet the boy in the corner of our picket fence, "bark" him to the end of the fence, then return to his post on the porch. One morning after a snowstorm, there were four-foot drifts in the corners of the fence bordering the sidewalk. Bearimore chased the paper boy as usual. But when he came to the corner of the fence, he could not break his speed, and before he knew it, he was over the drifts and onto the sidewalk, with nothing between him and the boy on the bicycle but the cold winter air. He yelped as if he had been struck; I ran to the rescue. But the only rescue he needed was from the shock of face-to-face confrontation!

Bearimore was a friend to strangers as well as friends. The joke in the family was that if a thief broke into the house, Bearimore would be the welcoming committee, escorting him from room to room with tail-wagging abandon.

On our last night on campus before moving to California, Sue and I took our usual walk around the reservoir for the last time. Bearimore followed us to the door, turned, walked down the steps, and disappeared. Despite all our efforts to find him, we never saw him again.

Kropotkin

He was a beautiful boxer puppy not more than ten weeks old. One of my students, who was raising puppies for a college fund for his son, gave him to me as a Christmas present. I named him for the Russian sociologist Peter Kropotkin. My insistence was that he must always be addressed by his full name—no play on words for him.

We were very close companions. Wherever I was in the house Kropotkin could always be found hard by. When he was six months old and had to have a city license, I went to the police station to secure it.

"Age of pup," barked the desk clerk.

"Six months."

"Sex of pup?"

"Male."

"Breed of pup?"

"Boxer."

"Name of pup."

"Kropotkin."

"Ah, named for the Russian sociologist."

This, from a Boston desk sergeant!

Kropotkin was a slow learner—beautiful, charming, friendly, but a bit stupid. It was impossible to teach him simple obedience. Always he recognized his name but beyond that he lived his very private life. He was a beautiful brindle-colored elegant creature. Wherever he appeared, people took special notice.

It was the first time in my experience with dogs that I noticed the development of a conscience. One day I found him resting on a bed in my room. When I came in, he looked up for a minute, then went back to his resting. Quietly I said, "Kropotkin, you know you should not be on the bed." He jumped down. It was all a quiet exchange. Another time he came into the room, started toward the bed, saw me, went to the bed, turned around, and came back and stretched out by my chair.

He enjoyed the whole family, including the stream of students and others who came in and out of 184 Bay State Road. Always he threatened to become a nuisance but did not ever quite succeed in bringing it off.

It was not until he was several months old that we discovered his affinity for little children. We had houseguests, DeReath Collins, wife of Dr. Daniel A. Collins of San Francisco, who was visiting us with our godson, Craig, the youngest of their four sons. He and

Kropotkin became close friends almost at once. It was wonderful to see how Kropotkin surrounded him with love. They were inseparable.

One evening when I came home from a late meeting, Kropotkin greeted me at the front door. It was clear at once that he had not been for a run all day and expected me not only to understand this but also to do something about it. I turned around and took him down along the Charles River for exercise. It was a cold, bitter Boston night with a high wind. I could endure it for only a few minutes.

I called him to me; he came immediately, stood in front of me looking up into my face for an extended minute, turned around, and trotted away toward downtown Boston. In my disgust I went home immediately without him.

I called an emergency house meeting, asking Anne to excuse herself from her evening's guest. I made a report about Kropotkin's behavior and suggested that he needed to go to an obedience school or else we would lose him. It was decided. Early the next morning a friend drove me to a neighboring suburb, where I sought to enroll Kropotkin for a four weeks' course in obedience training.

"What do you want me to train your dog to do?" the manager asked me.

"Nothing spectacular. I want him to come when I call him and to recognize his name under pressure. In addition, I want him to learn simple obedience. Nothing complicated or fancy."

"I have been training dogs fifteen years. My experience is that it takes me two weeks to teach the dog to trust me. After that, I can teach him anything else. I'll keep your dog for that length of time, and if I cannot teach him to trust me, I'll call you to come and get him. In that case, I'll charge you only the kennel rate for board."

Two weeks to the day, he called me to tell me to come to get Kropotkin because he could not teach him. "Your dog thinks that he is a human being. I am sorry."

I promised to pick him up in the late afternoon. Sue and I talked it over before I went to work.

When I returned in the evening, she said, "I have arranged for Kropotkin to be picked up and delivered to the airport tomorrow morning. He is being flown to San Francisco to live with the Collinses so that our godson, Craig, may have a companion."

And until Kropotkin's death, he and I visited together each time my travels brought me to San Francisco. Always he remembered and I did not ever forget.

Mr. Rosenwald and Mr. Gamble

I was elected during my junior year in college to represent the Morehouse student body at the national meeting of the Colored Men's Division of the national YMCA. The meeting was held in Cincinnati. Both the student and the city departments of the association were represented.

The occasion was memorable because I met for the first time Dr. Jesse Moreland, the senior secretary, a symbol of dignity, breeding, and courage, and Dr. John R. Mott, the legendary YMCA personality, who was at that time one of the world's leading Christian laymen.

The highlight of the meeting for me, however, was the Sunday afternoon session at which Julius Rosenwald addressed the assembly. Rosenwald was an owner of Sears Roebuck Company, which for me held childhood memories of days when we pored over the famous Sears catalog, which featured page after page of goodies we knew we could never own and, indeed, scarcely believed to exist.

As I grew older, I learned of Mr. Rosenwald's philanthropies. He offered a gift of twenty-five thousand dollars to any community that would raise another seventy-five thousand dollars for the construction of a building for a YMCA for black men and boys. Of course there were the Rosenwald schools established in various southern counties for the elementary education of poor youth, black and white.

All of us anticipated his speech at the mass meeting. Would he be boastful and arrogant, pointing with pride at what he had done for "the race," reminding us of our debt to him? We were curious, a bit awed, and mildly suspicious. The fact that Dr. Moreland, whom we trusted, had invited him was reassuring but did not forestall heated discussions among some of us.

Finally, the fateful Sunday afternoon arrived. At the conclusion of Dr. Moreland's introduction, Mr. Rosenwald walked to the podium. Suddenly, a young man stood up in the audience and said, "Pardon me, Mr. Chairman, but I am moved to speak," and he proceeded down the aisle. "Mr. Rosenwald," he said, "I want you to know that I speak on behalf of all the students here when I say that we hold you in high and venerable esteem. Where there was ignorance, darkness, and superstition, you have brought learning, light, and religion. Therefore, wherever we are privileged to come into your presence we take off our feet!" With this, he made a sweeping bow.

The whole audience, including Mr. Rosenwald, exploded with laughter. I have no recollection of what Mr. Rosenwald talked about when order had been restored, only the gales of laughter, the embarrassed retreat of the student, and the look of consternation on Moreland's face.

The trip to Cincinnati gave me the first opportunity to meet James N. Gamble of the Procter and Gamble soap company, who had befriended me during my second year in high school. I had known of his interest in the YMCA for a long time, and had written to tell him that I was coming as a delegate. Several weeks earlier I had proposed to him that he establish a fund that would provide grants to certain teachers in Negro colleges to study and complete their work for advanced degrees. The grantee would agree to repay, within a minimum of two years, through a monthly reduction from salary when he resumed his post. I had asked Mr. Gamble if he would assign the dividends of a certain number of shares of Procter and Gamble stock, the funds to be used for this purpose. When we met, he told me that my idea, while worthy, had come too late. He had recently entered into a similar arrangement with the general secretary of the YMCA.

Mr. Gamble came by in a chauffeured limousine to take me on a sightseeing trip. I sat with him in the back seat, and each time he addressed me as "Mr. Thurman," just as he had done in all of his letters. He had a kind and gentle face. He had a white beard and white hair; his eyes were the palest blue, but they were strong and direct. His face gathered me in when he looked at me. As we drove around the city, he pointed out places of particular interest and meaning to him; among them, the Rookwood Pottery and the large general hospital. At the hospital he introduced me to the chief of staff, who extended the first two fingers of his right hand when I reached out to shake hands!

Our last stop was 1430 Union Trust Building, where his office was located. He bade me good-bye and instructed his chauffeur, who was white, to drive me back to the YMCA. The chauffeur, not wishing to "drive" a black man, invited me to sit with him in the front. I, being a perfect gentleman, refused.

Peggy Strong

I have had a secret desire to paint pictures ever since I was a child. I like to doodle while my thoughts are otherwise engaged, to see where my unconscious mind will go. While at Howard University I took a few lessons from James A. Porter, a professor in the art department, but my workload was so heavy that I had to abandon them. A new opportunity came many years later in San Francisco.

Our home was located nineteen blocks from Fellowship Church. Each morning I walked the distance, choosing as many alternate routes as possible. Then, as now, I loved to savor the potpourri of sights and sounds, voices and smells of San Francisco. On any street one is apt to encounter an echo from a distant shore.

One day, as I walked full stride into the church office at 2041 Larkin Street, I stumbled over a wheelchair in front of the desk. In the midst of the laughter and my embarrassment, Lynn Buchanan, the church secretary, gave me the high sign to keep going into the inner office. Soon he followed me.

"The lady in the wheelchair is from Menlo Park. She called for an appointment. I told her there was no opening until next week, but she came anyway. What shall we do?" he asked.

"Ask her to come in," I said, "and buzz me in five minutes." As she wheeled herself in, she said, "My name is Peggy Strong. A friend of mine in Southern California suggested that we get acquainted."

239

I explained that I was expecting a visitor. I was startled when she replied, "I understand that, but he won't show. If he doesn't, may I have the time? Let's shake on it."

Just as we shook hands, my appointment called to cancel. When I hung up the telephone she was convulsed with the most contagious laughter I had ever heard.

Peggy and her friends began attending church each Sunday. During the day she lived in her wheelchair; she lived alone. A superbly gifted artist and portrait painter, she was one of the most resourceful human beings I have ever known. One of the fruits of our long and rich friendship is her portrait of me, which she gave to Sue and is now on loan to Boston University, hanging in the Thurman Lounge at Marsh Chapel.

It was she who urged me to paint. Once a week she would pick me up in San Francisco and drive me back to her studio cottage in Menlo Park. Our understanding was that she would not try to teach me to paint. She prepared the canvas, gave me paints and brushes, and left the rest to me. There is a heady quality of power and omniscience one feels making the stroke of a brush translate in color a time-space vision available to anyone with eyes to see. The infinite range of shadings of color was a revelation. To look at a forest of green trees and see numberless variations of a single hue opened a new world of meaning to me.

There was the additional pleasure of the ceremony that always took place when I brought a finished painting home from Peggy's studio. I would walk into the house and proclaim in a loud voice, "Is anybody home? Come at once to behold the greatest oil painting it will ever be your privilege to see!" What pure release—to be able to express un-self-conscious pride, even arrogance, concerning one's own work, completely oblivious of the standards or opinions of others!

My greatest joy has come from painting penguins. The initial inspiration came upon me during a visit to Vancouver. A penguin was hatched in the city zoo amid great excitement. On my way back east, I began sketching penguins. These developed into a series of oils, appropriately named "A Penguin on His First Date," "Two Drunk Penguins," "Penguin Politicians," and so on. Several of my friends sent me illustrated books about penguins, hoping,

I suspect, that some similarity might develop between my paintings and the real thing. But to no avail. I paint the Penguin's View of Himself! When my friends say, "That doesn't look like a penguin to me," my answer is "Maybe not. But it does to the penguin."

On the windowsills in my library-office there are dozens of penguins—ceramic, glass, metal, wood, of every conceivable size and shape—each of them the loving gift of a friend. When I receive a new one, I put him on my desk. When I feel the time is right, and they have given their permission, then and only then does the newcomer join the others.

First Murder Victim

Henrietta and I were walking home one day when we heard that a woman had been murdered by her boyfriend. We knew the fellow. He worked at the bicycle shop in Midway, a part of town into which we rarely ventured. Generally, the people who lived in Waycross regarded those who lived in Midway as "worldly."

As the murder occurred downtown, we turned around and ran some twelve blocks to see for ourselves. She was lying on the sidewalk, her face and torso covered by a man's coat. There was blood seeping from beneath the coat and soaking the ground at the sidewalk's edge. People had gathered around, staring at the body, talking in hushed tones. Then someone lifted the coat and we saw her face, grotesquely distorted with pain. In her still open eyes, panic was frozen into a stare.

We hurried home in silence, trying to make up for lost time, for we were long overdue. I had seen a dead person before, but the sight of this woman affected me in a way that I could not understand. I could not know then that death by human hands violates and ravishes the spirit, that it is unclean, that the mind recoils from it. By contrast, death at the hands of nature, however hapless and tragic, is never sordid. It leaves the spirit whole, though diminished by sadness for a time.

Henrietta and I swore secrecy. We could not let Grandma know where we had been, and we were sure that no one there knew who we were. That night I could not sleep. Every time I closed my eyes I could see that face and those frozen eyes. At last, in panic,

241

I begged Grandma to let me sleep in her bed. Then I confessed the whole story to her. And Grandma knew that there was no need for further punishment.

Meeting with the Federation of Indian Chiefs; Saskatchewan, 1962

We sat together in a small room in a motel on the outskirts of the town of Fort Qu-Appelle, the town in which the next day the meeting of the Federation of Indian Chiefs of Saskatchewan would take place. There were five of us: Ray, the executive of the Provincial Committee on Minority Groups (a paleface); Jonas, a chief from the north country up near the Arctic Circle; John, also a chief, and acting president of the federation; Wilf, employed professionally by the Division of Indian Affairs; and myself. Ray made the introductions, and the next half-hour was spent in easy, casual conversation. It was the first face-to-face encounter these men had had with a black man or, indeed, with an American academician. The three Indians were important leaders in the group. They wanted to get acquainted with me in some personal way before the meeting convened the following morning. At first, they seemed to be overwhelmed by my presence, but this lasted only a short time. Part of their apparent self-consciousness may have been their knowing that they were in a primary relationship with a man of prestige who had no power to grant them favors, a man who nevertheless was seeking to understand them and to be understood by them. This was exhilarating for them and for me. It was new.

In response to my questions, they spoke of the difference between Indians and "metis." Metis, in common language, are half-breeds, they said. "They are a group apart and tend to live in communities among themselves." In some ways they were less fortunate than the Indians, particularly "Treaty Indians" whose forebears had entered into treaties with Queen Victoria. There were eleven treaty agreements between that monarch and the Indians of British North America. The Royal Proclamation of 1763, issued by the British government following the acquisition of Canada, provided that no Indian could be dispossessed of lands without his consent and the consent of the Crown. This document had guided the relationship between the government and the Indians in principle if not in fact.

The three Indians with whom I met were Cree. Two of them understood and spoke English with facility. One of them knew only about fifty English words. I found from the outset that it was necessary for me to use as many images as possible in my conversation, the pictorial being more easily communicated than the conceptual and abstract. Once I got the drift, our discussion moved rather quickly into areas of mutual concern.

I wanted to know how the three Indian chiefs in the room viewed themselves. Were they Canadians first and Indians second in their own eyes, or the reverse? Did they regard themselves as Indians only? John, the acting president, announced that he was Indian first and said it was important for the Indian to keep his sense of self as an Indian whose roots reach back to a time before the coming of the paleface. He insisted that the best way to maintain a sense of identity was to keep alive the rhythm of the Indian spirit by participating in meaningful activities of the group: the dances and the basic folk celebrations. He had taught his children to do this to continue a living tradition which supported and sustained them as persons. "Once they are safely anchored in that sense," he said, "it will be far easier for them to share the general life of Canada without being swept away from their moorings." John was himself an example of this. He was steeped in all the ancient Cree traditions, yet he was so well integrated into the life of Canada that he was regarded as the finest interpreter among the chiefs, who could translate with ease the nuances of English and Cree to those who could speak and understand only one or the other language.

I watched him work. At the meeting the next day, he interpreted the speeches given by representatives of both the central and provincial governments. These messages had been carefully prepared and were read from text, for these men were speaking in their official capacities. These texts were then given to John, who read them aloud, translating the English into Cree. He conveyed not only the content of each speech, but nuances of humor as well. When John was elected president, I listened in utter rapture as he gave his acceptance address in Cree, though I did not understand the language. When he had finished, one of the Chippewa Indians, who did not understand Cree but did understand English, asked

John to repeat his speech in English. With some embarrassment he did so. Once again I was moved, but differently. When he spoke in English, I dealt with the ideas in his address, the need for cooperation, for working hard, for sharing responsibility—but when I had heard the same ideas expressed in Cree, I had felt the pull of his spirit and the mood of the group.

Jonas lived a very simple life on a reserve in the north country. He had an open countenance, a ready smile, and gentle peaceful eyes. There was an untroubled, yet hardly shallow, quality about the man. He did not understand what I meant by asking if one felt oneself to be an Indian first or a Canadian first. He could not make room in his mind for such a concept. He lived intimately with the wind and the trees and the flowing waters and the winter snow, gathering from them his strength and vitality. In their rhythm was the pulse of his own spirit. How I wish that I could have spoken his language for the good of my own soul!

Wilf was a Canadian first. He was a veteran of the Second World War and had traveled beyond the boundaries not only of the reserve or the province but outside Canada. His children attended a residential school, supported by the Catholic Church. He said to me, "I want to have a good house on a good street, and I want my wife and my children and myself to wear nice things. I want what any Canadian wants, but with this difference. As an Indian, I want to feel that when a Canadian looks at my work, at my appearance, at my home or my family, he cannot distinguish what he sees from the work, the home, the family, of any other acceptable Canadian, Indian or otherwise. I do not want my children to bother with Indian lore, myths, and dances. These things belong to the past and are symbols of a life that we must leave behind to fully integrate ourselves into the present."

These three men represented the basic attitudes expressed by the membership of the federation at the annual meeting. For a moment I was at another kind of meeting at home—in my own country. How familiar it was, how sadly the same were the recitations of isolation and abuse. Roads were well paved up to the boundaries of the reserves, then suddenly they turned into rock and became well-nigh impassable. Electricity was available and inexpensive up to the boundaries of the reserves, which were then bypassed entirely.

Police brutality was unacknowledged and unpunished; jobs were denied, though there was work to be done; living quarters, when available, were squalid and dehumanizing. And always, there were subtle insults to daze and confuse the unsophisticated, and confound the spirit of the worldly. Here were repeated all the familiar patterns of discrimination so much a part of the past and contemporary history of Western culture and civilization. But here, too, was something new. Indians were sharing their experiences and together they were finding a common tongue—even though the words for prejudice and discrimination did not exist in their languages.

The Federation of Chiefs gave to individual Indians a voice and a sense of voice. The provincial government made a grant of seventy-five hundred dollars for the work of the federation. This sum was expected to include the cost of the annual conference, the travel expenses and board and lodging for all who attended the conference, as well as any operating expenses of the president and the councillors during the year. The miracle is that so much could be done at so little cost.

Each year the federation became more and more autonomous. The year before, a remarkable thing happened. One of the major tasks of the federation meeting was to prepare recommendations for the federal and provincial governments relating to the grievances and needs of the Indians as they themselves perceived them. For some time there had been a feeling that these recommendations were largely ignored. So the previous year a request had been made by the federation through its executive committee that they be permitted to present their recommendations in person to the premier and his council. The premier granted an audience of one hour, the implication being that the presentation would be a shambles, and an hour was more than enough time to waste on it. Indians could not present an orderly and structured statement of their needs, it was assumed, but the fact that they had had an audience with the premier and his council would serve at least a political purpose. All this and more was expressed by the premier to the executive director, and he in turn, in what may be regarded as a mood of recklessness, told the executive committee of the federation precisely what the premier had said. The result was that the executive committee worked all night after the close of their meeting to prepare their presentation. All recommendations were examined and divided into six major categories, and each category was presented in a four-minute statement by one of the chiefs and backed by two two-minute statements from the floor. The presentation was opened by a prayer in Cree, and at the close of the meeting the premier was presented with a Cree Bible. The whole affair ended before the hour was out and it was conducted with such shrewd and intelligent attention to detail that one hard-boiled politician confessed that it was the best presentation he had ever heard in the legislative chambers. From that time on, the recommendations of the federation were taken more seriously—at least for a time.

My first lecture came in midmorning of Monday. As I was being introduced I made a sudden decision to dispense with the interpreter. When I told him of my wish, he was completely astounded. "Only two or three of us will understand what you are talking about," he said. "But I'll listen very carefully and then summarize your address for the men when you have finished." At first the atmosphere was tense and disconcerting. It was quite clear that the men didn't understand my words and were puzzled by the unusual procedure. My words went forth, but they seemed to strike an invisible wall, only to fall back to meet other words flowing from my mouth. The tension was almost unbearable. Then, suddenly, as if by some kind of magic, the wall vanished and I had the experience of sensing an organic flow of meaning passing between them and me. It was as if together we had dropped into a continuum of communication that existed *a priori* long before human speech was formed into sounds and symbols. Never before had I found a common path through such primeval woods. When I finished, there was a long breath of silence as if together we were recovering our separate rhythms.

Presently, the men dispersed and I found myself alone with a white representative from Ottawa, who began telling me in profoundest detail about elements of his personal life that had landed him where he was at the moment. He told me of the anatomy of his sense of failure, not as a government official, but as a human being.

On the last night of the conference, I was awakened by a man who brought a message that the men wanted me to say a few words in the morning before they left for home.

When I came down for breakfast, the dining room was empty. The men were standing around in clusters, chatting and smoking. Their cars were packed and they were ready to leave. While I was having my coffee and toast it was announced that I would make a closing speech. When I finished, each man came by my chair. Some took my hand, some gripped my shoulder with unspoken feeling, and at last an old chief, his two long braids falling over his shoulders, looked down at me, his eyes holding mine, as he stroked the top of my head with his right hand. And through it all, no man uttered a word.

The Language of Music and Speech

The miracle of a man's life is life itself. I look back upon my own path, which began three-quarters of a century ago, and I am now aware of certain aspects of that journey for the first time. For instance, I have always wanted to play a musical instrument. More than wanting to play an instrument, I wanted to *make* music. It is an expression of beauty with all the subtle nuances of meaning for the ear that can listen, to hear. Certain of its sounds are only open to the exquisite hunger of the self. The gift of intimacy is revealed by the magic music creates when a person who is so blessed makes an instrument sing. Sue has such a gift—always when she plays the piano something more than music flows forth. It is as if there is a happy blending of all harmonies created since time began. The sounds I *hear* with my inner ear are so complete, so glorious, that what I am able to achieve seems a sacrilege.

On a fateful Christmas morning while I was at Howard University, the family presented me with a large package. In it was a B-flat clarinet. The ROTC band instructor promised to give me lessons, but I lacked the incentive, or time, to study and soon gave it up. Nevertheless, through the years the hope that someday I would learn the instrument was kept alive. Finally, I studied the clarinet seriously for four months at the Boston University School of Music. For me it was long past high noon; I was sixty years old.

There was no time to devote to the skill and the art of mastering the clarinet, but I learned to play simple scales and to read the score of uncomplicated melodies.

The semester of study at Boston University gave me courage, however. As a signal of the new order of beginning, I purchased a very good French clarinet. What I enjoy most now is creating tunes that seem to me to be a part of melodies I have heard all my life. Occasionally, when the rhythm settles into a steady beat, I make awkward music on my beautiful instrument.

There has always been a running discussion in our family on favorite composers. Ever since our daughters were small, we have celebrated the birthday anniversary of Sue's beloved Mozart. Mozart is not my favorite composer, however. I revel in his music, but he is not the angel who soothes troubled waters. Now Beethoven! That is a different matter. There is a massive vitality in Beethoven's music that consumes all foibles and mediocrities, leaving only a literal and irreducible reality. For years I have worked at unlocking the doors to understanding the late quartets. One of the private ambitions of my life is to feel as much at home with them as I do now with the Seventh and Ninth symphonies. One night I sat in the San Francisco Opera House listening to Myra Hess. The "Moonlight Sonata" flowed through her spirit to the keyboard. Until that night, I did not know that an artist could become a perfect, complete, and utter channel for creative flow, an instrument of its hands. If I could share the mystery of the lonely giant Beethoven I would have the clue to my own solitariness. This can never be done, alas, because I have no active companionship with the tools he used.

The language of music and speech are different from that of the mountains and the sea. The language of the mountains is awesome, stark, and solitary. For me, the loneliness of the mountain peak against the background of the sky—day or night—is excruciating and glorious! It strips and lays bare the spirit. I have often felt that if I were a psychoanalyst I would live under the shadow of a mountain range and use direct exposure to the mountains in all their changes as a part of my therapy. I am sure that they would serve as a magnet pulling up from the depths of the psyche the underside of life, thus making the work of therapy and healing incredibly shorter.

The periods of greatest personal renewal in my life have been spent on the ocean. I love the sea and know it to be the womb from which all living things have come. There is something ominous about the phrase "the waters covered the face of the earth." Crossing the Atlantic for the first time was like a homecoming of the spirit. There were times when standing alone on deck, the boundaries of the self dimmed and almost disappeared, and then again affirmed themselves. I felt that I was outside of time, yet watching myself in time.

All life seems to come to attention when the waters are troubled, when the winds rage, and the ship is a thorn in the exposed flank of the waters.

Dilemmas of Survival

Continuously I have wrestled with the moral dilemma of reverence for life—at first with a quiet unease, and later with an acute sense of urgency. I was never able to resolve the issue in a manner that would bind me. As a boy, frightened as I was by rattlesnakes, I hated to kill one. All during my early years it was my job to kill the chickens we ate on Sunday by breaking their necks with a quick twist of the wrist. Finally, I made such a fuss over having to do it that Grandma stopped insisting. But every Saturday morning during the summer months when I worked as a delivery boy for the market, I had to kill many chickens, pluck the feathers, cut off their heads, and bring them in to the butcher for weighing and dressing.

As traumatic as that experience was, it did not compare with what awaited me when I took a job at a slaughterhouse. It was there that I learned how to kill sheep and watch them as they seemed complacently to offer their throats to be cut by the sharp knives.

None of these experiences, however, turned me into a vegetarian. Over and over I have echoed the words of the Apostle Paul (Romans 7:21, Moffatt's): "I desire to do what is right but wrong is all that I can manage." The most persistent struggles of my life have always centered on the gray areas of compromise. It may be that a man cannot live in a situation or a society of which he cannot approve, or to which he cannot assent, without compromise. After all, this is the issue upon which the survival of the weak turns when the fight is for survival itself. Many years ago when the implications of the dilemma were first taking shape in a formal way in my thought, I wrote these words:

The little birds know this:

> Feeding in meadows under sun-drenched skies
> The shadow of the Hawk appears.
> Time stops! All else forgot,
> Conditioned feet gather dead brown grass.
> A quick somersault and all is changed.
> High above, the Hawk clears his eyes,
> Shifts his course and seeks his meal
> In other fields.
> One with grass and root, they live
> For yet another day.

Little children know this:

> When parental will looms threateningly
> To deter or interfere,
> Defiance is not wise.
> By route direct and unabashed
> A steely web of chaste deception
> Trips and holds in firm embrace
> The parental power
> Until at last it yields to the little will
> As if it were its own.

The weak know this:

> All victims of Might
> Draw from this churning source —
> By the waters of Babylon they mingled tears
> With flowing streams.
> Into their midst Ezekiel came
> To comfort, soothe, make unafraid.

Words like liquid fire gushed forth at eventide—
Flaming words, but hidden in a vibrant code,
Crystal clear to all with ears to hear.
Distant Tyre, and far-off Egypt named he them.
But all the biting anger of prophetic ire
Bespoke in deftest phrase of Babylon.
The exiles knew and were consoled,
While Babylon kept watch, unconscious of the work
    the prophet wrought.
Who said, "I am God"—
Poor old Hiram of struggling Tyre?
Hardly.
It was the mighty king of Babylon.
The captives knew and found fresh strength.
It is an age-old way the weak have found
To fight the strong with hidden tools.

The African slave had learned this lesson well:

    The master's priest with fervid tones,
    Splashed on a canvas broad and high,
    The glories of another world where God would add
    New comforts to the blest of earth.
    The slave listened well; and deep within his soul
    A melody stirred:
    "Everybody talkin' 'bout Heaven ain' goin' there";
    There must be two heavens—he queried.
    No, for there is only one God.
    "Ah!" an old man said,
    "I'm having my hell now;
    When death calls me I go to Heaven.
    He is having his Heaven now;
    When death calls him, he goes to hell."
    Next day 'neath withering sun, deep in the rows of
        blossoming cotton,
    He cried: "I got shoes—you got shoes
    All God's chillun got shoes."
    His eyes fell on all his fellows acres 'round—
    "But everybody talkin' 'bout Heaven"—
    His eyes held the big house for one elastic minute—
    "Ain' goin' there."

But the word would not be stilled:

> Let your motive be simple;
> Your words, yea, yea; nay, nay.
> Hypocrisy for self-defense—
> Is that the sinless sin?
> Does it degrade the soul at last
> And sweep the raft against the hidden rocks?
> Deceive, and live for yet another day!
> Declare, and run the risk of sure destruction!

The Hair Shirt

Besides a loathing for killing creatures, a hair shirt that I have always worn is shyness and acute self-consciousness. One of the physical characteristics that contributed to this was the fact that as a child I was pigeon-toed. My right foot turned sharply inward as I walked, so much so that at times my right toes would sometimes rub against my left heel. I could not run as fast as, or with the ease of, other boys. I was odd man out in all games that required being fast of foot. One Sunday as we were being chased by a dog, I tripped and fell in a ditch, breaking my arm, while the dog ran by me, chasing the boys who could run, who could be chased.

One of the truly important moments of my young life came one morning when I went on an errand to Mrs. Brinkley's grocery store. When I looked up she was watching me as I approached the front steps. As I mounted the steps, she looked down at my feet and said: "Why don't you practice turning your right foot *out* when you walk? Practice it all the time, even when you go to bed. Think when you walk. Your foot will do what you make it do. That is why God gave you a brain." It was the moment of birth of a new self for me. I improved my gait. And yet often when I am in deep concentration or absorption I discover after all these years that my right foot turns to greet my left heel in response to an old memory.

This shyness is a nemesis in many ways. Strangely, it has not hindered my preaching or lecturing. But it has created an urgency in me to do my preparation with as much thoroughness and concentration as I can. My private necessity is to get the facts as accurately as possible—then chart my own flight pattern in my interpretation of their meaning. It is in that realm that I must feel the sweep of the up and down drafts. For me there is no feeling comparable to full flight in pursuit of a creative idea. During those moments self-consciousness is entirely forgotten.

My Sisters

I have often wondered, as I contemplate the experiences of loneliness and shyness, how different my orientation to life would have been had I grown up with brothers rather than sisters—or had my father lived longer. But from the beginning I was surrounded by women. In addition to my mother and grandmother, I had two sisters, Madaline, who was six years my junior, and Henrietta, two years older. There were our two stepfathers, but their influence on my life in the home was limited.

My relationship with Madaline was very close. I was her babysitter. I fashioned a cushioned crate with holes cut in the front for her legs and fastened this to the handlebars of my bicycle, so she could ride with me on my errands and sit comfortably in the crate as my bicycle leaned against a tree while I shot marbles or played croquet. I could always calm Madaline in her distress, help her to sleep when she was restless. I combed and braided her hair, changed her clothes, and served in general as her nursemaid. Looking back, I sense no feeling of having been burdened by this arrangement. It was totally acceptable to me and to my friends.

There was never the same intimacy between Henrietta, my older sister, and me. It was not merely the difference in our years. She had, even at an early stage, her own group of friends, and to her I was the "little brother," a condition I found most difficult to handle, and was forever trying to live down. One day she and I were going huckleberry-picking. It was early morning, under a hot Florida sun. Just in front of us, crossing the road in the sand, was a baby snake, not more than six inches long. I knew how she feared snakes of any kind so I called her attention to the little fellow and, noting her reaction, I said, "Look, I am not afraid of it. I'll stand on it with my bare feet." I proceeded to do this as she looked on with horror *and* amazement. I was very pleased with myself.

Henrietta took piano lessons and at an early age showed unusual talent in music and art. I was not allowed to have piano lessons. This training was considered suitable only for girls, a fact that perhaps contributed to our rivalry. At a time in our lives when we might have grown closer together, she went away to Fessenden Academy, a church school in another part of the state. Later, when she returned home to be married, I was away in school. I did not ever know her husband.

Near the end of my second year at Jacksonville, she developed typhoid fever. I had a summer job at the academy, substituting for the school bookkeeper who had become ill. One morning as I opened the office windows, I had an overwhelming impulse to pray. As I prayed, the picture of Henrietta lying in bed with her eyes closed in suffering came to my mind. Soon I was praying for her, and I began to weep. Moments later, a messenger knocked on the door and handed me a telegram. It was from Mamma telling me to come home at once, Henrietta was dying. By the time I arrived, she was dead.

Martin

Martin King's father, familiarly known as "Daddy King," and I were students at Morehouse College at the same time. I was an undergraduate in the college department while he was a student in the theological division. Sue and Alberta King, his wife, were in high school at Spelman during the same period. They remained in touch with each other long years afterward, until Alberta's tragic death.

My first year at Boston University was their son Martin's final year of study for his Ph.D. Our contacts were informal. We watched the world series on television at our house. Sue and Martin discussed very seriously the possibility of his coming to Fellowship Church; it was then she discovered his commitment to Montgomery.

Only one time during the phenomenal dynamism of the civil rights movement did we meet personally for serious talk. It was while he was recovering in the Harlem hospital after the stabbing that nearly cost him his life. His wife, Coretta, and aides had come up from Atlanta to be with him. Many times through the years I have had strange visitations in which there emerges at the center of my consciousness a face, a sense of urgency, a vibrant sensation involving some particular person. On a certain Friday afternoon, Martin emerged in my awareness and would not leave. When I came home I said to Sue, "Tomorrow morning I am going down to New York to see Martin. I am not sure why, but I must talk to him personally if the doctors will permit."

When we were alone, I asked, "What do the doctors say about the length of your convalescence before they will okay the resumption of your work?"

When he told me I urged him to ask them to extend the period by an additional two weeks. This would give him time away from the immediate pressure of the movement to reassess himself in relation to the cause, to rest his body and mind with healing detachment, and to take a long look that only solitary brooding can provide. The movement had become more than an organization; it had become an organism with a life of its own to which he must relate in fresh and extraordinary ways or be swallowed up by it.

We did not ever discuss in depth the progress, success, or failure of the movement itself. Lerone Bennett, the historian, in his book, *What Manner of Man*, states that Martin carried *Jesus and the Disinherited* in his briefcase as he journeyed up and down the land.

I joined my friend Frank Wilson in the memorable March on Washington and was a part of the vast throng who heard and felt the unearthly upheaval of triumphant anguish: "Free at last! Free at last! Thank God A'mighty, I am free at last." Perhaps the ultimate demand laid upon the human spirit is the responsibility to select *where* one bears witness to the Truth of his spirit. The final expression of the committed spirit is to affirm: I choose! and to abide. I felt myself a fellow pilgrim with him and with all the host of those who dreamed his dream and shared his vision.

Postlude

I have often wondered if my dabbling with a paintbrush, or studying the clarinet with serious effort at times, is not a reflection of a hidden longing going far back into my past to find an outlet for self-expression in the arts.

Neither of our daughters followed my sisters or Sue in the field of music. With their rather considerable artistic gifts, as they grew up, both chose painting as a hobby only. Their professions widened the range of the interests and concerns of the Thurman family. Olive is a librarian and a professional costume designer for the theater. Anne is an editor, a journalist, and an attorney-at-law. Through the years they have held my absorbing interest and comprehensive love. I enjoy them. As far as their parents are concerned, in their own right, they make the case for daughters. They are very good for us and to us, bringing a single flower on a visit or remembering some expensive thing we had wished for casually and forgotten, only to have it appear when least expected. They have given me some of the happiest moments of my life.

IX

The Binding Commitment

When we reestablished our residence in San Francisco, I was free to devote my total energies to the wide range of services with which I had been involved since my early years. During the period just prior to my formal retirement from Boston University, I was engaged in what has been defined as a wider ministry, serving as minister-at-large with a home base at the university. Relieved of administrative responsibilities, I was more than ever completely available to the central commitment of my life. Whatever personal ambitions had monitored my activities and guided me to goals of ego fulfillment were now receding into the background. In work and vocation I was being rounded out. The sand was no longer hot under my feet. At last I had retired formally from place and position and my time was my own. My physical health was good and my creative powers of mind and spirit had not diminished.

The Howard Thurman Educational Trust now became my focus. It had been incorporated in California three years earlier as a non-profit charitable institution and now I would be working again with Gene Walker, who had been the chairman of the board of trustees of Fellowship Church back when we had retired the thirty-thousand-dollar loan for the purchase of its permanent home. Gene, Sue, and I were the original incorporators of the Trust, with Gene serving as treasurer. The retirement gift from hundreds of friends and alumni from both universities I had served amounted to ten thousand dollars and on this foundation of resources we built the Trust. The Trust was dedicated to the education of black youth in colleges all over the country, but primarily in the Deep South; it was also dedicated to the enrichment of the religious and spiritual commitment of individuals who would be helped by the collection and classification of my written and taped messages and materials that were the distilled essence of my spiritual discoveries—what I had gleaned from the collative fruits of more than forty years.

Professional responsibilities were now of my own choosing and one of the major struggles of my life was neutralized, if not resolved. I had a new clear freedom of movement and involvement as far as what I chose to do or not to do. Not being a member of the staff of any academic community, I was now able to relate to various institutions on my own terms and in accordance with the inner promptings of my spirit and intellectual concerns.

In the first two years of retirement I accepted an assignment as visiting professor at the Presbyterian Theological Seminary in Louisville, Kentucky, and at the newly organized School of Religion at Earlham College. With reference to the latter it was more than the usual academic venture for me to be present and a part of the paradox created by a Quaker graduate school dedicated to the formal training of ministers for the ministry of the Society of Friends. Soon after, there followed a radically different adventure for me. I was selected to serve as member-at-large of the committee responsible for making recommendations to the United States State Department for the promotion of men and women in the Foreign Service. The three months in Washington were unique in our experience. Whereas Sue and I had spent years in the national capital in an academic post, we were now private citizens living in a furnished apartment, and for the first time we had no responsibility for our family life and the university work in which I was engaged. We walked the tree-lined streets and enjoyed the beauty of the city. We did not entertain and seldom ventured out for social occasions. It was a private life in Washington that we relished like tourists on a holiday.

Before leaving the East Coast permanently it was possible for us to follow through with an exciting plan that had engaged our interest for some time. We went to Salisbury, North Carolina, to dedicate the Poets and Dreamers Garden, located on the grounds of Livingstone College. On an earlier visit to the campus, Sue had proposed to the president, Samuel E. Duncan, and the board of trustees that such a garden be cultivated at the spacious entrance of this historic institution. They gave warm acceptance. We were joined in the dedicatory ceremony by a fine local committee and Mrs. Dana

M. Greeley, of Boston, Miss Margaret Thomas of the Greene Herb Gardens in Rhode Island, and Mrs. Carlton E. Byrne of Los Angeles, all associate members of the Garden, the latter making the gift of the Phillis Wheatley Fountain, in memory of her mother, Mrs. Ralph Smith. I have dedicated chapels and hundreds of children, but preparing a litany of poetry and music for this beautiful Garden was a rare and deeply cherished experience.

Our return to San Francisco was some help at this critical point. It brought back the fluid years of a seven-year-old Florida boy who times without number watched, with unbridled imagination, the ships at a distance in the Atlantic. I had a chance for the first time consciously to assess the journey from boyhood when I so long ago had rejected the church which had condemned my dead father and so grievously traumatized my young life. Walking by the water's edge, gazing out at the Pacific, I had time finally to think about the life commitment that I made a scant five years later to the very church I had seen as enemy but now knew to be the Way, the only Way for which I was born. I believe the seven-year-old has been hard at work all this time to understand that which subconsciously I have never been able fully to accept. He is at home with me and through God's grace, I with him. Now from my apartment window I could see other ships coming through the Golden Gate. On occasion I would go meet them at the dock and often I set sail myself across the broad expanse of the Pacific. The great and glorious bonus was having my caring and intensely close family together for the first time on the West Coast. Our daughters, Olive and Anne, and their children, Emily and Anton Wong and Suzanne Chiarenza, my sister Madaline, all of us could now assemble on a few hours' notice for happy family get-togethers or the more serious house meetings that had nourished us all through the years. We were home.

At the time of this writing more than five hundred people scattered all over the United States and Canada regularly contribute to the work of the Trust. In a few short years scholarships have been established in eighteen colleges, seminars conducted at Trust headquarters all through the year, and listening rooms based on the extensive collection of tape recordings sent from San Francisco have been located in many parts of the United States and in seventeen foreign countries, the latest of these, South Africa, where Mrs. Ellen Klemperer, a member of the Trust's board of trustees, delivered the equipment of tapes and books in person.

Nevertheless, the fantastic growth and support of the Trust slowly created for me the old dilemma, the lifelong struggle to maintain the inner integrity of my search for a meaningful self, even as I became more and more identified with the Trust and its goals. I was faced again with a problem that has never let me out of its sight. It concerned the conflict between the realization of the aims and goals of the Trust, and the narrow demands of my essential need for spiritual privacy which again forced the issue between my inner life and the demands of external authority and power. If I responded to human need as revealed in the unfolding of the program of the Trust, could the integrity of my own commitment maintain its essential autonomy? It was my old struggle with the demands of the organization to take over and possess my life. The conflict was yet another manifestation of the war zone in which my life had been lived and from which retirement from responsibility in institutions had delivered me.

The source of one of my major conflicts at Boston University was precisely this point. As dean of chapel I was a member of the university council, the president's cabinet. There were times when a member of the community would need to see me because of a personal crisis. Often the timing was very bad: I would have to make a choice between two necessities. Inevitably I leaned toward the immediate need if it could not be postponed. This meant being absent from the cabinet meeting. In making such a choice, which at times seemed to come with demonic frequency, increasing difficulties arose with the administration. And understandably so. There is no simple reaction to the sensitivity of this issue. My bias growing out of my interpretation of my commitment landed me inevitably on the side of the human situation. During the years of my tenure much time was spent with President Case in our effort to find a satisfactory solution. I am not sure what *my* attitude would have been toward me if the situations had been reversed.

After all, who and what bears witness to a man's life? Is it his deeds or is it what he creates with his mind, his dreams, his imagination? When a way of meaningful life confirms a person in his work and his achievement, is he the determining factor? Dare he lay claim to the illumination that lights up his path, putting words in his mouth, images in his mind, compassion in his heart? May he ever say: this belongs to me, as me, and no other? Can such things ever be sorted out? How may he separate himself from his gifts? It is an eternal question.

One day, how early in my life I do not recall, I discovered a little scar tissue in the center of both ear lobes. When I asked about it, I was told that my ears had been pierced when I was a baby. I was told that at the time of my birth my eyes were covered by a film. This meant, according to the custom, that I was gifted with "second sight"—a clairvoyance, the peculiar endowment of one who could "tell" the future. No parent wanted a child so endowed. It spelled danger and grief. If the ears were pierced, however, the power of the gift would be dissipated. How deeply I was influenced by this "superstition" I do not know. Who is there who can understand such things? One thing I do know, there are times when I am visited by the emergence of a quick memory, the vivid recollection of a face, a person, an event that shoots up from the unconscious on its own errand. Or it may be an insight or an inspiration, an "opening," to use a phrase from the Society of Friends. It is idea and more than idea. We say this thought came into our minds or we had a "hunch" that this was going to happen; our language is full of such references.

Again and again, I find myself turning to a seminal passage from a book, the words of a poem never memorized. If it is to something that I have written, no matter; there is no sense of authorship. Some need or urgency in me "mines" all experience to find what is useful for my condition. This is the root of all meditation—name it as we will. For years I have carried with me a copy of *The Inward Journey*. Often I turn to a page to read a paragraph or a sentence or an entire meditation to find my way in and through the darkness. For this reason I am never embarrassed or surprised when someone speaks of a particular need in him which was met by something that I have written. It is all of a piece, belonging to no one, located nowhere. No one understands the miracle and only the foolishly arrogant dare to lay claim to it as a personal or private possession. I experienced the sense of detachment when I watched the BBC documentary "Conversations with Howard Thurman," when for two hours I was interviewed by Landrum Bolling, then president of the Lilly Endowment; or when Ron Eyre of BBC discussed Protestantism with me for "The Long Search." When word comes of some formal course of study on my Life and Thought in a college or seminary, the same psychological distance obtains.

However, in quest of a life of meaning I have had to deal with my own fact. Often in desperation I have been driven to hold to any validation, however fragmented or authentic, that could confirm me in a world of "alien corn." The existential nature of environment may force a man to lay private claim to some grace, gift, talent, or visitation of inspiration in a radical effort to affirm himself, or even to build a moat around his ego. Or it may make him boastful and overbearing in his behavior, particularly with his peers. There is hardly a greater discipline, I have found, than to resist the urge to lay personal claim to that which at times is "channeled" through the mind or which rushes through the swinging doors of the heart.

Despite the nature of the dilemma or the paradox, my own life has been circumscribed by a sense of vocation, of "calling." It is so easy to look back over the years and credit a gathered accumulation of wisdom and experience as the crucial element in making early decisions. Yet when Dr. Stockings offered to give me a medical education if I would choose such a career, I refused. I do not know why. I do know that it was not even a temptation. My bias was on the side of religion—of this I was certain, although the reasons are hidden to me still.

A man's life is a single statement. This does not seem to be the case because we measure our lives episodically, in terms of events, particular circumstances, and experiences. But every incident is but a partial rendering of the total life. Some events are marked by dramatic intervals, by pain or joy which may cause us to mark the place and to memorialize it for all our days. They are watershed moments. At such intervals the whole life is seen as a single entity in time. There is the special role of the moment that becomes *the* moment—a current of energy, power, illumination—

there are many names for it. But life takes on a "whiff" of density —a moment of raw sanction given to the very idiom of the life itself.

When I was a little boy I gave a declamation as a part of the "Children's Day" exercise of our Sunday School. When the program was over "old lady Murray" came up to me, placed her hand on my head, looked down into my upturned face, and said, "Howard, God's spirit has surely touched you. You must ask Him not to pour more of His spirit upon you than you can manage." I was puzzled by this and asked Grandma what she meant. Her reply was, "You know how Sister Murray is." Well, I did not know how Sister Murray was. All I knew was that her words gave me a "funny" feeling. I put it together with other "funny" feelings that were a part of my bewildered youth. Even the sense of isolation and loneliness which was the quintessence of that time was not separate from this strange and hungry feeling. If only I could have known how to draw upon a wide frame of reference to contain all of this. But not so. It is only in retrospect that the totality of the early years becomes a part of the single statement of my life.

It was not until my experience with Halley's Comet that there began to emerge a faint but growing sense of personal destiny, religious in tone and spiritual in accent. Since that far-off time nearly four-score years ago I have never been totally cut off from a sense of the guidance of my life. Of such were the raw materials of religious experience that fertilized my very being. More than any other single factor lacing the fabric of my self-estimate was this dimension of life. I felt marked. It was more than mere ego-affirmation, as important as that is—it was a clue to my self-worth in the profoundest sense. It was the shield against the denigration of my environment; but much, much more.

Tangentially, my joining the Fellowship of Reconciliation as an undergraduate contained some of the same element. I had no particular interest in the peace movement per se. But in my encounter with the FOR, as exemplified in the life of one of its secretaries, Shorty Collins, I found a place to stand in my own spirit—a place so profoundly affirming that *I* was strengthened by a sense of immunity to the assaults of the white world of Atlanta, Georgia. A mixture of adolescent confusion, the affirmation of mind and personality fostered by my college experiences, a sense of calling going back to earlier times, and the vast possibilities of reconciliation between black and white all gave me the feeling of knowing a "secret." In this lay the strength to affirm my own life and the way that I should take to walk.

It is important in this accounting that at bottom all of this was a part of my meaning of God in the common life. God was everywhere and utterly identified with every single thing, incident, or person. The phrases "the God of Abraham, Isaac, or Jacob," or again, "the God of Jesus" were continuously luminous to me in my journey.

I prayed to God, I talked to Jesus. He was a companion. There was no felt need in my spirit to explain this companionship. There never has been. God was a reality. Jesus was a fact. From my earliest memories, Jesus was religious subject rather than religious object. It was Jesus with whom I talked as I sat under my oak tree fingering the bruises and scars of my childhood. Such was the pretheological ground for me when both life and time spread out before me.

The older I have grown, the more it is clear that what I needed to hold me to my path was the sure knowledge that I was committed to a single journey with but a single goal—a way toward life. In formal and religious terms this meant for me the disclosure of the Will of God. And from this flowed an inescapable necessity: to be totally involved. What I did with my life had to be secure in the inclusive sense that only the word "total" can signify.

The ground of many of the boyhood experiences I have described stands out clearly as part of this single fabric. The fact was that worship encounters in unfamiliar settings or even at Jewish temples at home and beyond our borders did not give me a sense of spiritual alienation. Strangeness, yes, but alienation, no.

I have been at home in many houses of worship. In the summer of 1926 Sherwood Eddy invited me to give a vesper address at his summer conference on the campus of Olivet College in Michigan. A few minutes before the service, he said, quite casually, "By the way, Howard, I neglected to tell you that many of the people at the vesper this afternoon will be Jewish." In that moment I suddenly imagined that I was a Jew. What would be my reaction, my thoughts! Instantly I felt a sensitivity I had never known and have never forgotten. I reshaped my address with that imaginative leap. It was a fresh, new moment in my life, the residue of which has never left me.

But it was not until I moved to San Francisco that I preached a sermon in a Jewish religious service. It was at Temple Emanu-El, the oldest Jewish temple west of the Rockies. Even now it is difficult to convey the timbre of my experience. As the service proceeded I felt increasingly stripped naked. It seemed to me that there was no veil between the worshipper and God. Mark you, I speak of the pervading atmosphere, the ambience of worship. It seemed utterly stark. I had entered the service as a guest, as an outsider, despite all attempts to make me feel at home and to surround me with a vibrant sense of welcome.

Yet, I missed the familiar psychic cushions which according to my custom absorb the anguish of the spirit. Instead, I felt surrounded by a climate of religious security which seemed to embolden these worshippers to assume that it was their essential prerogative, rooted in their birthright, to face the King of the Universe and to struggle toe to toe with Him. I could see Jacob wrestling with the angel and I could hear the angel say, "Daylight is coming, I must go," and Jacob's reply, "*I do not release you until you bless me.*" Those worshippers in Temple Emanu-El that night seemed deep within the invisible folds of a covenant that left me an outsider; a stranger, though not estranged. They seemed, audaciously, to stand on the same ground, men though they were, with the King of all the Universe! What bound them to Jehovah bound Jehovah to them. In a deep place in my spirit beyond all assessing I shuddered! The significance of this experience took root as I shared in worship on many occasions in various temples in the city and elsewhere. Always the moment came in the service when the presence of God gathered us all and we were part of Him even as He was part of us. These experiences were undergirded by hundreds of hours of talk, of probings of the mind, of sharing the spirit and simple, beautiful friendships with many rabbis and their families.

The test for me lay in the fact that we were free to talk about

Jesus and we did. They were not merely academic exchanges among professionals, but many acute moments of moving around in the hidden chambers of the self whose doors open only from the inside. I pause to name a few rabbis of those who are my private reserve, my treasures of the spirit. The late Dudley Weinberg, Irving Reichert, Alvin Fine, Joseph Glaser, the youngest of them all, Saul White, Roland Gittelsohn—and Elliot Burstein, who was present at the inaugural service of Fellowship Church and who invited me years later to be the narrator in the oratorio *Queen Esther* by Lavry, written especially for the centennial celebration of Temple Beth Israel, the composer coming from Israel to be present for the premiere performance.

Through all of this I was on my own scent. The sacred and the secular were aspects of a single reality, a single meaning. At no point could a line of separation be drawn. At long last it seems to me that the customary distinction between religion and life is a specious one. As I have felt my way back through the twists and turns of my own journey over the years, every facet of my way *belongs*, inherently. There is not a single experience that does not have a secret door opening out on the panorama of all my past; and I am confident that this is also true of my future. Even the most trivial event provides some clue of meaning to the broad expanse of the road over which I have already come. It points the way to that which may yet await me around some turn in the road ahead. "Nothing walks with aimless feet" is not to say that I am bound and held fast by the mystery of a kismet or even a predestination. But it is to say that all life, indeed all experience, is heavy with meaning, with particular significance. As was said of Tycho Brahe, the Danish astronomer: "They thought him a magician, Tycho Brahe—He was a magician—There is magic all around us—in the rocks, the trees and the minds of men . . . and he who strikes the rock aright may find them where he will."

Much of the agony of the personal life is due to a lack of awareness of this central aspect of all experience. At long last it is clear to me that it is essentially a false reading of life to say that life is good as contrasted with evil. No! Life is good in the sense that it contains both good and evil. This is the essential idiom of my own religion and the quality of my own experience. There can be no

cultivation of the mind, no opening of the heart to the flow of
the living spirit of the living God, no raw laceration of the nervous
system created by the agony of human suffering, pain, or tragedy;
there can be no thing that does not have within it the signature
of God, the Creator of life, the living substance out of which all
particular manifestations of life arise; there is no thing that does
not have within it as part of its essence, the imprimatur of God,
the Creator of all, the Bottomer of existence. The hunger of my
mind that through all the years has never been satisfied and the
hunger of my heart that remains always unsatiated, are *not* the personal dramatizations of the unyielding dualism inherent in the
very structure of life itself. My testimony is that life is against all
dualism. Life is One. Therefore, a way of life that is worth living
must be a way worthy of life itself. Nothing less than that can
abide. Always, against all that fragments and shatters and against
all things that separate and divide within and without, life labors
to meld together into a single harmony.

Therefore, failure may remain failure in the context of all our
strivings, hatred may continue to be hatred in the social and political arena of the common life, tragedy may continue to yield its
anguish and its pain, spreading havoc in the tight circle of our
private lives, the dead weight of guilt may not shift its position
to make life even for a brief moment more comfortable and en-
durable, for any of us—all this may be true. Nevertheless, in all
these things there is a secret door which leads into the central
place, where the Creator of life and the God of the human heart
are one and the same. I take my stand for the future and for the
generations who follow over the bridges we already have crossed.
It is here that the meaning of the hunger of the heart is unified.
The Head and the Heart at last inseparable; they are lost in wonder in the One.

The years, the months, the days, and the hours have flown by my open window. Here and there an incident, a towering moment, a naked memory, an etched countenance, a whisper in the dark, a golden glow—these and much, much more are the woven fabric of the time I have lived. What I have written is but a fleeting intimation of the outside of what one man sees and may tell about the path he walks. No one shares the secret of a life; no one enters into the heart of the mystery. There are telltale signs that mark the passing of one's appointed days. Always we are on the outside of our story, always we are beggars who seek entrance to the kingdom of our dwelling place. When we are admitted, the price exacted of us is the sealing of the lips. And this is the strangest of all the paradoxes of the human adventure: we live inside all experience, but we are permitted to bear witness only to the outside. Such is the riddle of life and the story of the passing of our days.

Index

INDEX

King, Martin Luther, Sr. ("Daddy
  King"), 254
Klemperer, Ellen, 262
Kropotkin (dog), 234–237
Kropotkin, Peter, 234, 235

Lannam, Allan, 171, 179
Lavry (composer), 268
Lawson, Dr. Warner, 90
Lee, Oscar, 109
Leonard, Dr. J. Paul, 151
Lester, Muriel, 107–108
Lincoln, Abraham, 124
Livingstone, David, 124
Logan, Dr. Rayford, 88
Loucks, Grace, 59
Luce, H. W., 123–124
Luce, Henry, 123

MacCracken, Henry, 98
MacMillan, Hugh, 58
Makechnie, George, 191
Malin, Patrick, 90
Mary, Aunt, 231, 232
Masaoka, Joe Grant, 151
Mathews, Evelyn, 82
Mathews, Red, 51, 52, 82
Mays, Benjamin E., 34, 41, 42
Miller, Dr. Max, 171, 179
Milton, Lorimer, 42
Mitropoulos, Dimitri, 157
Moehlman, Dr. Conrad, 54
Moffatt, James, 66
Mohammed, Mahmud, 198
Moore, Gary, 41–42, 43
Moreland, Dr. Jesse, 237, 238
Mori, Toshio, 153
Morton, Dr. Robert R., 78
Mott, Dr. John R., 237
Mozart, Wolfgang Amadeus, 248
Muelder, Walter, 167
Mukas, Balamu, 37–38
Murray, Mrs., 265
Muste, A. J., 139

Nabrit, James, 34, 35
Naidu, Sarojini, 136
Nehru family, 135

Niebuhr, Gustav, 149
Niebuhr, Hulda, 149
Niebuhr, Reinhold, 85, 149
Niebuhr, Richard, 149

Ogunbameru, Adun, 203
Oldfield, Barney, 8
Otto, Walter, 95
Owen, Dr. S. A., 17, 57

Palmer, Joseph, 191, 207, 208
Pandit, Madame Vijaya Lakshmi, 135
Paton, Alan, 145
Paul (apostle), 82, 190, 249–250
Pavlova, Anna, 54
Pilate, 198
Pizeah, Uncle, 231, 232
Porter, Dorothy Burnett, 91
Porter, James A., 239
Price, Betty McCree, 130

Ram, Mr. and Mrs. Rallia, 123
Randolph, A. Philip, 82, 85
Ray (Indian), 242
Read, Florence, 79–80
Redpath, Mrs., 110
Reichert, Rabbi Irving, 268
Richardson, Dick, 34
Rinder, Cantor, 152
Robins, Dr. Henry Burke, 54
Rockefeller family, 9
Rodzinski, Artur, 157
Roosevelt, Eleanor, 91, 141
Roosevelt, Franklin D., 91
Rosenwald, Julius, 237–238

Saint-Gaudens, Augustus, 91
Sams, Mr. (stepfather), 16, 96, 253
Sams, Alice ("Mamma Alice"), 5, 6,
  11, 12, 13–16, 21, 23, 24, 25, 28–29,
  82, 96, 155–156, 231, 232, 253, 254
Schooler, Jack, 53
Schreiner, Olive, 59, 75, 225–226
Scopes, John T., 58
Shakespeare, William, 53, 82
Shaw, Robert Gould, 188
Sia, Henry Nemle, 194

273

Printed in the USA
CPSIA information can be obtained
at www.ICGtesting.com
LVHW031128310824
789807LV00003B/97